INTRODUCTION TO AUTOMATA THEORY, LANGUAGES, AND COMPUTATION

Mauricio Alberto Ortega Ruiz

Toronto Academic Press

INTRODUCTION TO AUTOMATA THEORY, LANGUAGES, AND COMPUTATION

Mauricio Alberto Ortega Ruiz

Toronto Academic Press
4164 Lakeshore Road
Burlington ON L7L 1A4
Canada
www.tap-books.com

Email: orders@arclereducation.com

ISBN: 978-1-77956-301-9

ABOUT THE AUTHOR

Mauricio Alberto Ortega-Ruíz is an Electrical Engineering graduated from UNAM at Mexico, with experience in technical support for electronics equipment, field service and training services. This experience accomplishes instrumentation equipment, photo-lab and automation industry. Mauricio's academic journey includes a M. Sc. in signal processing at the Imperial College of Science Technology and Medicine and a PhD at City University of London, both are UK Universities. His main Research interest is in AI applications for medical imaging analysis and particularly in digital histopathology for breast cancer grading, he has published Scientific papers on this topic and participated in the Automated Gleason Grand Challenge 2022 in which he developed Deep Learning methods for Prostate cancer image grading and obtained the 10th place in the final ranking. He is cofounder of DigPatho, a research group for the LATAM region. Besides his passion for Research in the medical image field he has also demonstrated interest in signal processing, and other imaging applications. He dedicates time to culture and music, and as an amateur violist, he was member of the Imperial College Chamber orchestra during his masters.

Table of Contents

List of Figures

List of Table

PREFACE

Automata Theory, Languages, and Computation form the cornerstone of theoretical computer science, exploring the fundamental principles that govern computation. This field revolves around abstract models of computation known as automata, which are essential for understanding the capabilities and limitations of algorithms and programming languages.

This book comprises eight chapters, each focusing on distinct aspects of automata theory and its applications. Chapter one introduces the basics of automata theory, tracing its historical development and laying out foundational concepts such as finite automata, pushdown automata, Turing machines, and their relevance in understanding computability and complexity theory. Chapter Two delves into finite automata and regular expressions, detailing deterministic and nondeterministic models, equivalence between different automata types, and the use of regular expressions to describe and manipulate regular languages.

Chapter Three expands on computational complexity, examining various measures such as time and space complexity using mathematical notations like Big Oh, Omega, and Theta. It explores different classes of time complexity and their implications for algorithm efficiency, providing a rigorous foundation in the analysis of algorithmic performance. While fourth introduces context-free grammars and languages, illustrating how formal grammatical rules can define languages that extend beyond the capabilities of regular expressions. It covers derivation trees, ambiguity, and normalization techniques, offering insights into the structures and constraints of context-free languages.

Chapter Five focuses on pushdown automata, which augment finite automata with a stack-based memory mechanism. It explores relationships between pushdown automata and context-free languages, demonstrating their ability to recognize and generate languages that are beyond the scope of regular languages. Chapter Six delves into decidability, addressing concepts of solvability and unsolvability within automata theory. Seventh chapter introduces Turing machines, the foundational model of computation capable of simulating any algorithmic process. It details the components and operational principles of Turing machines, illustrating their role in defining computable functions and languages. Chapter Eight explores computability and undecidability, probing the limits of what can be computed using Turing machines and related formalisms. It covers properties of recursively enumerable languages, unrestricted grammars, and key undecidable problems, offering deep insights into the complexity of theoretical computer science.

This book is designed for students and professionals seeking a rigorous understanding of automata theory and its applications in computer science and related disciplines. It serves as a comprehensive guide, blending theoretical rigor with practical insights, and is intended to equip readers with the foundational knowledge necessary for advanced studies and research in theoretical computer science.

—Author

CHAPTER 1

Introduction to Automata

LEARNING OBJECTIVES

After studying this chapter, you will be able to:

- Understand the basic concepts of automata theory and its significance in computer science.
- Differentiate between various types of automata: finite automata, pushdown automata, and Turing machines.
- Explain the historical development and key contributions to automata theory.
- Recognize the importance of computability and complexity theories.
- Understand mathematical notions and terminologies used in automata theory.
- Analyze the computational power of different types of automata.
- Understand the practical applications of automata theory in compiler design, text processing, and artificial intelligence.

KEY TERMS FROM THIS CHAPTER

Automata theory
Computability theory
Deterministic finite automata (DFA)
Nondeterministic finite automata (NFA)
Regular languages
Complexity theory
Context-free languages
Finite automata
Pushdown automata
Turing machines

UNIT INTRODUCTION

Three key topics in the theory of computation are covered in this chapter: automata, computability, and complexity. Every field is essential to comprehending the basic powers and constraints of computers, an issue that has intrigued mathematicians and computer scientists since the 1930s (Hopcroft et al., 2001).

Automata theory explores into the mathematical models of computation, laying the groundwork for a multitude of applications in the field of computer science. Models like finite automata and context-free grammars play a vital role in various fields including text processing, compiler construction, programming languages, and artificial intelligence. Computability theory explores the scope of problems that can be tackled by computers (Montanari & Pistore, 1998).

This theory, which was developed early on by eminent mathematicians like as Alan Turing, Alonzo Church, and Kurt Gödel, has shown that certain problems are fundamentally difficult by computer algorithms. Compilation problems are categorized according to their difficulty by complexity theory. Sorting is an example of a computationally simple job, although certain scheduling challenges are difficult (Thathachar & Sastry, 2002).

This chapter also covers the fundamental mathematical concepts and terminology that form the basis of computing theory. The mentioned elements encompassed sets, sequences, functions, relations, graphs, and strings. These basic concepts are essential for comprehending the more advanced topics (Lynch et al., 2003).

Did you know?

Alan Turing's conceptual model of a computing machine, known as the Turing machine, was developed in 1936 and remains a foundational concept in computer science.

1.1. OVERVIEW OF AUTOMATA THEORY

Automata theory is a core discipline in theoretical computer science and mathematics that specifically examines abstract machines and the computational issues that can be addressed by these machines. Automata, often called abstract machines, are mathematical models that explain the computational functions and information processing of machines (Ying, 2000). Automata theory offers a conceptual foundation for comprehending the abilities and constraints of various computing models. The subject matter delves into the essence of computation, establishing the criteria for a problem to be capable of being solved by a machine, and categorizing issues according to their computational complexity (Shannon, 1958).The theory is based on formal languages, which consist of sets of strings across an alphabet that are determined by precise rules. Automata are used for the recognition of these languages, functioning as the core components for the creation and analysis of computer processes. Automata encompass a range of forms, each associated with a distinct category of languages and computational capabilities. These include finite automata, pushdown automata, and Turing machines (Baader, 1996). Automata theory is not just a theoretical concept, but it also has practical applications in various areas of computer science. It forms the foundation for compiler design, artificial intelligence, formal verification, and the creation of efficient algorithms (Stern, 1985). By exploring the complex structure of automata, individuals can acquire valuable knowledge about the inner workings of various computational models. This understanding enables them to craft algorithms that effortlessly function within these models, while also ensuring their accuracy and efficiency through strict proof (Alur & Dill, 1994).

1.1.1. Historical Background

Automata theory has a rich history that can be traced back to the early 20th century. Throughout its development, numerous mathematicians and computer scientists have made significant contributions to this field. Alonzo Church and Alan Turing laid the foundation for the concepts of computability and formal languages in the 1930s. Turing's groundbreaking research on Turing machines established a formal definition of computation, which continues to be a fundamental aspect of automata theory (Chakraborty et al., 2011). Warren McCulloch and Walter Pitts' introduction of regular languages and finite automata in the 1940s and 1950s marked significant advances in the discipline. It was due to their work on neural networks and mathematical modeling of brain activities that basic computing models could be understood. During this time, also the work of Stephen Kleene's enhanced the theory by offering a framework for characterizing regular languages (Yokomori & Okubo, 2021).

In the 1960s, there was a notable period of establishing and expanding of this field, during which Noam Chomsky introduced a classification system for languages based on their ability to generate different structures. Chomsky introduced context-free grammars, which have become an essential component of syntactic analysis in programming languages. The research conducted by Michael Rabin and Dana Scott on nondeterministic finite automata and its equivalence to deterministic finite automata offered profound insights into the fundamental principles of computation (Helmreich, 1992). Over the following decades, the theory progressed further through the examination of pushdown automata, context-sensitive grammars, and more complicated computational models. The field also started to overlap with other domains of computer science, including algorithm design, formal verification, and complexity theory. Currently, automata theory continues to be a dynamic field of study, with continuous progress that expands our comprehension of computation (Chrétien et al., 2015).

1.1.2. Basic Definitions and Concepts

Automata theory is founded upon a collection of essential definitions and concepts that serve as the basis for comprehending various forms of automata and their respective languages. An automaton consists of several key elements: states, alphabet, transition function, beginning state, and set of accepted states (Barnes, 1972). A state refers to a unique arrangement of the automaton at certain times. An alphabet refers to a limited collection of symbols that an automaton can identify and manipulate. The transition function determines the movement of the automaton between states, depending on the input symbols. The initial state refers to the state from which the automaton begins its calculation, whereas the set of acceptable states denotes the states that signify successful computations (Arbib, 1966). Finite automata are the most basic form of automata, characterized by a limited number of states. Regular languages, which can be defined by regular expressions, are recognized by them. Pushdown automata improve finite automata by including a stack, enabling them to understand context-free languages, which are more complicated than normal languages (Huckenbeck, 1989). Turing machines are highly advanced automata that possess the ability to simulate any computation that can be executed by a computer. The components of these systems include a never-ending tape, a device that both reads and writes symbols, and a collection of states and transition functions. Recursively enumerable languages are recognized by Turing machines, covering all languages that can be recognized by any algorithm (Ahsan et al., 2012). The concept of non-determinism is a basic aspect of automata theory. A nondeterministic automaton has the ability to select from numerous transitions for a given input, which represents various possible processing paths. Although nondeterministic finite automata are difficult, they are equally powerful as deterministic finite automata. This is because any nondeterministic automaton may be transformed into an equivalent deterministic one (Vafashoar et al., 2021). The fundamental definitions and concepts serve as the basis for examining and comprehending various forms of automata, their computational capabilities, and the languages they may identify. By acquiring proficiency in these principles, individuals can acquire profound understanding of the essence of computation and the development of effective algorithms and systems (Priese, 1983).

1.2. TYPES OF AUTOMATA

1.2.1. Finite Automata

Finite automata are the most basic type of automata, characterized by a limited number of states, a limited set of symbols, a function that determines state transitions, an initial state, and a set of states that are considered accepted. They identify regular languages, which are defined by regular expressions. Nondeterministic finite automata (NFA) and Deterministic finite automata (DFA) are the two types of finite automata. For every state and input symbol, a deterministic finite automaton (DFA) ensures that there is only one transition that leads to a new state (Elgot, 1961).

On the other hand, an NFA has the ability to have multiple transitions for the same state and input symbol, or even transitions without any input (epsilon transitions). Although it may seem complex, both DFAs and NFAs are equivalent when it comes to the languages they recognize. Finite automata have extensive applications in various fields such as lexical analysis, text processing, and network protocol design (Tsetlin, 1961).

1.2.2. Pushdown Automata

Pushdown automata enhance finite automata by including a stack, which offers supplementary memory. Pushdown automata can recognize context-free languages, which are more detailed than regular languages. The stack allows the automaton to maintain an unlimited amount of data, which is crucial for identifying nested patterns like balanced parentheses or matching tags in HTML/XML documents (Muller & Schupp, 1985). Pushdown automata can be classified as either deterministic (DPDA) or nondeterministic (NPDA). However, in contrast to finite automata, deterministic pushdown automata are less capable than their nondeterministic counterparts. This means that there exist context-free languages that can be recognized by a nondeterministic pushdown automaton (NPDA) but cannot be recognized by a deterministic pushdown automaton (DPDA). Pushdown automata play a crucial role in the process of parsing and syntax analysis in the field of compiler design (Valiant, 1975).

1.2.3. Turing Machines

Turing machines are the most potent form of automata, with the ability to simulate any computation that a computer can execute. The components of a Turing machine include an unending tape, a tape head that both reads and writes symbols, a limited number of states, and a transition function. A Turing machine operates by inspecting the symbol on the tape at the current position of the head, performing a state transition, writing a new symbol (which may be the same as the previous one) on the tape, and moving the tape head either to the left or right (Goldin et al., 2004).

Turing machines can be categorized as either deterministic or nondeterministic, and both varieties have the ability to recognize recursively enumerable languages. The concept of a Turing machine is the fundamental basis for contemporary computers, establishing the boundaries of computability. Turing machines play a crucial role in the examination of computability and complexity theory, offering valuable insights into the characteristics of algorithms and the limitations of computing problems (Rogozhin, 1996).

1.3. COMPUTABILITY AND COMPLEXITY THEORY

1.3.1. Complexity Theory

Computer issues can manifest in several forms, ranging from simple to complex. For example, the sorting problem is simple. Assume for a while that you have to put certain integers in ascending order. A million digits can be efficiently sorted by even a little computer (Mason, 2008).

Contrast that with a scheduling dilemma. It is necessary to obtain a timetable for all the classes offered by the university, while ensuring that no two sessions are scheduled in the same room at the same time, among other reasonable limits. The scheduling problem appears to be far more challenging than the sorting challenge. With a mere 1,000 classes, the task of establishing the optimal timetable could take centuries, even with the assistance of a supercomputer (Grobman, 2005).

- **What Distinguishes Easy from Difficult Computational Problems?**

The main query in complexity theory is this one. Interestingly, after more than 40 years of intensive research, we still don't know the answer. We examine this interesting query and some of its implications later. One significant advance in complexity theory nowadays is the simple scheme that has been found by academics to categorize issues based on their computing difficulty. Comparable to the periodic table, it allows elements to be arranged based on their chemical characteristics. With the use of this methodology, one can show how to provide evidence that some issues are computationally difficult, even in cases where we cannot provide proof of this (Morrison, 2008).

When you come across an issue that seems to be computationally difficult, you have a few choices. First, you might be able to change the problem in a way that makes it easier to solve by identifying whatever component of it is the source of the difficulty. Second, you might be able to accept a less-than-ideal resolution to the issue. Finding solutions that are only slightly better than the ideal one might be rather simple in some situations (Horn, 2008).

Furthermore, several problems exhibit difficulty only in the worst-case scenario, while being quite simple in the majority of cases. Depending on the specific use case, you may find it acceptable for a method to have rare instances of slowness, as long as it generally operates at a fast pace. Additionally, it is worth considering different forms of computation, such as randomized computation, which have the potential to accelerate specific activities (Dekker et al., 2011).

Cryptography, an ancient topic, has been directly impacted by complexity theory. Generally, in most domains, a computationally simple challenge is more desirable than a complex one due to the lower cost associated with solving simpler problems. Cryptography is unique in that it particularly necessitates the utilization of computationally challenging issues, as opposed to simple ones. Secret codes should possess a high level of resistance to decryption in the absence of the secret key or password. Cryptographers have been guided by complexity theory towards computationally challenging issues, which they have utilized to create breakthrough new codes (Teisman & Klijn, 2008).

1.3.2. Computability Theory

In the early 20th century, mathematicians such Alan Turing, Kurt Godel, and Alonzo Church made a significant discovery that computers are not capable of solving certain fundamental problems. A prime example of this phenomena is the challenge of determining whether it is true or false of a mathematical proposition. It is the fundamental and essential work of mathematicians. Due to its tight adherence to mathematical principles, this problem appears to be well-suited for computer-based solutions (Downey, 1998).

However, no algorithm on a computer can do this. The invention of concepts for theoretical computer models that ultimately aided in the development of actual computers was one of the significant outcomes of this discovery.

There is tight relationship between the theories of complexity and computability. The goal of complexity theory is to categorize issues as either easy or hard, while the goal of computability theory is to classify problems as either solvable or not. Many of the ideas found in complexity theory are introduced in computable theory (Alfonseca et al., 2021).

1.4. MATHEMATICAL NOTIONS AND TERMINOLOGY

In every mathematical discipline, it is usual to start by examining the fundamental mathematical entities, instruments, and symbols that we expect use (Edwards & Ward, 2004).

1.4.1. Sets

A set is a group of items that are joined as a single entity. A vast variety of things, including symbols, numbers, and even other sets, can be included in sets. The items contained within a set are referred to as its elements or members. Sets can be formally described in multiple ways (Yao, 1998).

Listing the components of a set inside brackets is one method.

S = {7, 21, 57}

Therefore, the set comprises the elements 7, 21, and 57. The symbols "∈" and "∉" represent the concepts of belonging to a set and not belonging to a set, respectively. One can express that 7 is an element of the set {7, 21, 57}, and that 8 is not an element of the set {7, 21, 57} (Mikhailov, & Shoitov, 2003).

A set A is considered a subset of another set B, denoted as A ⊠ B, if every element in A is also an element in B. A is considered a proper subset of B, denoted as A ⊠ B, when A is a subset of B but not equal to B. The order and repetition of members in a set are irrelevant (Lawvere, 1964). The set S is obtained by representing {57, 7, 7, 7, 21}.

When considering the frequency of member occurrences, the group is referred to as a multiset rather than a set. Therefore, {7} and {7, 7} may be distinct when considering multisets, but they are equivalent when considering sets. A set that is infinite has an endless number of elements. It is not possible to provide a comprehensive list of all the elements in an infinite set. Therefore, the notation "..." is often used to indicate that the sequence continues indefinitely (Knowles & Corne, 2002). Therefore, the set of natural numbers N can be expressed as;

{1, 2, 3, . . . }.

One way to represent the set of integers Z is by writing it as;

{ . . . , −2, −1, 0, 1, 2, . . .}.

The collection that has no elements is referred to as the empty set and is symbolized by ∅. A set containing only one element is referred to as a singleton set, while a set containing two elements is known as an unordered pair.

The notation {n|rule about n} is used to express a collection that contains elements based on a certain rule. The expression $\{n|\ n = m^2 \text{ for some } m \in N\}$ denotes the collection of numbers that may be expressed as the square of an integer (Solovay, 1978).

The union of two sets A and B, denoted as A∪B, is the set obtained by merging all the items from A and B into a single set. The intersection of sets A and B, denoted as A ∩ B, refers to the collection of elements that exist in both A and B. The complement of set A, denoted as $\bar{A}$, refers to the set of all items that are not included in set A (Cronbach, 1946).

As is frequently observed in mathematics, the use of a visual representation aids in clarifying a topic. Venn diagrams are utilized to represent sets. It depicts sets as bounded areas delineated by circular boundaries. The set START-t is defined as collection of all English words that have their initial letter as "t". For example, circle in diagram (Figure 1.1) symbolizes the set START-t. Multiple elements of this set are depicted as points within the circle (Dekker & Myhill, 1958).

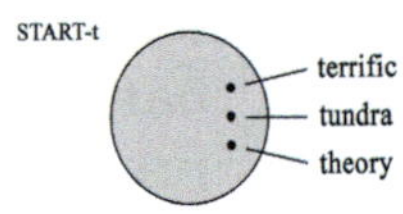

Figure 1.1. *Illustration of Venn diagram for the set of English words starting with "t".*

Source: Micheal Sipser, Creative Commons License.

Similarly, the set END-z, which consists of English words that have the letter "z" at the end, is shown in the image below (Figure 1.2).

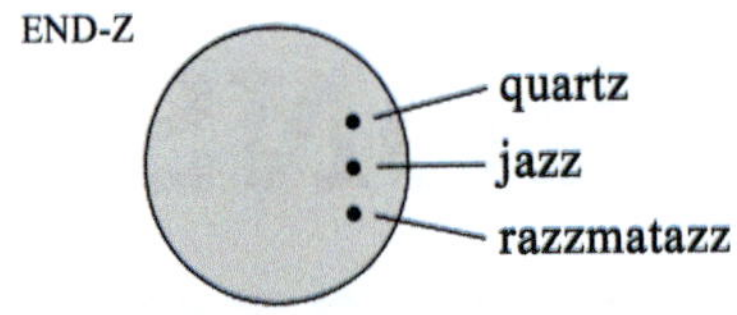

Figure 1.2. *Illustration of Venn diagram for the list of words in English that begin with "z".*

Source: Micheal Sipser, Creative Commons License.

In order to depict both sets in a single Venn diagram, it is necessary to draw them in a manner that demonstrates their intersection, demonstrating the presence of shared elements, as shown in the subsequent diagram (Figure 1.3). For example, the term "topaz" is present in both collections. The diagram also includes a circular shape representing the set START-j. The circle for START-t does not overlap because there are no words that belong to both sets (Maki et al., 1999).

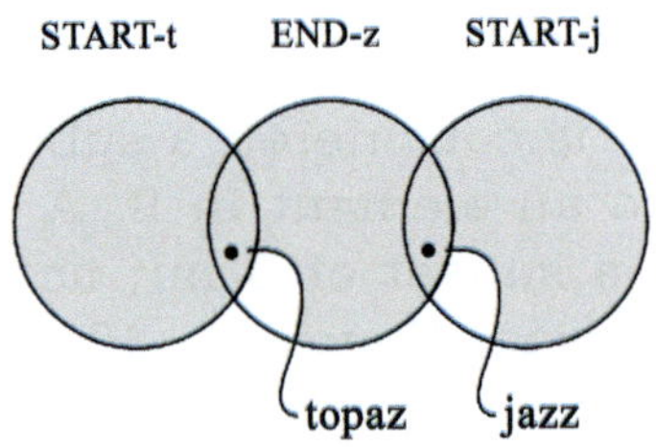

Figure 1.3. *Schematic of common elements indicated by the overlapping circles.*

Source: Manuel Blum, Creative Commons License.

The intersection and union of sets A and B are shown in the following two Venn diagrams (Figure 1.4).

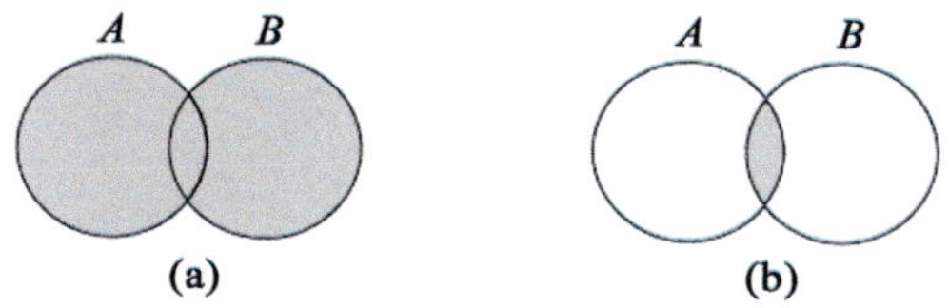

Figure 1.4. *Diagrams for (a) A∪B and (b) A ∩ B.*

Source: Manuel Blum, Creative Commons License.

1.4.2. Sequences and Tuples

A sequence is a structured arrangement of items in a specific order. A common practice is to indicate a sequence by enclosing the list in parentheses. As an example, the sequence 7, 21, 57 could be expressed;

(7, 21, 57).

In a sequence, the order matters, but in a set, it doesn't. Therefore, (7, 21, 57) and (57, 7, 21) are not the same. In the same way, repetition matters in a sequence but not in a set. As a result, while the set {7, 21, 57} is the same as the set {7, 7, 21, 57}, (7, 7, 21, 57) is distinct from both other sequences (Zhong & Weihrauch, 2003).

Sequences can be endless or finite, just like sets. Tuples are a common term for finite sequences. A k-tuple is a sequence consisting of k elements. As a result, (7, 21, 57) is a triple. An ordered pair is another name for a 2-tuple (Ginsburg & Tanaka, 1986). Sequences and sets can be elements of other sequences and sets. As an example, the collection of all of A's subsets is its power set. The set { ∅, {0}, {1}, {0, 1} } is the power set of A if A is the set {0, 1}. The set { (0, 0), (0, 1), (1, 0), (1, 1) } contains all ordered pairs with 0s and 1s as its elements.

The Cartesian product, or cross product, of two sets A and B, denoted as A × B, is the set of all ordered pairs where the first member belongs to A and the second element belongs to B (Rogozhin, 1996).

1.4.3. Functions and Relations

The foundation of mathematics is functions. An object that establishes an input–output relationship is called a function. An output is generated by a function given an input. The same input always gives the same result in every function. When the input value is a and the function f has an output value of b, we write;

f(a) = b.

Another name for a function is a mapping; if f(a) = b, then f maps a to b.

For example, the absolute value function, abs, accepts an integer x as its input and outputs x if x is positive, or -x if x is negative. Hence, the magnitude of 2 is equivalent to the magnitude of -2, which is 2. Another example of a function is the operation of addition, denoted as "add". The addition function accepts a pair of numbers in a particular sequence and yields their total (Kiryakova, 2000). The function's domain refers to the set of possible inputs it can accept. The results of a function are derived from a collection known as its range. The notation used to indicate that f is a function having a domain D and a range R is:

f: D→R.

For the abs function, while dealing with integers, the range and domain are represented by Z, hence we express it as . The domain and range of the addition function of integers are respectively the set of integer pairs and Z. Therefore, we represent it as add: Z × Z→Z. It is important to understand that a function may not always utilize every element inside the given range (Rabkin, 2007). The function abs does not include the value of -1, despite -1 being an element of Z. Being onto the range is the term used to describe a function that makes use of every element in the range. There are multiple ways to describe a particular function. There is a method for calculating an output based on a given input. Another approach involves utilizing a table that comprehensively outlines all potential inputs and their corresponding outputs (Paës et al., 2012).

A predicate or property is a function that only takes on the values of TRUE or FALSE. Let's consider the property "even" which evaluates to TRUE if the input is an even number and FALSE if the input is an odd number. The statement "even (4) = TRUE and even(5) = FALSE" is true (Benjamin et al., 2008). A property that applies to a set of k-tuples is a relation on set A, and is denoted as A × · · · × A and is referred to as a k-ary relation. One example that frequently arises is a 2-ary relation, which is commonly referred to as a binary relation. Infix notation is usually the best option when writing an expression with a binary relation. As an example, the relation "less than" is commonly expressed using the infix operation symbol < (Mel'cuk, 1996).

1.4.4. Graphs

A graph is an arrangement of points joined by lines. The lines in the given diagram are called edges, while the points are called nodes or vertices (Tutte, 1952).

A node's degree is determined by how many edges it has. Every node in Figure 1.5(a) has a degree of 2. Every node in Figure 1.5(b) has a degree of 3. Any two nodes can have no more than one edge between them. Depending on the circumstances, we might permit a self-loop, or edge from a node to itself (Fàbrega & Fiol, 1996).

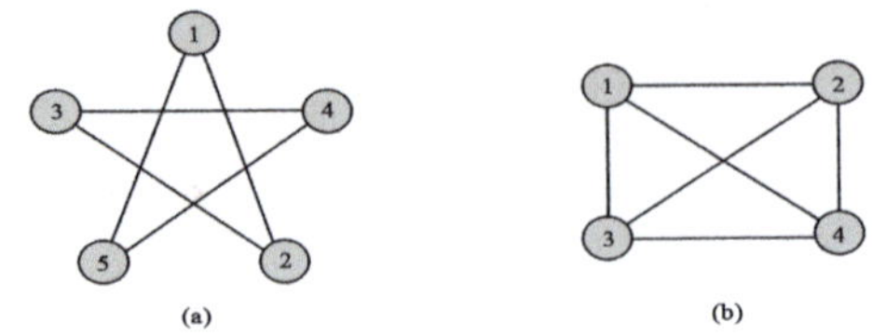

Figure 1.5. *Examples of graphs.*

Source: Richard Karp, Creative Commons License.

Within a graph G, the connection between nodes i and j is represented by the pair (i, j). In an undirected graph, the order of i and j is irrelevant. Therefore, both the pairs (i, j) and (j, i) represent the same edge. Undirected edges can be represented using set notation, such as {i, j}, where the order of the elements does not matter. When considering a graph, we denote the set of nodes as V and the set of edges as E. The graph can then be represented as G = (V, E). There are different ways to represent a graph, such as using a diagram or providing a formal description with V and E. For example, a detailed depiction of the graph in Figure 1.5(a) can be provided, while a formal description of the graph in Figure 1.5(b) can also be given (Sumner, 1974)

({1, 2, 3, 4, 5}, {(1, 2), (2, 3), (3, 4), (4, 5), (5, 1)}),

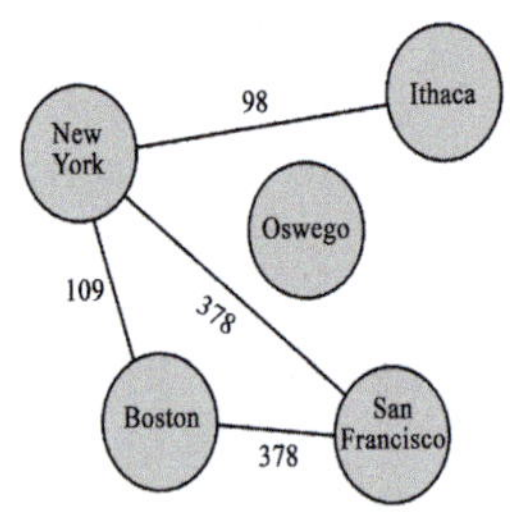

Figure 1.6. *Illustration of cheapest nonstop airfares between various cities.*

Source: Richard Karp, Creative Commons License.

A graph G is a subgraph of graph H if its nodes are a subset of H's and its edges are similar to H's edges, but only between the corresponding nodes. The diagram (Figure 1.7) illustrates a graph H and a subgraph G.

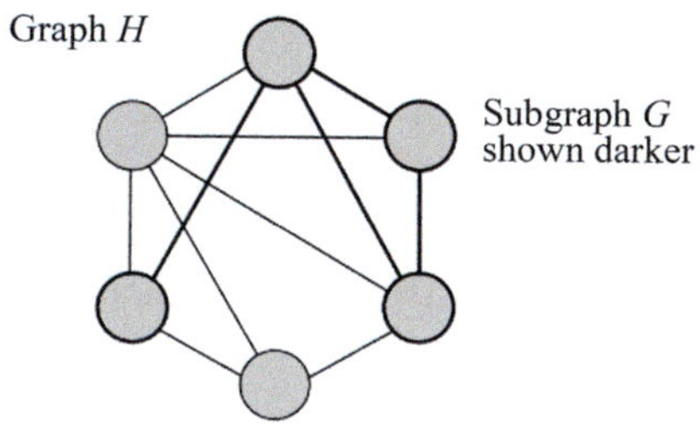

Figure 1.7. *Representation of graph G (shown darker) is a subgraph of H.*

Source: John Addison, Creative Commons License.

In a graph, a path is a series of nodes joined by edges. A path that has no repeating nodes is called a simple path. Any path connecting any two nodes in a graph is said to be linked. If a path begins and finishes at the same node, it is considered a cycle (Wu & Ye, 2011). A simple cycle is one in which just the initial and last nodes are repeated and there are at least three nodes. As seen in Figure 1.8, a graph is a tree if it is linked and devoid of simple cycles. There may be a root, or uniquely identified node, in a tree. The term "leaves" refers to a tree's degree 1 nodes that are not the root (Whitney, 1931).

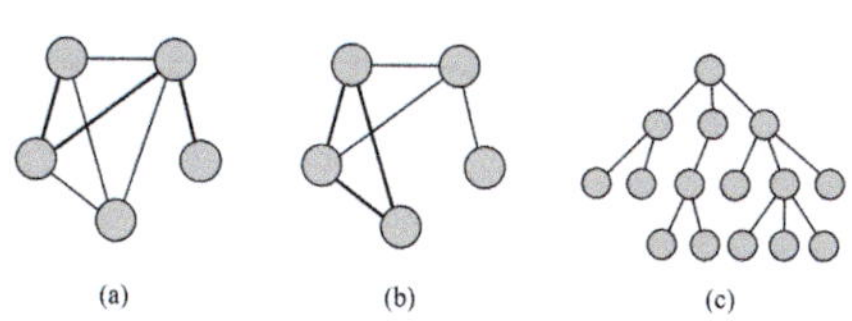

Figure 1.8. *Illustration of (a) path in a graph, (b) cycle in a graph, and (c) a tree.*

Source: John Addison, Creative Commons License.

As seen in the following diagram (Figure 1.9), a directed graph is one in which the connections between nodes are represented by arrows rather than lines. An object's outdegree is the number of arrows heading away from it, while its indegree is the number of arrows pointing towards it (Gilbert, 1959).

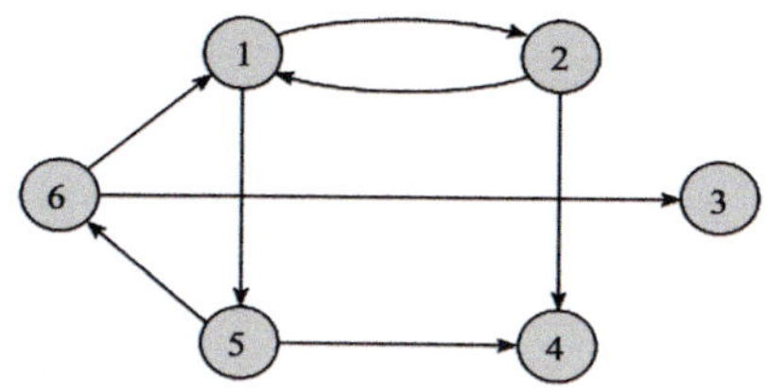

Figure 1.9. *Example of a directed graph.*

Source: Thang Bui, Creative Commons License.

An edge from i to j in a directed graph is represented as a pair (i, j). A directed graph G is formalized as (V, E), where V denotes the node set and E denotes the edge set. The graph in Figure 1.9 has the following formal description:

$$(\{1,2,3,4,5,6\}, \{(1,2), (1,5), (2,1), (2,4), (5,4), (5,6), (6,1), (6,3)\}).$$

A path that has all of its arrows pointing in the same direction as its steps is said to be directed. When a directed path connects each pair of nodes in a directed graph, the graph is said to be strongly linked. Directed graphs are a useful tool for showing binary relations. When considering a binary relation R with a domain of D × D, one way to represent it is through a labeled graph G = (D, E). In this representation, the set E consists of pairs (x, y) where *xRy* (Aalbersberg & Welzl, 1986).

1.4.5. Strings and Languages

In computer science, character strings are the fundamental building components.

Depending on the application, the alphabet over which the strings are defined may change. Any nonempty finite set is what we use to define an alphabet. The symbols that make up the alphabet are its members. Typically, we represent alphabets using the uppercase Greek letters "σ" and "Γ" and use a typewriter style for alphabetic symbols (Csuhaj et al., 2007). Here are some examples of alphabets:

Σ1 = {0,1}

Σ2 = {a, b, c, d, e, f, g, h, i, j, k, l, m, n, o, p, q, r, s, t, u, v, w, x, y, z}

Γ = {0, 1, x, y, z}

A string over an alphabet is a limited series of that alphabet's symbols, typically written side by side without commas in between. 01001 is a string over Σ1 if Σ1 = {0,1}. Abracadabra is a string over Σ2 if Σ2 = {a, b, c,..., z} (Boehm et al., 1995).

The length of a string, denoted as |w|, indicates how many symbols it contains if w is a string over Σ. The empty string, denoted by ε, is a string of length zero. In context of number system, the empty string represents 0. One can write w = $w_1w_2 \cdots w_n$ where each wi ∈ Σ if w has length n. The string that results from writing w in the opposite sequence is the reverse of w, denoted as w R (i.e., $w_nw_{n-1} \cdots w_1$). If z exists within w in a consecutive manner, then string z is a substring of w. For example, the substring "cad" of abracadabra (Enaganti et al., 2017).

The string obtained by appending y to the end of x, as in $x_1 \cdots x_my_1 \cdots y_n$, is the concatenation of x and y, written xy, if we have strings x of length m and y of length n. The superscript notation x^k is used to concatenate a string with itself several times. This means

$$\overbrace{xx\cdots x}^{k}.$$

Strings are arranged in the same lexicographic order as the well-known dictionary arrangement. Occasionally, we will use a modified lexicographic order that is the same as lexicographic order but with shorter strings coming before longer strings (Parys, 2011). This is known as shortlex order or just string order. Hence, for every string across the alphabet {0,1}, the string ordering is

(ε,0,1,00,01,10,11,000,...).

Assume that if a string z exists with xz = y, then string x is a prefix of string y; furthermore, if x ≠ y, then x is a legitimate prefix of y. A collection of strings is a language. If there are no members that properly prefix another member, then a language is prefix-free (Maurer et al., 1982).

1.4.6. Boolean Logic

A mathematical theory based on the binary variables TRUE and FALSE is known as Boolean logic. This approach was first thought to be simply mathematical, but it is today regarded as the foundation of digital electronics and computer design. Boolean values, or TRUE and FALSE, are commonly represented by the numbers 1 and 0 (Ashkenasy & Ghadiri, 2004). When there are two possible outcomes, like a wire that could have a high or low voltage, a statement that could be true or untrue, or a question that could have a yes or no response, we use Boolean values (Darwiche & Marquis, 2021). Boolean operations enable the manipulation of Boolean values. The negation operation, represented by the symbol ¬, is the fundamental Boolean operation. The negative of a Boolean value is its opposite value. Hence, the negation of 0 is 1 and the negation of 1 is 0 (Miyamoto et al., 2013). The symbol ∧ represents the logical conjunction or AND operation. The combination of two Boolean values is equal to 1 only when both of those values are equal to 1. The logical action of disjunction, often known as the OR operation, is represented by the symbol ∨. If any of the two Boolean values are equal to 1, then their disjunction is also equal to 1 (Heuvelink & Burrough, 1993). In summary, we present this information as follows:

$0 \wedge 0 = 0$	$0 \vee 0 = 0$	$\neg 0 = 1$
$0 \wedge 1 = 0$	$0 \vee 1 = 1$	$\neg 1 = 0$
$1 \wedge 0 = 0$	$1 \vee 0 = 1$	
$1 \wedge 1 = 1$	$1 \vee 1 = 1$	

Similar to how addition and multiplication build complicated arithmetic expressions, Boolean operations combine simple statements into more complex ones. For example, let's consider the Boolean values P and Q. P represents the truth of the statement "the sun is shining" and Q represents the truth of the statement "today is Monday".

One can use the notation P ∧ Q to express truth value of statement "the sun is shining and today is Monday". Similarly, one can use P ∨ Q with "and" replaced by "or". P and Q are commonly referred to as the operands of the operation (Herman et al., 2012). Occasionally, several more Boolean operations are observed. The ⊕ sign stands for the operation or-exclusive, also referred to as XOR (Waterman, 1984). It only evaluates to 1 when one of its two operands is 1, not when both are 1. The equality operation, denoted by the symbol ↔, evaluates to 1 when both operands have the same value 1. The implication operation, denoted by the symbol →, evaluates to zero when the first operand is 1 and the second operand is 0. Otherwise, → evaluates to 1. In conclusion, we provide this data as follows (Fenno et al., 2014).

$0 \oplus 0 = 0$	$0 \leftrightarrow 0 = 1$	$0 \rightarrow 0 = 1$
$0 \oplus 1 = 1$	$0 \leftrightarrow 1 = 0$	$0 \rightarrow 1 = 1$
$1 \oplus 0 = 1$	$1 \leftrightarrow 0 = 0$	$1 \rightarrow 0 = 0$
$1 \oplus 1 = 0$	$1 \leftrightarrow 1 = 1$	$1 \rightarrow 1 = 1$

There are multiple relationships that can be established among these operations. It is possible to represent all Boolean operations using the AND and NOT operations, as demonstrated by the following identities. There are two equal phrases in every row. The operation in each row is expressed in terms of the operations above it, along with the use of AND and NOT (Wang et al., 2023).

$P \vee Q$	$\neg(\neg P \wedge \neg Q)$
$P \rightarrow Q$	$\neg P \vee Q$
$P \leftrightarrow Q$	$(P \rightarrow Q) \wedge (Q \rightarrow P)$
$P \oplus Q$	$\neg(P \leftrightarrow Q)$

When working with Boolean expressions, the distributive law for AND and OR is useful. It is comparable to the addition and multiplication distributive law, which says that a × (b + c) = (a × b) + (a × c) (Zhao et al., 2021). There are two versions of the Boolean version:

i. P ∧ (Q ∨ R) equals (P ∧ Q) ∨ (P ∧ R), and its dual
ii. P ∨ (Q ∧ R) equals (P ∨ Q) ∧ (P ∨ R).

Did you know?

Kurt Gödel's incompleteness theorems caused significant disruption in the mathematical community throughout the 1930s by demonstrating the existence of true mathematical statements that cannot be proven inside a given system.

1.5. APPLICATIONS OF AUTOMATA THEORY

Numerous real-world applications of automata theory can be found in computer science and related disciplines. Designing and implementing compilers and interpreters for computer languages is one of its main uses. Regular expressions and finite automata are frequently used in lexical analysis to identify patterns and tokens in source code. Pushdown automata and context-free grammars are essential tools for syntactic analysis because they allow programming languages to be processed and abstract syntax trees to be created (Hopcroft et al., 2001).

Automata theory is used in formal verification to confirm that software and hardware systems are valid. Model checking is a verification technique that involves using automata to model system activity and validating properties stated in temporal logic. This method guarantees that systems follow their specifications, which is essential for creating durable and dependable systems (Obaidat et al., 2002).

Automata theory is also applicable in the fields of artificial intelligence and machine learning. Automata-based models are used to depict and analyze sequential decision-making processes. Finite automata and context-free grammars are used in natural language processing to analyze and synthesize human language. This enables the completion of tasks such as syntactic parsing, speech recognition, and machine translation (Vafashoar et al., 2021).

Furthermore, automata theory is utilized in the development of optimized algorithms and data structures. Automata theory techniques are used to enhance pattern matching algorithms, which play a crucial role in text processing, search engines, and bioinformatics. Automata are utilized in network protocols to model and analyze communication protocols, hence ensuring dependable data delivery (Maji et al., 2003).

Automata theory is widely applicable in diverse fields, underscoring its significance as a fundamental subject in computer science. Through comprehending and utilizing the ideas of automata, scholars and professionals can create systems that are more effective, dependable, and intelligent (Misra et al., 1990).

SUMMARY

- The fundamental ideas of automata theory are covered in this chapter, along with the examination of pushdown automata, Turing machines, and finite automata. Regular languages are recognized by context-free languages by pushdown automata, recursively enumerable languages by Turing machines, and finite automata, which are equivalent to modern computers in functionality. The chapter outlines the evolution of these ideas across time, starting with Alan Turing and Alonzo Church's fundamental work and ending with Noam Chomsky and others' formalization attempts.
- The chapter also discusses complexity theory, which groups problems according to their computational difficulty, and computability theory, which deals with the solvability of problems by computers. To offer a strong basis for comprehending these advanced topics, key mathematical concepts and terminology are introduced, including sets, sequences, functions, and relations. Readers will have a thorough understanding of the theoretical foundations of computation and the real-world applications of these ideas in computer science by the end of the chapter.

REVIEW QUESTIONS

1. What are the main differences between finite automata, pushdown automata, and Turing machines?
2. Describe the historical development of automata theory and the contributions of key figures such as Alan Turing and Alonzo Church.
3. Explain the significance of computability theory and provide an example of a problem that cannot be solved by any computer algorithm.
4. Discuss the concept of complexity theory and its importance in classifying computational problems.
5. How do nondeterministic finite automata (NFA) differ from deterministic finite automata (DFA), and why are they considered equivalent in terms of computational power?
6. Who are the key historical figures in the development of computability theory, and what were their main contributions?

MULTIPLE CHOICE QUESTIONS

1. Which of the following is used in the design of compilers?

a. Turing machine

b. Finite automaton

c. Pushdown automaton

d. Cellular automaton

2. **What is the primary focus of automata theory?**
   a. The study of algorithms
   b. The study of abstract machines and the computational problems they solve
   c. The development of computer hardware
   d. The analysis of software engineering principles
3. **Who introduced the concept of Turing machines?**
   a. Kurt Gödel
   b. Alonzo Church
   c. Alan Turing
   d. Stephen Kleene
4. **What type of languages do pushdown automata recognize?**
   a. Regular languages
   b. Context-free languages
   c. Context-sensitive languages
   d. Recursively enumerable languages
5. **What is the significance of nondeterministic finite automata (NFA)?**
   a. NFAs are more powerful than deterministic finite automata (DFA)
   b. NFAs and DFAs are equivalent in terms of the languages they recognize
   c. NFAs are less efficient than DFAs
   d. NFAs can only recognize context-free languages
6. **Which theory addresses the classification of problems based on their computational difficulty?**
   a. Automata theory
   b. Computability theory
   c. Complexity theory
   d. Information theory

Answers to Multiple Questions

1. (b); 2. (b); 3. (c); 4. (b); 5. (b); 6. (c)

REFERENCES

1. Aalbersberg, I. J., & Welzl, E. (1986). Trace languages defined by regular string languages. *RAIRO-Theoretical Informatics and Applications, 20*(2), 103–119.
2. Ahsan, J., Mordeson, J. N., & Shabir, M. (2012). Fuzzy semirings with applications to automata theory. *Studies in Fuzziness and Soft Computing, 278*, 18–43.

3. Alfonseca, M., Cebrian, M., Anta, A. F., Coviello, L., Abeliuk, A., & Rahwan, I. (2021). Superintelligence cannot be contained: Lessons from computability theory. *Journal of Artificial Intelligence Research, 70*, 65–76.
4. Alur, R., & Dill, D. L. (1994). A theory of timed automata. *Theoretical Computer Science, 126*(2), 183–235.
5. Arbib, M. A. (1966). Automata theory and control theory—A rapprochement. *Automatica, 3*(3, 4), 161–189.
6. Ashkenasy, G., & Ghadiri, M. R. (2004). Boolean logic functions of a synthetic peptide network. *Journal of the American Chemical Society, 126*(36), 11140–11141.
7. Baader, F. (1996). Using automata theory for characterizing the semantics of terminological cycles. *Annals of Mathematics and Artificial Intelligence, 18*, 175–219.
8. Barnes, B. H. (1972). A programmer's view of automata. *ACM Computing Surveys (CSUR), 4*(4), 221–239.
9. Benjamin, M., Kaiser, E., & Milz, S. (2008). Structure-function relationships in tendons: A review. *Journal of Anatomy, 212*(3), 211–228.
10. Boehm, H. J., Atkinson, R., & Plass, M. (1995). Ropes: An alternative to strings. *Software: Practice and Experience, 25*(12), 1315–1330.
11. Chakraborty, P., Saxena, P. C., & Katti, C. P. (2011). Fifty years of automata simulation: A review. *ACM Inroads, 2*(4), 59–70.
12. Chrétien, R., Cortier, V., & Delaune, S. (2015). From security protocols to pushdown automata. *ACM Transactions on Computational Logic (TOCL), 17*(1), 1–45.
13. Cronbach, L. J. (1946). Response sets and test validity. *Educational and Psychological Measurement, 6*(4), 475–494.
14. Csuhaj-Varjú, E., Petre, I., & Vaszil, G. (2007). Self-assembly of strings and languages. *Theoretical Computer Science, 374*(1–3), 74–81.
15. Darwiche, A., & Marquis, P. (2021). On quantifying literals in Boolean logic and its applications to explainable AI. *Journal of Artificial Intelligence Research, 72*, 285–328.
16. Dekker, J. C. E., & Myhill, J. (1958). Retraceable sets. *Canadian Journal of Mathematics, 10*, 357–373.
17. Dekker, S., Cilliers, P., & Hofmeyr, J. H. (2011). The complexity of failure: Implications of complexity theory for safety investigations. *Safety Science, 49*(6), 939–945.
18. Downey, R. G. (1998). Computability theory and linear orderings. In *Studies in Logic and the Foundations of Mathematics* (Vol. 139, pp. 823–976).
19. Edwards, B. S., & Ward, M. B. (2004). Surprises from mathematics education research: Student (mis) use of mathematical definitions. *The American Mathematical Monthly, 111*(5), 411–424.
20. Elgot, C. C. (1961). Decision problems of finite automata design and related arithmetic's. *Transactions of the American Mathematical Society, 98*(1), 21–51.
21. Enaganti, S. K., Ibarra, O. H., Kari, L., & Kopecki, S. (2017). On the overlap assembly of strings and languages. *Natural Computing, 16*, 175–185.

22. Fàbrega, J., & Fiol, M. A. (1996). On the extra connectivity of graphs. *Discrete Mathematics, 155*(1–3), 49–57.

23. Fenno, L. E., Mattis, J., Ramakrishnan, C., Hyun, M., Lee, S. Y., He, M., & Deisseroth, K. (2014). Targeting cells with single vectors using multiple-feature Boolean logic. *Nature Methods, 11*(7), 763–772.

24. Gilbert, E. N. (1959). Random graphs. *The Annals of Mathematical Statistics, 30*(4), 1141–1144.

25. Ginsburg, S., & Tanaka, K. (1986). Computation-tuple sequences and object histories. *ACM Transactions on Database Systems (TODS), 11*(2), 186–212.

26. Goldin, D. Q., Smolka, S. A., Attie, P. C., & Sonderegger, E. L. (2004). Turing machines, transition systems, and interaction. *Information and Computation, 194*(2), 101–128.

27. Grobman, G. (2005). Complexity theory: A new way to look at organizational change. *Public Administration Quarterly, 29*(3), 351–384.

28. Helmreich, S. (1992). The historical and epistemological ground of von Neumann's theory of self-reproducing automata and theory of games. In Varela and Bourgine (Eds.), *Toward a Practice of Autonomous Systems: Proceedings of the First European Conference on Artificial Life* (pp. 385–391). MIT Press.

29. Herman, G. L., Loui, M. C., Kaczmarczyk, L., & Zilles, C. (2012). Describing the what and why of students' difficulties in Boolean logic. *ACM Transactions on Computing Education (TOCE), 12*(1), 1–28.

30. Heuvelink, G. B., & Burrough, P. A. (1993). Error propagation in cartographic modelling using Boolean logic and continuous classification. *International Journal of Geographical Information Systems, 7*(3), 231–246.

31. Hopcroft, J. E., Motwani, R., & Ullman, J. D. (2001). Introduction to automata theory, languages, and computation. *ACM SIGACT News, 32*(1), 60–65.

32. Horn, J. (2008). Human research and complexity theory. *Educational Philosophy and Theory, 40*(1), 130–143.

33. Huckenbeck, U. (1989). Euclidean geometry in terms of automata theory. *Theoretical Computer Science, 68*(1), 71–87.

34. Kiryakova, V. S. (2000). Multiple (multiindex) Mittag–Leffler functions and relations to generalized fractional calculus. *Journal of Computational and Applied Mathematics, 118*(1, 2), 241–259.

35. Knowles, J., & Corne, D. (2002). On metrics for comparing nondominated sets. In *Proceedings of the 2002 Congress on Evolutionary Computation (CEC'02)* (Vol. 1, pp. 711–716). IEEE.

36. Lawvere, F. W. (1964). An elementary theory of the category of sets. *Proceedings of the National Academy of Sciences, 52*(6), 1506–1511.

37. Lynch, N., Segala, R., & Vaandrager, F. (2003). Hybrid I/O automata. *Information and Computation, 185*(1), 105–157.

38. Maji, P., Shaw, C., Ganguly, N., Sikdar, B. K., & Chaudhuri, P. P. (2003). Theory and application of cellular automata for pattern classification. *Fundamental Informaticae, 58*(3, 4), 321–354.

39. Maki, H., Rao, K. C., & Gani, A. N. (1999). On generalizing semi-open sets and preopen sets. *Pure and Applied Mathematica Sciences, 49*(1, 2), 17–30.

40. Mason, M. (2008). Complexity theory and the philosophy of education. *Educational Philosophy and Theory, 40*(1), 4–18.

41. Maurer, H. A., Rozenberg, G., & Welzl, E. (1982). Using string languages to describe picture languages. *Information and Control, 54*(3), 155–185.

42. Mel'cuk, I. (1996). Lexical functions: A tool for the description of lexical relations in a lexicon. In L. Wanner (Ed.), *Lexical Functions in Lexicography and Natural Language Processing* (pp. 37–102). John Benjamins Publishing.

43. Mikhailov, V. G., & Shoitov, A. M. (2003). Structural equivalence of s-tuples in random discrete sequences. *Discrete Mathematics and Applications, 13*(6), 541–568.

44. Misra, S., Das, A. K., Chowdhury, D. R., & Chaudhuri, P. P. (1990). Cellular automata—Theory and applications. *IETE Journal of Research, 36*(3, 4), 251–259.

45. Miyamoto, T., Razavi, S., DeRose, R., & Inoue, T. (2013). Synthesizing biomolecule-based Boolean logic gates. *ACS Synthetic Biology, 2*(2), 72–82.

46. Montanari, U., & Pistore, M. (1998). An introduction to history dependent automata. *Electronic Notes in Theoretical Computer Science, 10*, 170–188.

47. Morrison, K. (2008). Educational philosophy and the challenge of complexity theory. *Educational Philosophy and Theory, 40*(1), 19–34.

48. Muller, D. E., & Schupp, P. E. (1985). The theory of ends, pushdown automata, and second-order logic. *Theoretical Computer Science, 37*, 51–75.

49. Obaidat, M. S., Papadimitriou, G. I., & Pomportsis, A. S. (2002). Guest editorial learning automata: Theory, paradigms, and applications. *IEEE Transactions on Systems, Man, and Cybernetics, Part B (Cybernetics), 32*(6), 706–709.

50. Paës, G., Berrin, J. G., & Beaugrand, J. (2012). GH11 xylanases: Structure/function/properties relationships and applications. *Biotechnology Advances, 30*(3), 564–592.

51. Parys, P. (2011). Application of automata theory to processing of XML documents. In *Proceedings of the 28th International Conference on Very Large Data Bases* (VLDB, Vol. 2, pp. 95–106).

52. Priese, L. (1983). Automata and concurrency. *Theoretical Computer Science, 25*(3), 221–265.

53. Rabkin, S. W. (2007). Epicardial fat: Properties, function and relationship to obesity. *Obesity Reviews, 8*(3), 253–261.

54. Rogozhin, Y. (1996). Small universal Turing machines. *Theoretical Computer Science, 168*(2), 215–240.

55. Shannon, C. E. (1958). Von Neumann's contributions to automata theory. *Bulletin of the American Mathematical Society, 64*(3), 123–129.

56. Solovay, R. M. (1978). Hyper arithmetically encodable sets. *Transactions of the American Mathematical Society, 239*, 99–122.

57. Stern, J. (1985). Complexity of some problems from the theory of automata. *Information and Control, 66*(3), 163–176.

58. Sumner, D. P. (1974). Dacey graphs. *Journal of the Australian Mathematical Society, 18*(4), 492–502.

59. Teisman, G. R., & Klijn, E. H. (2008). Complexity theory and public management: An introduction. *Public Management Review, 10*(3), 287–297.

60. Thathachar, M. A., & Sastry, P. S. (2002). Varieties of learning automata: An overview. *IEEE Transactions on Systems, Man, and Cybernetics, Part B (Cybernetics), 32*(6), 711–722.

61. Tsetlin, M. L. (1961). On behaviour of finite automata in random medium. *Avtomat. i Telemekh, 22*(10), 1345–1354.

62. Tutte, W. T. (1952). The factors of graphs. *Canadian Journal of Mathematics, 4*, 314–328.

63. Vafashoar, R., Morshedlou, H., Rezvanian, A., & Meybodi, M. R. (2021). Cellular learning automata: Theory and applications (Vol. 307, pp. 1–365). *Studies in Computational Intelligence.*

64. Valiant, L. G. (1975). Regularity and related problems for deterministic pushdown automata. *Journal of the ACM (JACM), 22*(1), 1–10.

65. Wang, Y., Sun, Q., Yu, J., Xu, N., Wei, Y., Cho, J. H., & Wang, Z. L. (2023). Boolean logic computing based on neuromorphic transistor. *Advanced Functional Materials, 33*(47), 2305791.

66. Waterman, M. S. (1984). Some applications of information theory to cellular automata. *Physica D: Nonlinear Phenomena, 10*(1, 2), 45–51.

67. Whitney, H. (1931). A theorem on graphs. *Annals of Mathematics, 32*(2), 378–390.

68. Wu, Y. W., & Ye, Y. (2011). A novel abundance-based algorithm for binning metagenomic sequences using l-tuples. *Journal of Computational Biology, 18*(3), 523–534.

69. Yao, Y. Y. (1998). A comparative study of fuzzy sets and rough sets. *Information Sciences, 109*(1–4), 227–242.

70. Ying, M. (2000). Automata theory based on quantum logic. (I). *International Journal of Theoretical Physics, 39*, 985–995.

71. Yokomori, T., & Okubo, F. (2021). Theory of reaction automata: A survey. *Journal of Membrane Computing, 3*, 63–85.

72. Zhao, S., Yu, L., Yang, S., Tang, X., Chang, K., & Chen, M. (2021). Boolean logic gate based on DNA strand displacement for biosensing: Current and emerging strategies. *Nanoscale Horizons, 6*(4), 298–310.

73. Zhong, N., & Weihrauch, K. (2003). Computability theory of generalized functions. *Journal of the ACM (JACM), 50*(4), 469–505.

CHAPTER 2

Finite Automata and Regular Expressions

LEARNING OBJECTIVES

After studying this chapter, you will be able to:

- Define and differentiate between deterministic and non-deterministic finite automata.
- Explain the components and working of deterministic finite automata (DFA).
- Illustrate the construction and working of non-deterministic finite automata (NFA).
- Convert a non-deterministic finite automaton to an equivalent deterministic finite automaton.
- Describe and construct regular expressions and regular languages.
- Convert regular expressions to finite automata and vice versa.
- Define and explain two-way finite automata.
- Describe finite automata with output and the models of Mealy and Moore machines.

KEY TERMS FROM THIS CHAPTER

Deterministic finite automata (DFA)
Kleene star
Moore machine
Regular languages
Two-way finite automata
Input alphabet
Mealy machine
Regular expressions
transition function

UNIT INTRODUCTION

A mathematical representation of a system with discrete inputs and outputs is called a finite automaton. The system's state encompasses the necessary information from past inputs to forecast its behavior with future inputs. The system can be in any one of a finite number of internal configurations, or "states." An excellent instance of a finite state system is the elevator's control mechanism. Only the present floor, the mobility direction (up or down), and the collection of unfulfilled service requests are retained by that system; it does not retain track of all prior requests for service. Numerous instances of finite state systems may be found in computer science, and the theory of finite automata is a helpful tool for their design (Brüggemann, 1993).

A switching circuit, like the one in a computer's control unit, is a prime example. A switching circuit consists of a limited number of gates, typically identified by the numbers 0 and 1, each of which can be in one of two states. In terms of electronics, these situations may be two distinct voltage values at the gate output. Any one of the two assignments of 0 or 1 to the different gates is hence the state of a switching network with n gates (Gruber & Holzer, 2015).

While the voltage on each gate has the potential to take on any value from an infinite set, the electronic circuitry is specifically engineered to ensure that only the two voltages representing 0 and 1 are stable. Any other voltages will rapidly adapt themselves to one of these stable values. Switching circuits are intentionally built in this manner to allow them to be perceived as finite state systems. This separation enables the logical design of a computer to be distinct from its electrical implementation. Text editors and lexical analyzers, which are frequently utilized in compilers, are typically constructed as finite state systems (Antimirov, 1996).

For example, a lexical analyzer examines the symbols in a computer program in order to identify the sequences of characters that represent identifiers, reserved words, numerical constants, and other similar elements. During this procedure, the lexical analyzer is required to retain a limited amount of information, specifically the length of a prefix of a reserved word that it has encountered since the system was initiated. The theory of finite automata is extensively utilized in the development of efficient string processors for various purposes (Li & Pedrycz, 2005).

The computer can be considered a finite state system, although this perspective is not as practical as desired. In theory, the state of the central processor, main memory, and auxiliary storage can be described as one of a vast yet limited number of states. It is assumed that there is a predetermined quantity of disks, drums, cassettes, and other storage devices accessible for use, and it is not possible to infinitely expand the memory (Stearns & Hunt, 1985).

Considering a computer as a finite state system, though, is unsatisfactory both from a mathematical and realistic standpoint. It imposes an artificial constraint on the memory capacity, thereby failing to represent the true nature of computation. One might be compelled to perceive the human brain as a limited state system. The quantity of brain cells, also known as neurons, is constrained, likely reaching a maximum of 235. It is possible, despite the existence of opposing evidence, to describe the state of each neuron using a limited number of bits. If that is the case, then the principles of finite state theory are applicable to the brain (Choueka, 1978).

Nevertheless, due to the vast number of states involved, it seems doubtful that this technique will yield valuable insights into the workings of the human brain, just as finite state assumptions do not aid in comprehending big yet finite computer systems. The study of finite state systems is crucial due to their inherent naturalness, seen from their occurrence in various contexts. This indicates that we have successfully grasped the concept of a fundamental category of systems, which is characterized by its complex structure and potential for various uses (Kumar & Verma, 2014).

Two key ideas in automata theory are examined in this chapter: finite automata and regular expressions. Mathematical representations of discrete input/output systems that can exist in a limited number of states are called finite automata. These models are crucial for many applications, including as computer science, where they aid in the design of effective switching circuits and text processors. We will go through the differences between deterministic and non-deterministic finite automata as well as how to convert between them. We will also go over how to define regular languages using regular expressions and how to compose them (Melnikov & Melnikova, 2018).

2.1. DETERMINISTIC FINITE AUTOMATA (DFA)

2.1.1. Automata

An automaton is an abstract representation of a digital computer. An automaton is capable of processing input, which consists of a string that is composed of a specified set of characters. The input is stored in a "input file" that the automaton can read but cannot alter (Vayadande et al., 2022) (Figure 2.1).

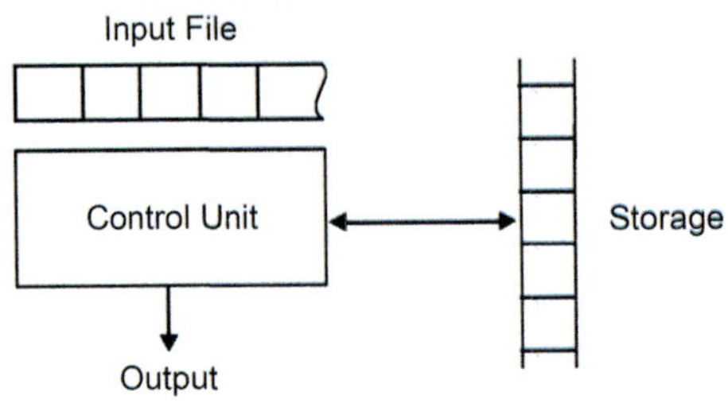

Figure 2.1. *Illustration of automation.*

Source: S.P Eguane, Creative Commons License.

The input file is partitioned into cells, with each cell capable of containing a single symbol. The automaton is equipped with a temporary "storage" device that contains an endless number of cells. The automaton has the ability to modify the contents of these cells. An automaton consists of a control unit that can be in one of a limited number of "internal states". The automaton has the ability to transition between states in a specific way (Omlin & Giles, 1996).

2.1.2. Automaton Types

There exist two distinct categories of automata

i. Deterministic Automata

ii. Non-deterministic Automata

A deterministic automaton is a system where the current configuration determines each transition from one state to another.

It is possible to predict the future behavior of automata by having knowledge of their internal state, input, and storage contents. If not, they are considered non-determinist automata. This is known as deterministic automata (Lucas & Reynolds, 2005).

An automaton that produces either a "yes" or "no" response is referred to as a "Acceptor".

2.1.3. Deterministic Finite Automaton Definition

A Deterministic Finite Automaton (DFA) is defined as a 5-tuple:

$M = (Q, \Sigma, \delta, q\ , F\ )$

Where; Q is the "Internal states" finite set; Σ is the "Input alphabet" and is a finite set of symbols; $\delta: Q \times \Sigma \rightarrow Q$ is the Transition Function; $q0$ ÎQ is the Initial state; and $F \subseteq Q$ is the Final states Set The input method only moves in one direction, from left to right, and it processes one symbol at a time. The transition from one internal state to another is determined by a specific function called the transition function δ. When the transition function $\delta(q_0\ , a) \rightarrow q_1$, the deterministic finite automaton (DFA) will transition from state to state when the current input symbol is a (De Giacomo & Favorito, 2021).

- **Example 2.1** Create a DFA, M that is capable of processing the specified language.

does not contain three consecutive b's).

Let $\mathbf{M} = (\mathbf{Q}, \Sigma, \delta, \mathbf{q}_0\ , \mathbf{F}\ )$

Where $Q = \{q0, q1, q2, q3\}$; $\Sigma = \{a, b\}$; q_0 is the initial state; and $F = \{q0, q1, q2,\}$ are initial states defined as follows:

Initial state q	Symbol σ	Final state Δ(q,σ)
q_0	a	q_0
q_0	b	q_1
q_1	a	q_0
q_1	b	q_2
q_2	a	q_0
q_2	b	q_3
q_3	a	q_3
q_3	b	q_3

- **Solution**

M does not have a preference for any particular language, as long as it has not encountered three consecutive b's.

It is important to mention that

1. After encountering a sequence of consecutive 'b's, M enters state (where i can be 0, 1, or 2). This sequence of 'b's can either start at the beginning of the input string or be preceded by a 'a'.
2. Machine M returns to its original state, if the input symbol is 'a' and it is in one of the following states: , , or M.

"Final states" are , and (as stated in the issue). Thus, any input string that does not have three consecutive b's in it will be recognized (Bensch et al., 2009).No matter what other symbol appears in the remainder of the string, M will stay in the state, which is not the ultimate state—if we receive three consecutive bs. It is argued that is in a "dead state" or that M is "trapped" at The following diagram (Figure 2.2) displays the DFA schematic as discussed earlier (Fernau et al., 2015).

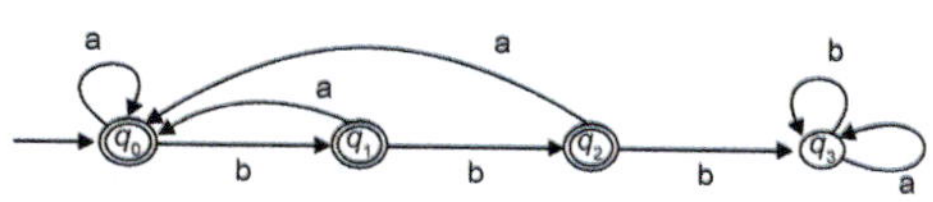

Figure 2.2. *Illustration of the finite automaton with four states.*

Source: Michel Siper, Creative Commons License.

Did you know?

Text editors and search engines use finite automata extensively for syntax highlighting and pattern matching. For example, when a word is searched in a document, a finite automaton can effectively locate every instance of that term.

2.2. NON-DETERMINISTIC FINITE AUTOMATA (NFA)

- **Definition**

A 5-tuple defines a Nondeterministic Finite Automata (NFA).

$M = (Q, \Sigma, \delta, q_0, F)$

Where $Q, \Sigma, \delta, q_0, F$ are defined as follows: Q = Internal states Finite Set; Σ = "Input alphabet" are known as finite set of symbols; $\delta = Q \times (\Sigma) \rightarrow P(Q)$; q_0 ÎQ is Initial states set; and $F \subseteq Q$ is Final states set

Regarding the range of δ, there is a difference between NFA and DFA. The range of δ in NFA lies in powerset *P(Q)*.

If there is a series of movements that gets the machine to the desired state at the end of the string, then an NFA will accept the string (Vayadande et al., 2022).

- **Example 2.2:** Create a Non-Deterministic Finite Automaton (NFA) that can identify a language made up of all strings that, when counted from the end, have a 1 in the third position over the alphabet {0,1}.
- **Solution**

are the beginning states. represents the ultimate or concluding stage (Holzer & Kutrib, 2009).

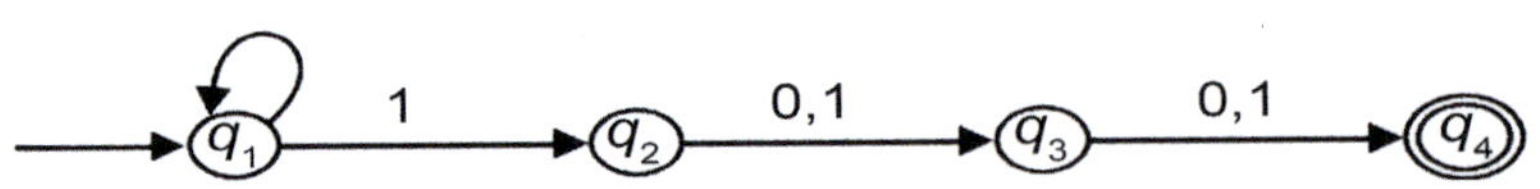

- **Example 2.3***:* Construct a non-deterministic finite automaton (NFA) that recognizes a language defined as |x| 3 and the third symbol of x from the right is 'a'.
- **Solution**

The conditions are

i. The two final symbols can only be either 'a' or 'b'.
ii. The third symbol from the right is the letter 'a'.
iii. The symbol can be 'a' or 'b' in any place except for the last three positions (Leung, 1998).

The NFA is shown in Figure 2.3 Below

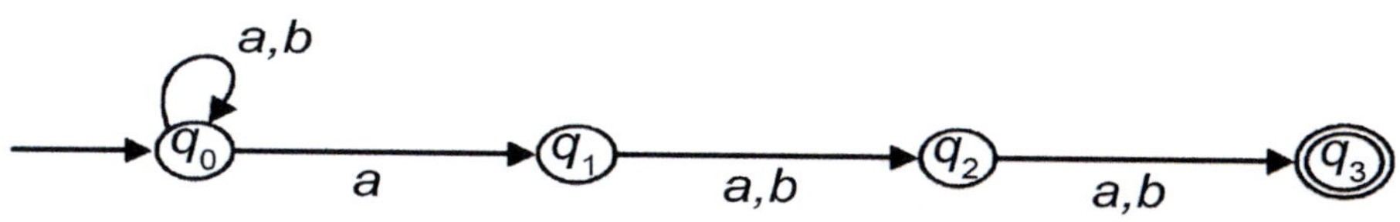

Figure 2.3. *Illustration of an NFA.*

Source: Xaivier L, Creative Commons License.

Did you know?

In the 1940s, Warren McCulloch and Walter Pitts made significant advances to the concept of finite automata by modeling neural networks and brain activities using them.

2.3. EQUIVALENCE OF DFA AND NFA

- **Definition**

and , two finite automata, are equal if

$L(M_1) = L(M_2)$,

i.e., assuming they use the same language

The same class of languages is recognized by both DFA and NFA. It is significant to remember that each NFA has a corresponding DFA. Let's use an example to demonstrate how to convert an NDA to a DFA (Câmpeanu et al., 2005).

- **Example 2.4.** Find a finite state automaton that is deterministic given the Unpredictable FSA.

$M = (\{q_0, q_1\}, \{a, b\}, \delta, q_0, \{q_1\})$

Using the state table diagram shown below

δ	a	b
q_0	$\{q_0, q_1\}$	$\{q_1\}$
q_1	Æ	$\{q_0, q_1\}$

- **Solution**

Let $M' = (Q', \Sigma, \delta', q_0', F')$ be a deterministic finite state automaton (DFA),

Where; $Q' = \{[q0], [q1], [q0, q1], [Æ]\}$; $q¢0 = [q0]$; and $F' = \{[q1], [q0, q1]\}$

Please keep in mind that [] only represents one state. Moving on, let's define δ' for the DFA (Jiang et al., 1991).

δ'	a	b
$[q_0]$	$[q_0, q_1]$	$[q_1]$
$[q_1]$	Æ	$[q_0, q_1]$
$[q_0, q_1]$	$[q_0, q_1]$	$[q_0, q_1]$
Æ	Ø	Æ

It is important to mention that

$$\delta'([q_0,q_1],a)=[q_0,q_1]$$

$$\delta'([q_0,q_1],a)=\delta(q_0,a)\cup\delta(q_1,a)$$

Since

$$=\{q_0,q_1\}\cup\ \emptyset$$

$$=\{q_1,q_1\}$$

And

$$\delta'([q_0,q_1],b)=[q_0,q_1]$$

Since

$$\delta'([q_0,q_1],b)=\delta(q_0,b)\cup\delta(q_1,b)$$
$$=\{q_1\}\cup\{q_0,q_1\}$$
$$=\{q_0,q_1\}$$

Here any subset containing is (Figure 2.4)

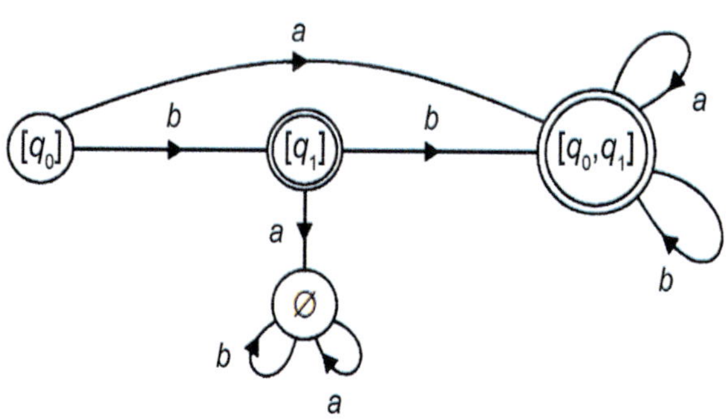

Figure 2.4. *Illustration of the final state in DFA. This is shown as below.*

- **Example 2.5**: Considering the NDA shown in Figure 2.5(a) and δ depicted in Figure 2.5(b).

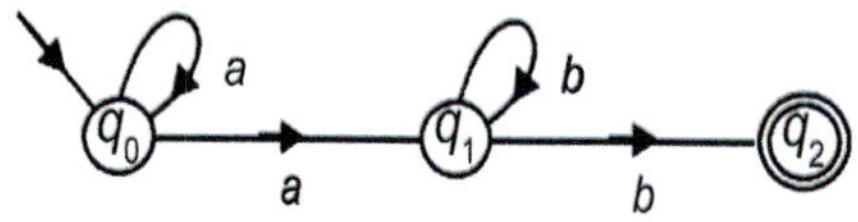

Fig. (a)

	a	b
q_0	$\{q_0, q_1\}$	$\emptyset$
q_1	$\emptyset$	$\{q_1, q_2\}$
q_2	$\emptyset$	$\emptyset$

Figure 2.5. *Illustration of the NDA.*

Find the comparable DFA for the NDA mentioned above.

- **Solution**

The conversion of a nondeterministic finite automaton (NDA) to a deterministic finite automaton (DFA) is achieved using the subset construction method, as seen in the State table diagram below (Bollig et al., 2009).

	a	b
$[q_0]$	$[q_0, q_1]$	$\emptyset$
$[q_0, q_1]$	$[q_0, q_1]$	$[q_1, q_2]$
$[q_1, q_2]$	$\emptyset$	$[q_1, q_2]$
$\emptyset$	$\emptyset$	$\emptyset$

Note that the final state in this case is any subset that contains .

ACTIVITY 2.1

For a given language, create a DFA and an NFA and show how they are equivalent. Select a moderately complicated language, like strings over {a, b} that don't have three consecutive 'a's. Draw the state diagrams for the NFA and DFA, and then demonstrate how to transform the NFA into a DFA equivalent step-by-step. Discuss about the benefits and drawbacks of using NFAs and DFAs in this situation.

2.4. REGULAR EXPRESSION

2.4.1. Regular Languages

Languages that can be built using the three basic set operations are referred to as regular languages: (a) Union, (b) Concatenation, and (c) Kleene star (Barrington et al., 1992).

A regular language can be defined as:

- **Definition:**

Consider an alphabet denoted by the symbol Σ. The class of "regular languages" over the alphabet Σ is defined inductively as follows:

1. The language represented by the symbol Ø is a regular language.
2. Every symbol σ in Σ is a regular language represented by {σ}.
3. For each natural number n greater than or equal to 2, if L_1, L_2, ..., L_n are languages, then the union of L_1, L_2, ..., L_n is also a language (Habarra & Jiang, 1991).
4. For each integer n greater than or equal to 2, if L_1, L_2, ..., L_n are languages, then $L_1 \circ L_2 \circ \ldots \circ L_n$ is also a language, where ∘ is the concatenation.
5. If L is a regular language, then L* is also a regular language. Both occurrences are regular, L* is the Kleen star of L.
6. No other language may be classified as a regular language unless it is constructed according to criteria (a) to (e).

The Kleen star is defined as: if *A* is a set of symbols (or an alphabet), the Kleene star of *A*, denoted as A^*, is defined as: $A^*=\{\epsilon\} \cup A \cup AA \cup AAA \cup \ldots$

Examples:

a. L is a regular language according to rule (a).
b. The language L = {a, ab} is a language over the alphabet Σ = {a, b} because both {a} and {b} are regular languages according to rule (b). According to rule (d), it can be deduced that the composition of sets {a} ∘ {b} = {ab} is a regular language. Applying rule (c), it can be observed that the union of {a} and {ab} is equal to L, which is a regular language (Denis, 2001).
c. The language over the alphabet {0, 1} consisting of strings that contain an even number of 0's can be represented by the regular expression (1*((01*) (01*))*) or simply 1*(01* 01*)*.

2.4.2. Regular Expressions

The purpose of regular expressions is to serve as a mathematical tool for representing regular languages (Bartoli et al., 2016). These are built using a variety of fundamental components and operations. This representation makes use of parenthesis, the operations +, *, and *, along with symbol strings from an alphabet Σ.

With the operations +, ∘ and * (which stand for union, concatenation, and Kleene star), the symbols {a, b, c}, the empty string ∊, and the empty set ∅ are combined to generate a regular expression (Asarin et al., 2002).

- **Examples**

0 + 1 represents the set {0,1}

1 represents the set {1}

0 represents the set {0}

(0 + 1) 1 represents the set {01, 11}

(a + b) · (b+ c) represents the set {ab, bb, ac, bc}

$$(0+1)^* = \in + (0+1) + (0+1)(0+1) + \cdots\cdots = \Sigma^*$$
$$(0+1)^* = (0+1)(0+1)^* = \Sigma^+ = \Sigma^* - \{\varepsilon\}$$

2.4.3. Generating Regular Expressions

Assume that Σ = {*a*, *b*, *c*}

"Zero or more a's" is indicated by the symbol a*.

Saying "zero or more ab's," such as { , ab, abab,..., requires saying (ab)*.

One or more: To express "one or more a's," you can use the notation aa* (or equivalently a*a), as a* denotes "zero or more a's." Similarly, you can represent "one or more ab's" as ab(ab)*, which means the set of strings {ab, abab, ababab, ...}.

Zero or one: It can be defined as an alternative 'a' with (a + λ) (Ye et al., 2020).

Any string at all: To represent any string using the alphabet Σ = {a, b, c}, you can utilize the regular expression (a + b + c)*.

Any string that is not empty: The characters used to write this are any character chosen from the set Σ = {a, b, c}, followed by any random string. ((a + b + c) (a ° b + c)*

Any string not containing: You can use (b + c)* to describe any string that does not contain a 'a' (with Σ = {*a*, *b*, *c*}),

Any string containing exactly one: To characterize any string with a single "a" in it. On either side of the 'a,' write "any string not containing an a," such as (b + c)* a (b + c)* (Flores et al., 2020).

2.4.4. Regular Expression-Defined Languages

Regular expressions and the languages they represent have a very basic correspondence (Mignot et al., 2017):

Regular expressions	L (Regular expressions)
x, for each x ∈ Σ	{x}
λ	{λ}
Æ	{ }
(r_1)	$L(r_1)$
r_1^*	$(L(r_1))^*$
$r_1 r_2$	$L(r_1)\ L(r_2)$
$r_1 + r_2$	$L(r_1) \cup L(r_2)$

2.4.5. Regular Expressions to NFA

a. The regular expression indicates the language {x} for each x in Σ. That language is precisely represented by the NFA, which has a single start state and a single final state as shown below (García et al., 2011).

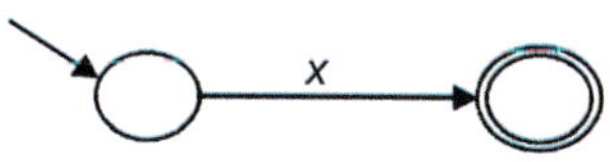

NFA for *x*

b. The language , or the language that only contains the empty string, is indicated by the regular expression .

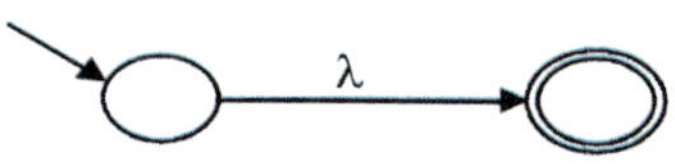

NFA for λ

c. The regular expression ∅ represents the language that has no strings, including the empty string (Navarro & Raffinot, 2005).

NFA for ∅

d. To achieve juxtaposition, where strings in L() are followed by strings in L( ), we connect the NFAs in a chain as demonstrated.

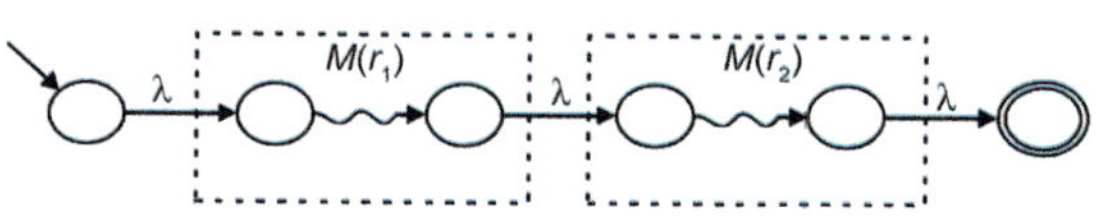

NFA for r_1r_2

e. In a regular expression, "+" stands for "or," thus we would use an NFA with several pathways.

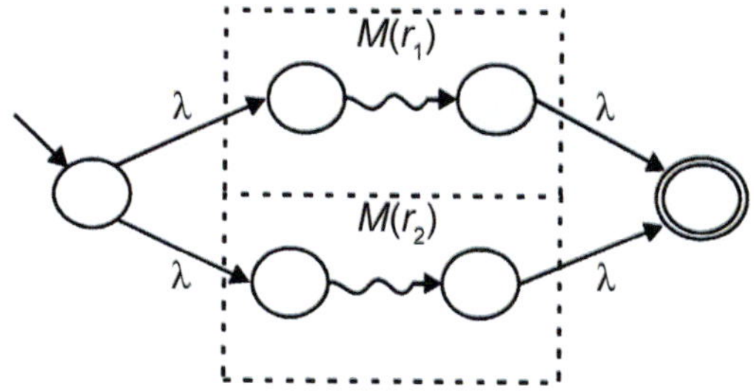

NFA for $r_1 + r_2$

f. Since the star (*) indicates that the regular expression has been applied zero or more times, an NFA loop must be established (Pao & Cheung, 2013).

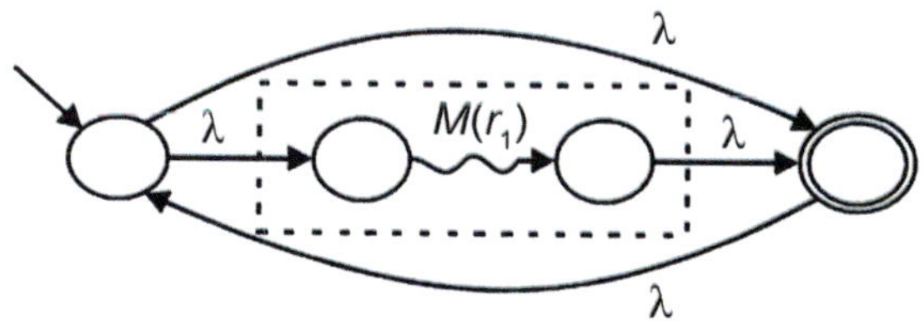

2.4.6. NFAs to Regular Expression

The following is the fundamental method for converting NFA to Regular Expressions:

i. Convert an NFA with several final states to one with just one final state. Create a λ-transition from each of the initial, nonfinal state to the new, single final state (Lee, 2008).

ii. The NFA can be regarded as a generalized transition graph, resembling an NFA but having the capability to provide labels to edges using any regular expressions. Each label on the edges of a Non-deterministic Finite Automaton (NFA) can be either λ or an element of a regular expression.

iii. The process involves systematically eliminating states from the NFA, while simultaneously relabeling the edges, until only the start and end states are left (Yamamoto et al., 2007).

iv. Derive the final regular expression from the two-state automaton that is generated.

The regular expression derived in the final phase identifies the identical language as the initial NFA.

Remember

Any NFA can be transformed into a DFA that is equal and capable of understanding the same language. Creating states in the DFA that match sets of states in the NFA is the procedure known as the subset building algorithm.

2.5. TWO-WAY FINITE AUTOMATA

Two-way finite automata are machines capable of processing input strings in both forward and backward directions. These machines are equipped with a "read head" that has the ability to travel in either the left or right direction along the input string (Geffert et al., 2007). Similar to finite automata, two-way finite automata consists of a Q of states finite set. They can either be nondeterministic (2NFA) or deterministic (2DFA). They exclusively accept regular sets, such as common finite automata. It is assumed that the symbols in the input string are placed in separate cells of a finite tape, with one symbol per cell, as shown in the diagram. The input string is separated by the left and right endmarkers |— and —|. The input alphabet excludes the endmarkers (Pighizzini, 2013).

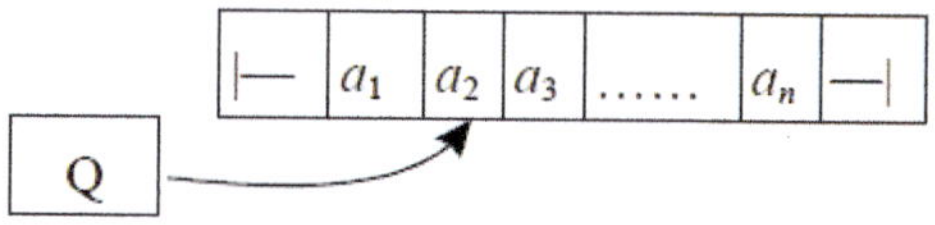

- **Definition**

A 2DFA is an octuple

$$M = (Q, \Sigma, |\!—, —\!|, \delta, s, t, r)$$

Where Q is the set of all possible states; Σ is an input alphabet's finite set; The left endmarker is |—; and the right endmarker is —| ∉ Σ , and the transition function δ Q × (Σ ∪ {|—, —|}) → (Q × {L, R}) is defined. The start state is denoted by s Q , accept state by t Q, and the reject state by r Q,

when r ≠ t, such that for any states q,

δ(q,t) = (u,R) for some u ∈ Q,

δ(q, —|) = (v,L) for some v ∈ Q,

and for all symbols $b \in \Sigma \cup \{|\!—\}$

$$\delta(t,b) = (t,R), \qquad \delta(r,b) = (r,R).$$
$$\delta(t,—\!|) = (t,L), \qquad \delta(r,—\!|) = (r,L).$$

The function δ takes two parameters: a state and a symbol and returns a new state and the head's direction of motion. For instance, if δ (p, b) = (q, d), the machine will move its head one cell in the direction of d and transition to state q when it is in state p and reading a tape cell with symbol b (Kapoutsis & Zakzok, 2021).

2.6. FINITE AUTOMATA WITH OUTPUT

2.6.1. Definition

The components of a finite-state machine M are as follows: an initial state (), a transition function (δ) that assigns an output to each state and input pair, an output function (λ) that assigns an output to each state and input pair, a finite set Q of states, a finite input alphabet (Σ), and a finite output alphabet (O) (Tao & Chen, 2000).

Let M be a finite state machine with $M = (Q, \Sigma, O, \delta, \lambda, q_0)$. For each pair of states and input, the values of the output function λ and the transition function δ are indicated using a state table (Khaleel et al., 2016).

2.6.2. Mealey Machine

Finite automata often produce binary output, meaning they either accept or reject a given string. The determination mostly depends on whether the initial state leads to the attainment of the ultimate state. By eliminating this limitation, we are attempting to explore a paradigm in which the outputs can be selected from a different set of symbols (Amato et al., 2010).

In the most common scenario, the values of the output function F(t) depend on the current input x(t) and state q(t) (Kalihari et al., 2013).

$$F(t) = \lambda(q(t), x(t))$$

Where the output function is denoted by λ.

"Mealey machine" is the name given to this model.

A six-tuple $(Q, \Sigma, O, \delta, \lambda, q_0)$ is called a "Mealey machine" if all of the symbols (aside from λ) have the same meaning as described in the sections before (Yang, 1996).

The function λ maps elements from the set Σ × Q to the set O.

2.6.3. Moore Machine

If the output function F (t) is entirely determined by the current state and is not influenced by the current input q (t), then the output function f (t) can be expressed as

$F(t) = \lambda(q(t))$

A six-tuple (Q, Σ, O, δ, λ, q_0) meaning for a symbol is called a Moore machine (Pavithran et al., 2022).

Remember

An NFA may have more than one transition for the same input symbol or may not have any transition at all, whereas a DFA has exactly one transition for each input symbol from every state.

- **Example 2.6**

Draw the state diagram given the state table below, which represents a finite-state machine with states $Q = \{q0 , q1 , q2 , q3\}$, input alphabet $\Sigma = \{0,1\}$ and output alphabet O = {0, 1}.

State	δ		λ	
	Input		Output	
	0	1	0	1
q_0	q_1	q_0	1	0
q_1	q_3	q_0	1	1
q_2	q_1	q_2	0	1
q_3	q_2	q_1	0	0

- **Solution**

The provided state table corresponds to a finite-state machine with output. Below is the state diagram that corresponds to the given information (Solov, 2013).

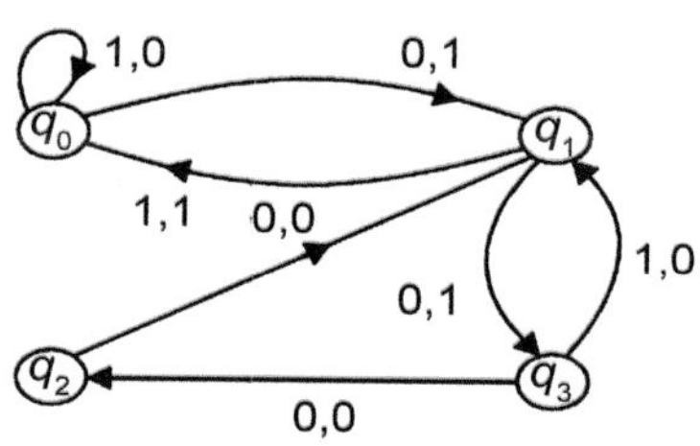

2.7. REGULAR SETS' (LANGUAGES) PROPERTIES

A regular set, often known as a regular language, is a set that can be accepted by a finite automaton (Diekert et al., 2022).

2.7.1. Closure

A set is said to be closed under an operation if, for any of the elements in the set, applying the operation will always yield another element that is also part of the set. For example, since x + y is always an integer when x and y are integers, the set of integers is closed under addition. Nevertheless, division of integers is not closed: when considering integers x and y, it is important to note that the result of dividing x by y may or may not be an integer (Lilly, 1992).

Numerous operations are defined on languages:

$L1 \cup L2$: strings in either or .

$L1 \cap L2$: strings in both and .

$L_1 L_2$: strings made up of one L_1 string, and one L_2 string

$-L_2$: All strings (over the same alphabet) not in (Altmann et al., 1998).

: Concatenated strings from L, zero or more

$L1$ $L2$: strings in that are not in .

: strings in , reversed.

We will demonstrate that for each of these processes, the set of regular languages is closed (Jeavons et al., 1997).

2.7.2. Union, Negation, Concatenation, Reverse, Kleene Star

The general method is as follows:

i. Create automata (NFA or DFA) for every language that is involved.
ii. Demonstrate how to merge the automata to create a new automaton that can understand the target language.
iii. We will determine that the language is regular since NFA/DFA represents it (Nagy, 2021).

2.7.2.1. Union of and

i. Establish a new state.

ii. From each of the initial start states to the new start state, perform a λ-transition (Colazzo et al., 2017).

2.7.2.2. Concatenation of and

i. Add a λ-transition between each of the ending state and the starting state.

ii. Make the first final states non-final (Dudakov & Karlov, 2021).

2.7.3. Set Difference and Intersection

Starting with automata for the original language and constructing a new automaton to represent the operation performed on the first language, it can be shown that regular languages are closed under intersection and set difference, similar to other operations (Deza et al., 1978). By using this structure, a brand-new machine is created, each of whose states is identified by an ordered pair of state names, with the first element from and the second from .

i. Create an initial state labeled as the combination of the start state of and the start state of .

ii. Continue repeating until no additional arcs can be added:

   a. Locate a state (A, B) that does not have a transition for a certain x in the set Σ.I

   b. Implement a transition on variable x that moves from the state (A, B) to the state (δ (A, x), δ (B, x)). (If this state is not currently in existence, please proceed to establish it) (Margalit & Knott, 1989).

2.7.3.1. Negation of

a. Begin with a fully completed DFA rather than an NFA.

b. Turn every state that is final into a nonfinal state and vice versa.

2.7.3.2. Kleene Star of

a. Create a new start state and use a λ-transition to link it to the initial start state.

b. Create a new final state and use λ-transitions to connect it to the previous one, which now becomes nonfinal.

c. Two λ-transitions are used to link the new final state and new start state (Pinkas et al., 2018).

2.7.3.3. Reverse of

a. Begin with a single final state automaton.

b. Set the final state to initial and the initial state to final.

c. Turn each arc around in the other direction.

The same construction is done for both intersection and set difference. The variations arise in the selection of the final states (Deuber et al., 1997).

2.7.3.4. Intersection

Make a state (A, B) as final if both

a. A is a final state in and

b. B is a final state in

2.7.3.5. Set Difference

If state A is a final state in language and state B is not a final state in language , then designate state A as final (Ressayre, 1988).

2.8. PUMPING LEMMA

2.8.1. Principle of Pumping Lemma

a. If a language that contains an endless number of words is regular, it can be described by a deterministic finite automaton (DFA).

b. The DFA possesses a finite quantity of states (let's assume).

c. Given that the language is limitless, it is unavoidable that certain strings within the language will have a length greater than n.

d. For a string with a length exceeding n to be accepted by the DFA, it is necessary for the path through the DFA to contain a cycle (Borchardt, 2004).

e. Any number of cycles should lead to another string that has the DFA's approval.

The "pumping lemma" for regular languages is a method used to demonstrate that a given infinite language is not regular (Boonyavatana & Slutzki, 1988). The proof is always conducted through the method of "contradiction". The technique is as follows:

a. Let's assume that the language L is regular.

b. According to the Pigeon-hole principle, if a string in L is long enough, it is bound to repeat a state in the DFA. As a result, the walk will contain a "cycle".

c. Show that a string that does not belong to L may be formed by "pumping" the cycle, or repeating it a specific number of times.

d. Determine that L is not a regular language (Fetaji et al., 2021).

2.8.2. Applying the Pumping Lemma

2.8.2.1. Pumping Lemma Definition

There exists a positive integer *m* such that every string w in L, i.e. *w*∈ *L,* and having a length of *m* or more, the pumping length, L can be divided into three parts, namely " ", if L is an infinite regular language (Câmpeanu et al., 2003).

i. .

ii.

iii. = z is also in L for all i = 0, 1, 2, 3, ...

Utilizing this lemma, we must demonstrate (de Mendívil & Garitagoitia, 2014).

- For any given value of m,
- Let's select a value of *w* from the set L, and we will ensure that *w* has a length of at least '*m*'.

- Given any decomposition of string *w* into substrings *xyz*, where the length of substring $|xy|$ is not higher than *m* and substring *y* is not ,
- we can always select an index such that the string z is not a member of language L (Kwee & Otto, 2017).
- **Example 2.7:** Prove that $L = \{a^n b^n : n \geq 0\}$ is not regular.
- **Solution**

i. Although *m* is unknown to us, let's assume that it exists.

ii. Select a string where $n > m$, so that the only *a's* can appear in any prefix of length '*m*'.

iii. Although the breakdown of *w* into *xyz* is unknown, *xy* must only include a's because $|xy| \leq m$. Furthermore, *y* is not empty (Lemma et al., 2012).

iv. Select $i = 0$. Without altering the quantity of *b's*, this eliminates $|y|$ *a's* from the string. The resultant string does not belong in L since it contains more *b's* than *a's*.

Consequently, L is not a regular language (Maletti, 2005).

SUMMARY

- Systems having discrete inputs and outputs, and a finite number of states can be effectively modeled using finite automata. Non-deterministic finite automata (NFA) permit several alternative moves from a given configuration, whereas deterministic finite automata (DFA) allow each step to be uniquely determined by the present configuration. Despite their differences, both Deterministic Finite Automata (DFAs) and Non-deterministic Finite Automata (NFAs) recognize the same category of languages, which are referred to as regular languages.
- Regular expressions offer a concise and versatile method for defining regular languages by the the use of union, concatenation, and the Kleene star operations. The chapter shows the process of constructing regular expressions and transforming them into finite automata, as well as the reverse process of converting finite automata back into regular expressions. In addition, we demonstrate two-way finite automata, which have the ability to read input strings in both directions, as well as finite automata with output, which are represented by Mealy and Moore machines.
- Understanding finite automata and regular expressions is essential for designing efficient string processors and gaining a solid grasp of the theoretical foundations of computer science. These concepts have practical applications and provide insights into the fundamental nature of computation and systems.

REVIEW QUESTIONS

1. Define deterministic finite automata (DFA) and non-deterministic finite automata (NFA). What are the key differences between them?
2. Explain the process of converting an NFA to an equivalent DFA.
3. What are regular expressions? How are they used to define regular languages?
4. Describe the Kleene star operation and provide an example.
5. How can regular expressions be converted into finite automata?
6. What is the significance of two-way finite automata, and how do they differ from one-way finite automata?
7. Explain the models of finite automata with output, specifically the Mealy and Moore machines.
8. Provide an example of a regular language and construct a corresponding DFA.

MULTIPLE CHOICE QUESTIONS

1. **Which of the following is a distinguishing feature of a deterministic finite automaton (DFA)?**

   a. It allows multiple transitions for a single input.

   b. It has a finite number of states.

c. It has exactly one transition for each input symbol from each state.

d. It can have an infinite number of states.

2. **What does the Kleene star operation denote in regular expressions?**

   a. Zero or more occurrences of the preceding element.

   b. One or more occurrences of the preceding element.

   c. Zero or one occurrence of the preceding element.

   d. Exactly one occurrence of the preceding element.

3. **What is the primary difference between DFA and NFA?**

   a. DFA can have multiple transitions for the same input symbol.

   b. NFA can have multiple transitions for the same input symbol.

   c. DFA has an infinite number of states.

   d. NFA has exactly one transition for each input symbol from each state.

4. **Which model of finite automaton is used to produce outputs in addition to accepting/rejecting strings?**

   a. DFA

   b. NFA

   c. Mealy Machine

   d. Two-way Finite Automaton

5. **How is a regular language defined?**

   a. A language that can be represented using a DFA.

   b. A language that cannot be represented using a DFA.

   c. A language that can only be represented using an NFA.

   d. A language that cannot be represented using regular expressions.

6. **What is the purpose of the transition function in a finite automaton?**

   a. To define the initial state of the automaton.

   b. To determine the next state for a given input symbol.

   c. To define the final states of the automaton.

   d. To count the number of states in the automaton

Answers to Multiple Questions

1. (c); 2. (a); 3. (b); 4. (c); 5. (a); 6. (b)

REFERENCES

1. Altmann, G. T., van Nice, K. Y., Garnham, A., & Henstra, J. A. (1998). Late closure in context. *Journal of Memory and Language, 38*(4), 459–484.
2. Amato, C., Bonet, B., & Zilberstein, S. (2010). Finite-state controllers based on Mealy machines for centralized and decentralized POMDPs. In *Proceedings of the AAAI Conference on Artificial Intelligence, 24*(1), 1052–1058.
3. Antimirov, V. (1996). Partial derivatives of regular expressions and finite automaton constructions. *Theoretical Computer Science, 155*(2), 291–319.
4. Asarin, E., Caspi, P., & Maler, O. (2002). Timed regular expressions. *Journal of the ACM, 49*(2), 172–206.
5. Barrington, D. A. M., Compton, K., Straubing, H., & Thérien, D. (1992). Regular languages in NC1. *Journal of Computer and System Sciences, 44*(3), 478–499.
6. Bartoli, A., De Lorenzo, A., Medvet, E., & Tarlao, F. (2016). Inference of regular expressions for text extraction from examples. *IEEE Transactions on Knowledge and Data Engineering, 28*(5), 1217–1230.
7. Bensch, S., Bordihn, H., Holzer, M., & Kutrib, M. (2009). On input-revolving deterministic and nondeterministic finite automata. *Information and Computation, 207*(11), 1140–1155.
8. Bollig, B., Habermehl, P., Kern, C., & Leucker, M. (2009). Angluin-Style Learning of NFA. In *IJCAI* (Vol. 9, pp. 1004–1009).
9. Boonyavatana, R., & Slutzki, G. (1988). The interchange or pump (di) lemmas for context-free languages. *Theoretical Computer Science, 56*(3), 321–338.
10. Borchardt, B. (2004). A pumping lemma and decidability problems for recognizable tree series. *Acta Cybernetica, 16*(4), 509–544.
11. Brüggemann-Klein, A. (1993). Regular expressions into finite automata. *Theoretical Computer Science, 120*(2), 197–213.
12. Câmpeanu, C., Kari, L., & P⊠un, A. (2005). Results on Transforming NFA into DFCA. *Fundamenta Informaticae, 64*(1–4), 53–63.
13. Câmpeanu, C., Salomaa, K., & Yu, S. (2003). A formal study of practical regular expressions. *International Journal of Foundations of Computer Science, 14*(6), 1007–1018.
14. Choueka, Y. (1978). Finite automata, definable sets, and regular expressions over ⊠n-tapes. *Journal of Computer and System Sciences, 17*(1), 81–97.
15. Colazzo, D., Ghelli, G., & Sartiani, C. (2017). Linear time membership in a class of regular expressions with counting, interleaving, and unordered concatenation. *ACM Transactions on Database Systems (TODS), 42*(4), 1–44.
16. De Giacomo, G., & Favorito, M. (2021). Compositional approach to translate LTLf/LDLf into deterministic finite automata. In *Proceedings of the International Conference on Automated Planning and Scheduling* (Vol. 31, pp. 122–130).
17. de Mendívil, J. R. G., & Garitagoitia, J. R. (2014). Fuzzy languages with infinite range accepted by fuzzy automata: Pumping Lemma and determinization procedure.

Fuzzy Sets and Systems, 249, 1–26.

18. Denis, F. (2001). Learning regular languages from simple positive examples. *Machine Learning, 44*, 37–66.
19. Deuber, W. A., Erd⊠s, P., Gunderson, D. S., Kostochka, A. V., & Meyer, A. G. (1997). Intersection statements for systems of sets. *Journal of Combinatorial Theory, Series A, 79*(1), 118–132.
20. Deza, M., Erd⊠s, P., & Frankl, P. (1978). Intersection properties of systems of finite sets. *Proceedings of the London Mathematical Society, 3*(2), 369–384.
21. Diekert, V., Fernau, H., & Wolf, P. (2022). Properties of graphs specified by a regular language. *Acta Informatica, 59*(4), 357–385.
22. Dudakov, S., & Karlov, B. (2021). On decidability of theories of regular languages. *Theory of Computing Systems, 65*(3), 462–478.
23. Fernau, H., Heggernes, P., & Villanger, Y. (2015). A multi-parameter analysis of hard problems on deterministic finite automata. *Journal of Computer and System Sciences, 81*(4), 747–765.
24. Fetaji, M., Fetaji, B., & Asilkan, Ö. (2021). Analyses of the case studies for the efficiency of pumping lemma for the context-free languages. *CRJ,* (1), 9–15.
25. Flores, C. A., Figueroa, R. L., Pezoa, J. E., & Zeng-Treitler, Q. (2020). CREGEX: A biomedical text classifier based on automatically generated regular expressions. *IEEE Access, 8*, 29270–29280.
26. García, P., López, D., Ruiz, J., & Álvarez, G. I. (2011). From regular expressions to smaller NFAs. *Theoretical Computer Science, 412*(41), 5802–5807.
27. Geffert, V., Mereghetti, C., & Pighizzini, G. (2007). Complementing two-way finite automata. *Information and Computation, 205*(8), 1173–1187.
28. Gruber, H., & Holzer, M. (2015). From finite automata to regular expressions and back—A summary on description complexity. *International Journal of Foundations of Computer Science, 26*(8), 1009–1040.
29. Habarra, O., & Jiang, T. (1991). Learning regular languages from counterexamples. *Journal of Computer and System Sciences, 43*(2), 299–316.
30. Holzer, M., & Kutrib, M. (2009). Nondeterministic finite automata—Recent results on the description and computational complexity. *International Journal of Foundations of Computer Science, 20*(4), 563–580.
31. Jeavons, P., Cohen, D., & Gyssens, M. (1997). Closure properties of constraints. *Journal of the ACM (JACM), 44*(4), 527–548.
32. Jiang, T., McDowell, E., & Ravikumar, B. (1991). The structure and complexity of minimal NFA's over a unary alphabet. *International Journal of Foundations of Computer Science, 2*(2), 163–182.
33. Kalihari, R., Verma, T., & Jaiswal, A. (2013). Concept of automated machine using mealy. *International Journal of Computer Applications Technology and Research, 2*(3), 335–339.
34. Kapoutsis, C., & Zakzok, M. (2021). Alternation in two-way finite automata. *Theoretical Computer Science, 870*, 75–102.

35. Khaleel, G., Turaev, S., Al-Shaikhli, I., & Tamrin, M. M. (2016). An overview of cryptosystems based on finite automata. *Journal of Advanced Review on Scientific Research, 27*(1), 1–7.

36. Kumar, A., & Verma, A. K. (2014). A novel algorithm for the conversion of parallel regular expressions to non-deterministic finite automata. *Applied Mathematics & Information Sciences, 8*(1), 95–101.

37. Kwee, K., & Otto, F. (2017). A pumping lemma for ordered restarting automata. In *Descriptional Complexity of Formal Systems: 19th IFIP WG 1.02 International Conference, DCFS 2017, Milano, Italy, July 3–5, 2017, Proceedings* (Vol. 19, pp. 226–237).

38. Lee, T. H. (2008). Hardware architecture for high-performance regular expression matching. *IEEE Transactions on Computers, 58*(7), 984–993.

39. Lemma, M. G., Coscioni, E., Tritto, F. P., Centofanti, P., Fondacone, C., Salica, A., & Genoni, M. (2012). On-pump versus off-pump coronary artery bypass surgery in high-risk patients: Operative results of a prospective randomized trial (on-off study). *The Journal of Thoracic and Cardiovascular Surgery, 143*(3), 625–631.

40. Leung, H. (1998). On finite automata with limited nondeterminism. *Acta Informatica, 35*(7), 595–624.

41. Li, Y., & Pedrycz, W. (2005). Fuzzy finite automata and fuzzy regular expressions with membership values in lattice-ordered monoids. *Fuzzy Sets and Systems, 156*(1), 68–92.

42. Lilly, D. K. (1992). A proposed modification of the germano subgrid-scale closure method. *Phys Fluids A, 4*, 633–635.

43. Lucas, S. M., & Reynolds, T. J. (2005). Learning deterministic finite automata with a smart state labeling evolutionary algorithm. *IEEE Transactions on Pattern Analysis and Machine Intelligence, 27*(7), 1063–1074.

44. Maletti, A. (2005). Relating tree series transducers and weighted tree automata. *International Journal of Foundations of Computer Science, 16*(4), 723–741.

45. Margalit, A., & Knott, G. D. (1989). An algorithm for computing the union, intersection or difference of two polygons. *Computers & Graphics, 13*(2), 167–183.

46. Melnikov, B., & Melnikova, A. (2018). Pseudo-automata for generalized regular expressions. *International Journal of Open Information Technologies, 6*(1), 1–8.

47. Mignot, L., Sebti, N. O., & Ziadi, D. (2017). Tree automata constructions from regular expressions: A comparative study. *Fundamenta Informaticae, 156*(1), 69–94.

48. Nagy, B. (2021). Union-Freeness Revisited—Between deterministic and nondeterministic union-free languages. *International Journal of Foundations of Computer Science, 32*(5), 551–573.

49. Navarro, G., & Raffinot, M. (2005). New techniques for regular expression searching. *Algorithmica, 41*, 89–116.

50. Omlin, C. W., & Giles, C. L. (1996). Constructing deterministic finite-state automata in recurrent neural networks. *Journal of the ACM (JACM), 43*(6), 937–972.

51. Pao, D., Or, N. L., & Cheung, R. C. (2013). A memory-based NFA regular expression match engine for signature-based intrusion detection. *Computer Communications, 36*(10, 11), 1255–1267.

52. Pavithran, P., Mathew, S., Namasudra, S., & Srivastava, G. (2022). A novel cryptosystem based on DNA cryptography, hyperchaotic systems and a randomly generated Moore machine for cyber-physical systems. *Computer Communications, 188*, 1–12.

53. Pighizzini, G. (2013). Two-way finite automata: Old and recent results. *Fundamenta Informaticae, 126*(2, 3), 225–246.

54. Pinkas, B., Schneider, T., & Zohner, M. (2018). Scalable private set intersection based on OT extension. *ACM Transactions on Privacy and Security (TOPS), 21*(2), 1–35.

55. Ressayre, J. P. (1988). Formal languages defined by the underlying structure of their words. *The Journal of Symbolic Logic, 53*(4), 1009–1026.

56. Solov'ev, V. V. (2013). Implementation of finite-state machines based on programmable logic ICs with the help of the merged model of Mealy and Moore machines. *Journal of Communications Technology and Electronics, 58*, 172–177.

57. Stearns, R. E., & Hunt III, H. B. (1985). On the equivalence and containment problems for unambiguous regular expressions, regular grammars and finite automata. *SIAM Journal on Computing, 14*(3), 598–611.

58. Tao, R., & Chen, S. (2000). Input-trees of finite automata and application to cryptanalysis. *Journal of Computer Science and Technology, 15*(4), 305–325.

59. Vayadande, K. B., Sheth, P., Shelke, A., Patil, V., Shevate, S., & Sawakare, C. (2022). Simulation and testing of deterministic finite automata machine. *International Journal of Computer Sciences and Engineering, 10*(1), 13–17.

60. Vayadande, K., Patel, K., Punde, N., Patil, S., Nikam, S., & Pathrabe, S. (2022). Non-deterministic finite automata to deterministic finite automata conversion by subset construction method using Python. *International Journal of Computer Sciences and Engineering, 10*(1), 1–5.

61. Yamamoto, H., Miyazaki, T., & Okamoto, M. (2007). Bit-parallel algorithms for translating regular expressions into NFAs. *IEICE Transactions on Information and Systems, 90*(2), 418–427.

62. Yang, W. (1996). Mealy machines are a better model of lexical analyzers. *Computer Languages, 22*(1), 27–38.

63. Ye, X., Chen, Q., Wang, X., Dillig, I., & Durrett, G. (2020). Sketch-driven regular expression generation from natural language and examples. *Transactions of the Association for Computational Linguistics, 8*, 679–694.

CHAPTER 3

Computational Complexity

LEARNING OBJECTIVES

After studying this chapter, you will be able to:

- Define and differentiate between decidable and intractable problems.
- Explain the concept of computational complexity and its significance.
- Identify and describe the different types of algorithmic complexities, including time and space complexities.
- Analyze algorithms to determine their time and space complexities.
- Describe polynomial-time algorithms and the classes P and NP.
- Understand and apply Big O, Big Omega, and Theta notations to algorithm analysis.
- Explain the significance of NP-complete problems and the Cook-Levin theorem.
- Discuss examples of NP-complete problems and their implications.
- Understand the significance of the Cook-Levin theorem in computational complexity theory.

KEY TERMS FROM THIS CHAPTER

Big O notation	Big omega notation
Computational complexity	Decidable problems
Intractable problems	NP-complete problems
polynomial time	Space complexity
theta notation	Time Complexity

UNIT INTRODUCTION

If there is a hypothetical algorithm that can solve a decision problem, it is said to be decidable. This chapter aims to identify the problems that can be solved by practical algorithms, which are capable of providing answers for instances of reasonable size within a reasonable time frame. These two concepts are not always identical. The satisfiability problem is computationally solvable, but, the existing methods do not significantly outperform the brute-force method, which involves examining an exponential number of examples individually (Goldreich, 2008). It has already been established that decidable issues involve algorithms. Multiple algorithms may exist for solving a decidable problem. Algorithms might vary in terms of their execution time and memory usage, even when given the identical input, resulting in different outcomes (Crossley et al., 2007). This phenomenon is commonly referred to as computational complexity. The question at hand relates to determining the most effective algorithm for addressing a choice problem. When addressing computational complexity, several fundamental aspects like as software, hardware, and data structure are typically disregarded (Stockmeyer, 1987). Computer science encompasses the fundamental principles of information, computing, and the practical methods used for their implementation and application. This chapter will explore various difficulties of algorithms, including polynomial time algorithms, the P and NP classes, and relevant examples (Blondel & Tsitsiklis, 2000). The set P consists of problems or languages that can be determined in polynomial time by a Turing machine or any equivalent computational model, based on the size of the instance. Nondeterministic polynomial time (NP) is defined similarly, but with relaxed restrictions on decision algorithms to allow for the use of nondeterministic approaches. There is a widely held belief that NP is a more extensive collection (García et al., 1987). This implies that the ability to make an informed guess and confirm it within a reasonable amount of time does not necessarily guarantee the existence of a regular algorithm that can solve the problem in polynomial time. However, there is currently insufficient evidence to support the idea that P is not equivalent to NP (Denef & Douglas, 2007). By using the concept of polynomial-time reduction, we examine NP-complete issues, which are the most challenging problems in the class NP. Additionally, we establish the Cook-Levin theorem, which states that the satisfiability problem belongs to this class of problems. This chapter delves into the topic of computational complexity, which is the categorization of computing issues based on the resources needed to solve them and their inherent difficulty. The first step in the chapter is to distinguish between intractable issues, for which there are no known efficient algorithms, and decidable problems, which contain algorithms that can potentially provide answers (Bossaerts et al., 2019). We explore algorithm efficiency measurement, presenting significant concepts like time and space complexity. We additionally examine at polynomial-time algorithms and the difference between P and NP complexity classes. The Cook-Levin theorem and numerous instances of NP-complete problems are used to show the importance of the idea of NP-completeness (Bossaerts & Murawski, 2017), which is also covered in this chapter.

3.1. TYPES OF COMPUTATIONAL COMPLEXITY

An algorithm's complexity is mostly quantified in two ways. These are:

1. Time complexity
2. Space complexity

When measuring algorithm complexity, worst-case possibilities are taken into account.

3.1.1. Time Complexity

The time complexity of a program is determined by the number of elementary instructions it requires to execute a given input. The value is calculated using the input's length (n). When analyzing the temporal complexity of algorithm 'A' for problem 'P', we denote the number of steps needed to produce the output from an input of size n as T(n). This indicates that the number of steps is either less than or equal to n. (In this scenario, we assume that each elementary instruction requires one processor instruction and one unit of time (Oliveto et al., 2007).

3.1.2. Space Complexity

The amount of memory required by a program to store basic objects while it is being executed is referred to as its space complexity. The length (n) of the input is used to calculate this number's value. S(n) represents the space complexity of algorithm 'A' for problem 'P'. It is ensured that an input of length *n* will not use more memory places than *n* to produce the output (Ben-Sasson & Galesi, 2003).

Remember

Big O Notation (O): used to express the worst-case scenario and the upper bound of an algorithm's time complexity.

3.2. VARIOUS NOTATIONS FOR TIME COMPLEXITY

Take four functions:

$f_1(n) = 2n$
$f_2(n) = n^2$
$f_3(n) = 2n^2$
$f_4(n) = 2n + 3$

Now, in the subsequent table, we are computing the values of the four functions for various values of *n* (Robinson, 1996).

Table 3.1. The Four Function Values for Various Values of n

Function	n = 0	= 2	= 10	= 50	= 100
	0	4	20	100	200
	0	4	100	2,500	10,000
	0	8	200	5,000	20,000
	4	7	1,027	11258999068 42627	12676506002282294014967 03205379

Source: John C Martin, Creative Commons License.

Among these, let's take a look at and . Both of them have a direct relationship with each other. When n is equal to zero, both of them produce identical outcomes. However, for values of . When comparing and , it becomes evident that they yield identical results for n = 0 and n = 2. However, for n = 2, the values of and are equal. It has been proven that the rate of growth for exponential functions surpasses that of polynomial functions (Lim et al., 2000). Based on this discussion, various growth rate notations can be derived. There are five widely recognized notations for growth rates of functions. These are:

i. Big oh notation, denoted as 'O'
ii. Big omega notation, denoted as
iii. Theta notation, denoted as
iv. Little-oh notation, denoted as 'o'
v. Little omega notation, denoted as ''

3.2.1. Big Oh Notation

Consider two functions, and , defined on the set of positive natural or real numbers. If a positive constant *C* and a value *k* exist such that, for all values of *n* higher than or equal to k, $f(n)$ is less than or equal to C multiplied by $g(n)$, then the function is said to be $O(g(n))$. The upper bound of an algorithm's worst-case time complexity is indicated by the notation "Big Oh" (Baber et al., 2014).

3.2.2. Rules Related to Big Oh

Take into consideration and , which have growth orders of $O(f(n))$ and $O(g(n))$, respectively.

i. + = max ($O(f(n))$, $O(g(n))$).

ii. * = O ($f(n)$* $g(n)$).

iii. C* = $O(f(n))$, where C is a constant (Mala & Ali, 2022).

3.2.3. Big Omega (Ω) Notation

Let us consider two functions defined on the set of positive natural numbers, $f(n)$ and $g(n)$. If there is a positive constant C and a value k such that for all values of n less than or equal to k, $f(n)$ is higher than or equal to C times $g(n)$, then $f(n)$ is said to have a lower bound of $g(n)$. Big omega indicates a function's asymptotic lower bound. It is the big oh notation's opposite (Angluin & Fisman, 2016).

3.2.4. Theta Notation (Θ)

Consider two functions, $f(n)$ and $g(n)$, defined for positive natural numbers (both real and integer).

$f(n)$ is called ($g(n)$) if there exist two positive constants and and a value k such that g(n)

$f(n)$ $g(n)$ for all n k (Srivastava, 2005).

The notation for a function to be in is defined as $f(n)$ $g(n)$ and $f(n)$ $g(n)$. Put simply, if two functions $f(n)$ and $g(n)$ satisfy the conditions $f(n) = O(g(n))$ and $f(n) = \Omega(g(n))$, then it may be stated that $f(n)$ = (g(n)) (Ishizeki et al., 2012).

3.2.5. Little-oh Notation (o)

Let $f(n)$ and $g(n)$ be two functions defined for positive natural numbers (real and integer). If a natural number k and a positive constant C exist such that $f(n)$ is always smaller than C multiplied by $g(n)$ for all values of n higher than or equal to k, then $f(n)$ is defined as being $o(g(n))$ (Sherman, 1991).

3.2.6. Little Omega Notation (ω)

Let $f(n)$ and $g(n)$ be two functions that can be real or integer values that are defined for positive natural numbers. $f(n)$ is defined as $\omega(g(n))$ if there is a natural number k and a positive constant C such that for all values of n greater than or equal to k, $f(n)$ is greater than C multiplied by $g(n)$ (Melnikov & Melnikova, 2020).

3.3. DIFFERENT TYPES OF TIME COMPLEXITY

We have already acquired knowledge about several notations of temporal complexity and distinct categories of issues. In order to address these issues, it is necessary to develop algorithms. To assess and determine the most suited method, it is necessary to calculate the temporal complexities of these algorithms. The design study of computational complexity theory and algorithms are closely related (Oliveto et al., 2007).

One aspect involves analyzing the resources utilized by a particular algorithm to solve a problem, such as time and space. The other aspect involves a more comprehensive investigation into all possible algorithms that could be used to solve the same problem. Various algorithms exhibit several sorts of time complexity. Within this part, we will explore many categories of time difficulties (Shah & Bhavsar, 2022).

3.3.1. Constant Time Complexity

An algorithm that operates independently of the input size is referred to as a constant time complexity algorithm. The algorithm exhibits constant time complexity, meaning that it takes an equal amount of time to execute regardless of the input size. The complexity is represented by the notation $O(1)$ (Thanh et al., 2016).

3.3.2. Logarithmic Time Complexity

A logarithmic time complexity algorithm is one that operates in logarithmic time as a function of the input. Because computers use the binary number system, logarithmic time complexity algorithms often have a foundation of 2. As a result, $log_2 n$ is often written as $log\ n$. Logarithmic time complexity is represented by the time complexity $O(log\ n)$ (Griewank, 1992).

3.3.3. Linear Time Complexity

An algorithm is said to be linear if its execution time increases linearly with the size of the input. The linear time complexity is represented by $O(n)$ (Kapovich et al., 2005).

3.3.4. Quasilinear Time Complexity

To delve into the concept of quasilinear time complexity, it is essential to have a solid understanding of linearithmic algorithms. The runtime of algorithms with a time-based complexity that exhibits a growth rate higher than linear but slower than logarithmic experiences an increase. The time-dependent complexity of an algorithm that evolves linearithmically is denoted by $O(n\ log\ n)$ (Najman & Couprie, 2006).

In 1978, Schnorr, Gurevich, and Shelah proposed the concept of quasilinear time complexity in their famous research work titled 'Satisfiability is quasilinear complete in NQL'. A quasilinear time complexity is given to an algorithm when its running time can be represented as *O(n (log n)k)*, where *k* is a value higher than or equal to 1. Quasilinear algorithm outperforms polynomial algorithms with degrees higher than 1 in terms of speed. Linearithmic algorithms are a specific type of quasilinear algorithm with a value of *k* equal to 1 (Bloch et al., 1998).

3.3.5. Average Case Time Complexity

Assume that the array's *kth* smallest element is the pivot element. Additionally, there are items that come before the spot where *k* is, and elements that come after the place where *k* is. As a result, is the time complexity for sorting the array's left half, and is the time complexity for sorting the array's right half (Ding et al., 2021).

The number of comparisons required to place the pivot element is equal to . The temporal complexity for the average case of quicksort on an array of n elements is:

$$T(n)=(n+1)+\frac{1}{n}\sum_{1\leq k\leq n} T(k-1)+T(n-k)$$

$$nT(n)=n(n+1)+\sum_{1\leq k\leq n} T(k-1)+T(n-k)$$

3.3.6. Polynomial Time Complexity

A polynomial in mathematics is a finite expression formed by combining variables and constants using subtraction, multiplication, addition, and non-negative integer exponents. An algorithm with polynomial time complexity is one whose maximum execution time is determined by a polynomial expression in the input's size. The complexity is represented by the notation *O(nk)*, where *k* is a fixed value (Dell et al., 2014).

3.3.7. Super Polynomial Time Complexity

This is occasionally referred to as exponential time complexity. A super polynomial time complexity algorithm is one that requires *2n* steps to run for an input of size n. The computational complexity of these methods exhibits exponential growth as the input size, n, rises (Potra & Stoer, 2010).

3.4. THE TURING MACHINES' TIME COMPLEXITY

When considering a Turing machine that decides a language , it is useful to view it as solving a decision problem: Is , given that ,? One way to determine the magnitude of the problem at hand is by considering the length of the input string. When dealing with decision problems involving different types of instances, it is typically assumed that the size of the instance can be measured by an integer that is closely linked to string length encoding the instance (Marion, 1994).

Determining a Turing machine's time complexity function is the first step towards characterizing and classifying the complexity of computing problems (Hartmanis, 1968).

- **Definition 3.1 the Turning Machines' Time Complexity**

Let us examine a Turing machine T with an input alphabet Σ that will ultimately stop on every input string. The time complexity of T can be denoted by the function , where N represents the set of natural numbers. The function computes the number of iterations it takes for an input string of length *n* in to halt, and returns the highest value as (n).

When discussing a Turing machine's time complexity, it is assumed that it will halt on every input (Woods & Neary, 2009).

3.4.1. Calculating Simple TM's Time Complexity

For example, the TM T recognizes the language L = . When n is even, we shall construct a formula for (n); in the other case, it is smaller.

There are three components involved in the computation of a string with a length of $n = 2k$. In the process, T identifies the middle point and converts the symbols to uppercase. The tape head is then moved back to its initial position and the first half is converted to lowercase. It concludes by comparing the two parts (Fincke & Pohst, 1985).

As part of the initial step, the tape head can be easily move to the first input symbol with just a single move. It takes $2k + 1$ steps to change the starting symbol and locate the symbol on the far right. Furthermore, there is an extra requirement of performing $2k$ moves to alter the symbol located at the far-right position and return the tape head to the leftmost lowercase symbol (Zenil et al., 2018).

The total number of moves is determined by deducting four from the number of moves for each succeeding pass.

$$1+\sum_{i=0}^{k}(4i+1)=1+(k+1)+4\sum_{i=0}^{k}i=k+2+4\frac{k(k+1)}{2}=2k^2+3k+2$$

The length of the input string is the single factor that determines the number of moves in the second phase, which is calculated by adding 1 to the value of k. The provided string determines the third portion's length.

However, there are more motions required for the strings in L. In the last step, every one of the k symbols from the first part of the computation for a string in L is processed in one pass.

Each pass has k rightward movements, k leftward movements, and one additional rightward movement. Since is the maximum number of moves in this section, we may deduce that

There are one or two steps that convert each symbol in the input string to the opposite case, and one move that compares the symbol to another symbol. The other steps, which include repeatedly moving from one end of the string to the other, lead the formula for (n) to be quadratic. By introducing new states, the number of these can be decreased (Ibarra, 1971) (Figure 3.1).

By enhancing the memory capacity of the Turing Machine to keep two symbols simultaneously, we can significantly reduce the number of iterations required. Furthermore, expanding the memory capacity beyond two symbols would further enhance performance, particularly for larger values of n.

Methods such as these have the potential to significantly decrease the time complexity of any Turing machine, by any desired constant factor. Nevertheless, it is impossible to entirely prevent the ongoing exchange of information in this situation. Furthermore, it can be demonstrated that any Turing Machine that processes this language has a time complexity of at least quadratic (Littman et al., 1998).

$$\tau_T(n)=\tau_T(2k)=4k^2+5k+4=n^2+5n/2+4$$

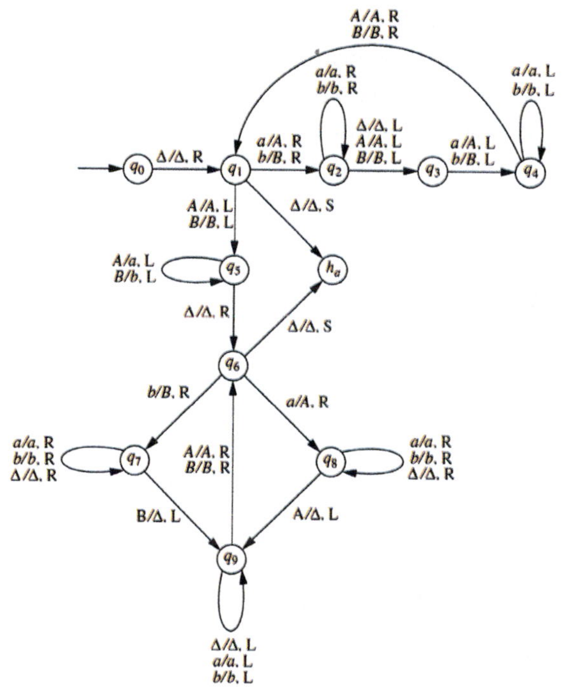

Figure 3.1. *Illustration of a Turing machine accepting .*

Source: John C Martin, Creative Commons License.

The quadratic formula is a key aspect of in this model. When considering the Turing Machine's time complexity, it is more convenient to concentrate on overall growth rate of the function instead of its value at a particular point.

This definition simplifies the discussion (Hutter, 2002). One way to rephrase the statement is to explain that, with the exception of a few values of n, f is generally not greater than *g*, except for a constant factor. At first glance, the expression may appear to be related to the number , but it actually has a different meaning. The notation may seem standard, but it can be a bit confusing initially. It has the same meaning as .

This approach allows for a comparison of the long-term growth rates of the two functions, but it does not provide specific details about the values of *f(n)* and *g(n)* for each given *n* (Currin et al., 2017). Under the given conditions of f and g being total functions, f being equal to O(g), and g(n) being positive for every $n \in N$, it can be inferred that there exists a positive constant *C*.

This constant ensures that *f(n)* is always less than or equal to *C* times *g(n)* for every *n*. In the context of function analysis, it is important to consider that $f = O(g)$ does not assume that *f* or *g* are defined for all values or that *g(n)* is always non-zero. There may be cases where *f* or *g* are undefined in certain places or where *g(n)* equals 0 for specific values of *n* (Fagin, 1974).

As an example;

$$n^2 + 5n/2 + 4 = O\left(n^2\right)$$

In the same way, we can examine a polynomial *f* that has a degree of *k*, and its formula can be expressed as

$$f\left(n\right) = a_k n^k + a_{k-1} n^{k-1} + \cdots + a_1 n + a_0$$

When dealing with large values of *n*, it is important to note that *f(n)* will always be positive if the leading coefficient s positive. In cases where the coefficient is negative, we can consider it as undefined. , based on a reasoning similar to the quadratic polynomial (Wang & Chew, 1991).

Despite our limited progress in categorizing decision problems by complexity, we can consider the task of determining the language as relatively simple.

There is a wide range of decision problems that seem to be significantly more challenging. One way to locate examples is by examining combinatorial problems that require considering a significant number of cases to find the solution. Following are two examples (Kruskal, 1983).

A mathematical phrase with the Boolean variables , which can be true or false, and the logical operators ∧, ∨, and ¬ is a common example of the satisfiability problem. Whether a truth value assignment to the variables exists that completes the expression or makes it true is the question at hand.

It is clear that this problem can be solved, as a brute-force algorithm may be used. Explore different truth value assignments, either until a satisfying expression is found or until all possible assignments have been tried (Chen, 2004).

ACTIVITY 3.1

Objective: To understand and analyze the time complexity of various algorithms.

Materials: Pen, paper, and a computer with access to algorithm examples.

Instructions:

a. Divide students into small groups.
b. Assign each group a different algorithm (e.g., binary search, quicksort, merge sort).
c. Have each group analyze their assigned algorithm to determine its time complexity.
d. Each group should prepare a brief presentation explaining their algorithm, the steps involved in the analysis, and the resulting time complexity.

Groups will present their findings to the class, followed by a discussion on the different complexities and their implications.

3.5. POLYNOMIAL VERIFIABILITY AND THE SET NP

The satisfiability problem appears to be difficult since no decision algorithm has been discovered that performs a great deal better than trying each potential assignment one at a time.

Testing is not difficult; we can quickly determine whether a particular truth assignment satisfies any logical way of defining a Boolean expression with *n* unique variables. The problem is that there are an endless number of possible assignments for every *n*. The total time needed would not be polynomial, even if we could test each one in a fixed amount of time, independent of *n* (Blondel & Olshevsky, 2014).

In other instances, non-determinism was used to streamline the creation of a TM when our primary concern was not the length of time required to test an input text, but rather whether a language was recursively enumerable. This is also a nondeterministic TM, where Satisfiable is accepted by assuming an assignment and then (deterministically) determining whether it satisfies the expression. Clearly, this method ignores the complexity problem (Yamakawa & Zhandry, 2024).

As we will see in more detail below, the steps required to guess and test an assignment can be completed in polynomial time. However, since the non-determinism removes the time-consuming aspect of the brute-force approach, the method does not appear to reveal much about how difficult the problem is.

Still, it offers at least an easy solution of the question raised by problems such as Sat (satisfiability): Is there any reason to assume that a language L is in P if it can be accepted in polynomial time by a nondeterministic TM?

First, we determine the Non-deterministic Turing Machine's (NTM) temporal complexity assuming (as defined in Definition 3.1) that no input string may produce an infinite loop. With the exception of having to account for the machine's maximum number of moves, the definition is essentially the same. This consideration applies not just to all strings of length *n*, but also to all conceivable sequences of moves that the machine may make on a specific input string of length *n*.

As before, we can say that a decision issue is in NP if the corresponding language is for a suitable manner of encoding instances (Philip et al., 2012).

P⊆NP is evident an ordinary Turing machine since it can be thought of an NTM. We first analyze two cases, including a more thorough examination of the satisfiability problem, before moving on to the opposite inclusion (Buhrman et al., 2010).

3.5.1. The Satisfiability Problem

The term "Sat" is often used as a symbol to denote the satisfiability problem. An instance is a mathematical phrase that contains Boolean variables , where v is a number greater than or equal to 1. The term "literal" can refer to either a variable x_i or the negation $\neg x_i$ of x_i. The given expression is believed to be in conjunctive normal form, also known as CNF (Hansen & Jaumard, 1990).

$$C_1 \wedge C_2 \wedge \cdots C_c$$

A conjunctive clause, or conjunct, is produced by combining disjunctions (using ∨ operators) of literals. Regarding this type of expression, Sat is questioning if it can be satisfied by any truth assignment to the variables (Kohli et al., 1994).

For example,

$$(x_1 \vee x_3 \vee x_4) \wedge (\overline{x}_1 \vee x_3) \wedge (\overline{x}_1 \vee x_4 \vee \overline{x}_2) \wedge \overline{x}_3 \wedge (x_2 \vee \overline{x}_4)$$

is a five-conjunct expression that the truth assignment satisfies.

$$x_2 = x_4 = true, \qquad x_1 = x_3 = false$$

To encode Sat instances, we will remove parentheses and ∨'s and use unary notation to indicate subscripts. For example, the expression given (Stewart, 1995).

$$(x_1 \vee \overline{x}_2) \wedge (x_2 \vee x_3 \vee \overline{x}_1) \wedge (\overline{x}_4 \vee x_2)$$

will be denoted by the string

$$\wedge x1\overline{x}11 \wedge x11x111\overline{x}1 \wedge \overline{x}1111x11$$

The language Satisfiable consists of all the encoded instances that are classified as "yes" and is defined over the alphabet .

If we define the size of a problem instance as the number of literals, denoted by k (which may not be distinct), and n as the length of the string that encodes the instance, then it follows that $k < n$. In addition, it is clear that the value of n is constrained by a quadratic function of k. Thus, if the problem of determining

Remember

Problems that are both as hard as any other problem in NP and fall under the NP complexity class, meaning that if an NP-complete problem can be solved in polynomial time, then so can all other problems in NP.

satisfiability (Satisfiable) belongs to the complexity class NP, it is logical to conclude that the choice problem Sat is also a member of NP (Selman et al., 1996).

When processing a Satisfiable input, the first step of an NTM T is to verify the validity of the input string as a legitimate CNF expression, additionally, it checks if there is a variable v such that the variables are , , ..., . If this is indeed the case, T aims to meet the requirement by maintaining a log of the fulfilled conditions and the assigned values for the unsatisfied conditions.

The iterative stage involves recognizing the initial conjunct that has not yet been fulfilled. Within that conjunction, a literal is chosen that does not have an assigned value. This is the only instance of procedural non-determinism. Then, a value satisfying the conjunct is assigned to the variable in that literal. The conjunct is marked as fulfilled, and all subsequent occurrences of that variable in unfulfilled conjuncts are assigned the same value. Any conjuncts that are satisfied because of the supplied value are also indicated (Gottlieb et al., 2002).

There are two ways the loop can end. There are two possible results: either the literals in the first unsatisfied conjunct are found to be untrue, or all conjuncts are fulfilled. T rejects the input in the second case although it accepts it in the first. There exists a set of movements that can enable T to guess a valid truth assignment if the expression is satisfiable. However, if the assertion is unsatisfactory, then no series of actions will result in acceptance (Alyahya et al., 2022).

Except for a few steps that require time proportional to n, the Turing Machine T can be constructed in such a way that all of its operations are merely slight modifications of the succeeding operation: Find any other occurrences of the input sequence that are also enclosed by the same non-1 symbol. The input sequence starts with a series of 1s (Garey & Johnson, 1978).

It is necessary to confirm that the number of such operations is polynomial and that one of these types of operations may be completed in a polynomial amount of time. We deduce that Sat and Satisfiable are NP-complex (Jeroslow & Wang, 1990).

3.5.2. Polynomial-Time Reductions and NP-Completeness

Similar to demonstrating the decidability of a problem by reducing it to another problem, one can establish that languages are in the complexity class P by reducing them to other languages within this class. (By using reductions, we can identify other languages that are not in the class P, in addition to the ones we already know.) In order to reduce language to language , it is important to find a computable function *f* that can help us determine whether *x* belongs to by checking if *f(x)* belongs to (Johnson, 1983).

In this particular situation, we have come to realize that the task of selecting the first language is equally as difficult as choosing the second language. Our analysis focused on two levels of difficulty: decidable and undecidable. In order to determine if *x* , we can simply calculate *f(x)* and check if it is a member of . It is worth noting that *f* is a computable function. Given that certain decidable languages may require more time to decide than others, it is necessary for a reduction to meet certain additional criteria. It is acceptable to believe that the function can be computed in polynomial time (Watanabe & Tang, 1992).

3.6. THE COOK-LEVIN THEOREM

In 1971 and 1972, Stephen Cook and Leonid Levin made a significant discovery regarding the satisfiability problem and its unique property. Before we dive into presenting and outlining the proof of the result, let's take a look at another problem that can be simplified to Sat. This problem may not be inherently interesting due to its finite set of instances, which eliminates the need for reduction in order to solve it. Nevertheless, this serves as helpful example of the overall principle utilized in the proof of the theorem and has the potential to be used in order to simplify other problems to Sat (Atserias, 2011).

Both in this simple example and in the demonstration of the theorem itself, it is advantageous to utilize a fact about logical statements. Any proposition that includes Boolean variables and their negations can be logically equated to another proposition. The proposition q is written in conjunctive normal form and includes these variables (Lutz & Mayordomo, 1996).

The problem at question is: Is the undirected graph linked given that it has three vertices? (Only when two of the three potential edges are truly existent can a graph with three vertices qualify as linked.) The initial stage in reducing the problem to Sat involves creating a function *f* that maps 3-vertex graphs to Boolean expressions. This function ensures that a graph G is connected if and only if *f(G)* can be satisfied. Polynomial-time computability for a finite issue such as this one is automatic (Araya et al., 2024). The numerals 1, 2, and 3 stand for the vertices of G. Three Boolean variables () are taken into consideration. We consider to be related to the statements "there is an edge from *i* to *j*." Based on this analysis of the three variables, a formula that "asserts" the graph's connectivity is

$$S:\left(x_{1,2}\wedge x_{1,3}\right)\vee\left(x_{1,2}\wedge x_{2,3}\right)\vee\left(x_{1,3}\wedge x_{2,3}\right)$$

The statement S is not in conjunctive normal form, which is one of the instances where we apply the aforementioned truth. The meaning of the variables does not now depend on the specific graph G, but rather provides a general assertion about the connectivity of a three-vertex graph (Yampolskiy, 2013) One important consideration is whether the statement remains valid when taking into account the restrictions that specify the edges that are absent in this specific problem case. It indicates that the edges from 1 to 2 and from 2 to 3 are absent from the graph that only has the edge from 1 to 3, but that at least two additional edges are there. Here is the corresponding expression:

$$\overline{x}_{1,2} \wedge \overline{x}_{2,3} \wedge S$$

Where the bars over the *x*, as usual, indicate negation. It does not matter what values are put in for the three variables to satisfy this expression (Krajíček, 2014).

The function *f* is derived precisely in this manner. The phrase *f(G)* consists of the conjunction of all words that correspond to the absent edges, along with the CNF form of the expression S that was generated before. G is considered linked if and only if the function *f(G)* may be satisfied by any truth assignment to the three Boolean variables (Ogiwara & Hemachandra, 1993).

This particular example, while basic, may be considered uncommon because it clearly demonstrates that as the number of edges in the graph increases, the probability of it being connected also increases. As a result, figuring out the expression *f(G)'s* satisfiability can be reduced to figuring out its truth value when every edge that is not specifically marked as missing is actually present. Typically, just a single assignment is not going to be sufficient for testing satisfiability (Müller, 2022).

To be more precise, it can be shown that the satisfiability of the formula *f(G)* is equal to the connectedness of *G*. We have already stated that is linked to the statement "there exists an edge from *i* to *j*". The manner in which we conceptualize the variable is not the main concern. Instead, we have formulated the expression S in such a way that its logical framework precisely reflects structure of claim "*G* is connected" in this simple scenario. The interpretation just enhances the clarity of this logical equivalency (Mohri & Pereira, 1998).

Another aspect of the expression *f(G)* highlights graph limitations due to the exclusion of specific edges. Thus, the issue at hand is whether it is possible to define the edges in a manner that adheres to these limitations, resulting in a connected *G*. In order to fulfill the entire expression *f(G)*, we need to determine if truth values can be assigned to the variables (Jones & Liskov, 1978).

SUMMARY

- An extensive analysis of computational complexity, a crucial field in theoretical computer science that investigates algorithm efficiency, is given in this chapter. To start, we define decidable and intractable problems, highlighting the usefulness of determining which problems are accessible to efficient solutions. The chapter provides an overview of time and space complexity and explains how these metrics are used to assess an algorithm's effectiveness.
- We examine various notations used to describe the time complexity of algorithms, including Big O, Big Omega, and Theta, and explain their use in measuring the efficiency of algorithms. The chapter provides an explanation of the difference between (class P) and (class NP), with a focus on the continuing P vs NP challenge.
- The chapter explores NP-complete problems, explaining their significance as some of the most difficult problems in NP and introducing the Cook-Levin theorem as a fundamental outcome in this field.
- The chapter aims to provide readers with a thorough comprehension of computational complexity by using examples and theoretical talks. This will enable readers to examine and categorize algorithms based on their performance characteristics.

REVIEW QUESTIONS

1. What is the difference between decidable and intractable problems?
2. Explain the concepts of time complexity and space complexity with examples.
3. Describe the classes P and NP and provide examples of problems in each class.
4. How is Big O notation used to analyze algorithms? Give an example.
5. What is the significance of NP-complete problems in computational complexity?
6. Discuss the Cook-Levin theorem and its implications in complexity theory.

MULTIPLE CHOICE QUESTIONS

1. What is the primary focus of computational complexity?

a. Hardware performance
b. Algorithm efficiency
c. Software development
d. Network security

2. Which notation represents the worst-case time complexity of an algorithm?

a. Big Omega (Ω)
b. Big Theta (Θ)
c. Big O (O)

d. Little Oh (o)

3. **What does NP stand for in complexity theory?**
   a. Nondeterministic Polynomial time
   b. Non-Polynomial time
   c. Numerical Polynomial time
   d. Normal Polynomial time
4. **Which problem is an example of an NP-complete problem?**
   a. Linear Search
   b. Binary Search
   c. Traveling Salesman Problem
   d. Matrix Multiplication
5. **What is the significance of the Cook-Levin theorem?**
   a. It defines the class P.
   b. It proves that P ≠ NP.
   c. It asserts that the satisfiability problem is NP-complete.
   d. It introduces the concept of space complexity.
6. **Which of the following notations is used to describe the asymptotic lower bound of a function?**
   a. Big O (O)
   b. Big Omega (Ω)
   c. Big Theta (Θ)
   d. Little Oh (o)

Answers to Multiple Questions

1. (b); 2. (c); 3. (a); 4. (c); 5. (c); 6. (b)

REFERENCES

1. Alyahya, T. N., Menai, M. E. B., & Mathkour, H. (2022). On the structure of the Boolean satisfiability problem: A survey. *ACM Computing Surveys (CSUR), 55*(3), 1–34.
2. Angluin, D., & Fisman, D. (2016). Learning regular omega languages. *Theoretical Computer Science, 650,* 57–72.
3. Araya, T., Celikbas, O., Cook, J., & Kobayashi, T. (2024). Modules with finite reducing Gorenstein dimension. *Beiträge zur Algebra und Geometrie/Contributions to Algebra and Geometry, 65*(2), 279–290.
4. Atserias, A. (2011). Stephen Cook and Phuong Nguyen. Logical foundations of proof complexity. Perspectives in Logic. Cambridge University Press, New York,

2010, 15+ 479 pp. *Bulletin of Symbolic Logic, 17*(3), 462–464.

5. Baber, J., Dailey, M. N., Satoh, S. I., Afzulpurkar, N., & Bakhtyar, M. (2014). BIG-OH: Binarization of gradient orientation histograms. *Image and Vision Computing, 32*(11), 940–953.
6. Ben-Sasson, E., & Galesi, N. (2003). Space complexity of random formulae in resolution. *Random Structures & Algorithms, 23*(1), 92–109.
7. Bloch, S. A., Buss, J. F., & Goldsmith, J. (1998). Sharply bounded alternation and quasilinear time. *Theory of Computing Systems, 31,* 187–214.
8. Blondel, V. D., & Olshevsky, A. (2014). How to decide consensus? A combinatorial necessary and sufficient condition and a proof that consensus is decidable but NP-hard. *SIAM Journal on Control and Optimization, 52*(5), 2707–2726.
9. Blondel, V. D., & Tsitsiklis, J. N. (2000). A survey of computational complexity results in systems and control. *Automatica, 36*(9), 1249–1274.
10. Bossaerts, P., & Murawski, C. (2017). Computational complexity and human decision-making. *Trends in Cognitive Sciences, 21*(12), 917–929.
11. Bossaerts, P., Yadav, N., & Murawski, C. (2019). Uncertainty and computational complexity. *Philosophical Transactions of the Royal Society B, 374*(1766), 20180138.
12. Buhrman, H., Fortnow, L., Koucký, M., Rogers, J. D., & Vereshchagin, N. (2010). Does the polynomial hierarchy collapse if onto functions are invertible? *Theory of Computing Systems, 46,* 143–156.
13. Chen, H. Y. (2004). Efficient time-bound hierarchical key assignment scheme. *IEEE Transactions on Knowledge and Data Engineering, 16*(10), 1301–1304.
14. Crossley, S. A., Louwerse, M. M., McCarthy, P. M., & McNamara, D. S. (2007). A linguistic analysis of simplified and authentic texts. *The Modern Language Journal, 91*(1), 15–30.
15. Currin, A., Korovin, K., Ababi, M., Roper, K., Kell, D. B., Day, P. J., & King, R. D. (2017). Computing exponentially faster: Implementing a non-deterministic universal Turing machine using DNA. *Journal of the Royal Society Interface, 14*(128), 20160990.
16. Dell, H., Husfeldt, T., Marx, D., Taslaman, N., & Wahlen, M. (2014). Exponential time complexity of the permanent and the Tutte polynomial. *ACM Transactions on Algorithms (TALG), 10*(4), 1–32.
17. Denef, F., & Douglas, M. R. (2007). Computational complexity of the landscape: Part I. *Annals of Physics, 322*(5), 1096–1142.
18. Ding, Y., Kunisky, D., Wein, A. S., & Bandeira, A. S. (2021). The average-case time complexity of certifying the restricted isometry property. *IEEE Transactions on Information Theory, 67*(11), 7355–7361.
19. Fagin, R. (1974). Generalized first-order spectra and polynomial-time recognizable sets. *Complexity of Computation, 7,* 43–73.
20. Fincke, U., & Pohst, M. (1985). Improved methods for calculating vectors of short length in a lattice, including a complexity analysis. *Mathematics of Computation, 44*(170), 463–471.

21. García, P., Vidal, E., & Casacuberta, F. (1987). Local languages, the successor method, and a step towards a general methodology for the inference of regular grammars. *IEEE Transactions on Pattern Analysis and Machine Intelligence,* (6), 841–845.

22. Garey, M. R., & Johnson, D. S. (1978). "Strong" NP-completeness results: Motivation, examples, and implications. *Journal of the ACM (JACM), 25*(3), 499–508.

23. Goldreich, O. (2008). Computational complexity: A conceptual perspective. *ACM SIGACT News, 39*(3), 35–39.

24. Gottlieb, J., Marchiori, E., & Rossi, C. (2002). Evolutionary algorithms for the satisfiability problem. *Evolutionary Computation, 10*(1), 35–50.

25. Griewank, A. (1992). Achieving logarithmic growth of temporal and spatial complexity in reverse automatic differentiation. *Optimization Methods and Software, 1*(1), 35–54.

26. Hansen, P., & Jaumard, B. (1990). Algorithms for the maximum satisfiability problem. *Computing, 44*(4), 279–303.

27. Hartmanis, J. (1968). Computational complexity of one-tape Turing machine computations. *Journal of the ACM (JACM), 15*(2), 325–339.

28. Hutter, M. (2002). The fastest and shortest algorithm for all well-defined problems. *International Journal of Foundations of Computer Science, 13*(3), 431–443.

29. Ibarra, O. H. (1971). Characterizations of some tape and time complexity classes of Turing machines in terms of multihead and auxiliary stack automata. *Journal of Computer and System Sciences, 5*(2), 88–117.

30. Ishizeki, R., Kruczenski, M., & Ziama, S. (2012). Notes on Euclidean Wilson loops and Riemann theta functions. *Physical Review D—Particles, Fields, Gravitation, and Cosmology, 85*(10), 106004.

31. Jeroslow, R. G., & Wang, J. (1990). Solving propositional satisfiability problems. *Annals of Mathematics and Artificial Intelligence, 1*(1), 167–187.

32. Johnson, D. S. (1983). The NP-completeness column: An ongoing guide. *Journal of Algorithms, 4*(2), 189–203.

33. Jones, A. K., & Liskov, B. H. (1978). A language extension for expressing constraints on data access. *Communications of the ACM, 21*(5), 358–367.

34. Kapovich, I., Myasnikov, A., Schupp, P., & Shpilrain, V. (2005). Average-case complexity and decision problems in group theory. *Advances in Mathematics, 190*(2), 343–359.

35. Kohli, R., Krishnamurti, R., & Mirchandani, P. (1994). The minimum satisfiability problem. *SIAM Journal on Discrete Mathematics, 7*(2), 275–283.

36. Krají⍰ek, J. (2014). On the computational complexity of finding hard tautologies. *Bulletin of the London Mathematical Society, 46*(1), 111–125.

37. Kruskal, J. B. (1983). An overview of sequence comparison: Time warps, string edits, and macromolecules. *SIAM Review, 25*(2), 201–237.

38. Lim, T. S., Loh, W. Y., & Shih, Y. S. (2000). A comparison of prediction accuracy, complexity, and training time of thirty-three old and new classification algorithms. *Machine Learning, 40*, 203–228.

39. Littman, M. L., Goldsmith, J., & Mundhenk, M. (1998). The computational complexity

of probabilistic planning. *Journal of Artificial Intelligence Research, 9*, 1–36.

40. Lutz, J. H., & Mayordomo, E. (1996). Cook versus Karp-Levin: Separating completeness notions if NP is not small. *Theoretical Computer Science, 164*(1, 2), 141–163.
41. Mala, F. A., & Ali, R. (2022). The Big-O of Mathematics and Computer Science. *Applied Mathematics and Computation, 6*(1), 1–3.
42. Marion, B. (1994). Turing machines and computational complexity. *The American Mathematical Monthly, 101*(1), 61–65.
43. Melnikov, B., & Melnikova, A. (2020). Some more on omega-finite automata and omega-regular languages. Part I: The main definitions and properties. *International Journal of Open Information Technologies, 8*(8), 1–7.
44. Mohri, M., & Pereira, F. C. (1998). Dynamic compilation of weighted context-free grammars. In *36th Annual Meeting of the Association for Computational Linguistics and 17th International Conference on Computational Linguistics* (Vol. 2, pp. 891–897).
45. Müller, A. F. (2022). Polynomial fill-in puzzles or how to make sense of the Cook-Levin theorem. *Elemente der Mathematik, 77*(2), 53–62.
46. Najman, L., & Couprie, M. (2006). Building the component tree in quasi-linear time. *IEEE Transactions on Image Processing, 15*(11), 3531–3539.
47. Ogiwara, M., & Hemachandra, L. A. (1993). A complexity theory for feasible closure properties. *Journal of Computer and System Sciences, 46*(3), 295–325.
48. Oliveto, P. S., He, J., & Yao, X. (2007). Time complexity of evolutionary algorithms for combinatorial optimization: A decade of results. *International Journal of Automation and Computing, 4*, 281–293.
49. Philip, G., Raman, V., & Sikdar, S. (2012). Polynomial kernels for dominating set in graphs of bounded degeneracy and beyond. *ACM Transactions on Algorithms (TALG), 9*(1), 1–23.
50. Potra, F. A., & Stoer, J. (2010). On a class of super linearly convergent polynomial time interior point methods for sufficient LCP. *SIAM Journal on Optimization, 20*(3), 1333–1363.
51. Robinson, P. (1996). Learning simple and complex second language rules under implicit, incidental, rule-search, and instructed conditions. *Studies in Second Language Acquisition, 18*(1), 27–67.
52. Selman, B., Mitchell, D. G., & Levesque, H. J. (1996). Generating hard satisfiability problems. *Artificial Intelligence, 81*(1, 2), 17–29.
53. Shah, B., & Bhavsar, H. (2022). Time complexity in deep learning models. *Procedia Computer Science, 215*, 202–210.
54. Sherman, M. T. (1991). On super polylogarithmic sub exponential functions (Part II). *ACM SIGACT News, 22*(2), 51–56.
55. Sperber, M., Dybvig, R. K., Flatt, M., Van Straaten, A., Findler, R., & Matthews, J. (2009). Revised6 report on the algorithmic language Scheme. *Journal of Functional Programming, 19*(S1), 1–301.

56. Srivastava, B. (2005). Ramanujan's mock theta functions. *Mathematical Journal of Okayama University, 47*(1), 163–174.
57. Stewart, I. A. (1995). Completeness of path-problems via logical reductions. *Information and Computation, 121*(1), 123–134.
58. Stockmeyer, L. (1987). Classifying the computational complexity of problems. *The Journal of Symbolic Logic, 52*(1), 1–43.
59. Thanh, V. H., Zunino, R., & Priami, C. (2016). Efficient constant-time complexity algorithm for stochastic simulation of large reaction networks. *IEEE/ACM Transactions on Computational Biology and Bioinformatics, 14*(3), 657–667.
60. Wang, Y. M., & Chew, W. C. (1991). Application of the fast recursive algorithm to a large inhomogeneous scatterer for TM polarization. *Microwave and Optical Technology Letters, 4*(4), 155–157.
61. Watanabe, O., & Tang, S. (1992). On polynomial-time Turing and many-one completeness in PSPACE. *Theoretical Computer Science, 97*(2), 199–215.
62. Woods, D., & Neary, T. (2009). The complexity of small universal Turing machines: A survey. *Theoretical Computer Science, 410*(4–5), 443–450.
63. Yamakawa, T., & Zhandry, M. (2024). Verifiable quantum advantage without structure. *Journal of the ACM, 71*(3), 1–50.
64. Yampolskiy, R. V. (2013). Efficiency theory: A unifying theory for information, computation and intelligence. *Journal of Discrete Mathematical Sciences and Cryptography, 16*(4, 5), 259–277.
65. Zenil, H., Hernández-Orozco, S., Kiani, N. A., Soler-Toscano, F., Rueda-Toicen, A., & Tegnér, J. (2018). A decomposition method for global evaluation of Shannon entropy and local estimations of algorithmic complexity. *Entropy, 20*(8), 605.

CHAPTER 4

Context-Free Grammar and Languages

LEARNING OBJECTIVES

After studying this chapter, you will be able to:

- Define and explain the components of a context-free grammar (CFG).
- Differentiate between regular grammars and context-free grammars.
- Construct CFGs for various languages, including those not possible with regular grammars.
- Derive strings from given CFGs and understand the concept of derivation trees.
- Comprehend and resolve ambiguity in context-free grammars.
- Simplify CFGs to minimize complexity and facilitate easier analysis.

KEY TERMS FROM THIS CHAPTER

Ambiguity	Context-free grammar (CFG)
Derivation	Derivation tree
Non-terminal symbol	Palindrome
Production rule	Start variable
Syntax	Terminal symbol

UNIT INTRODUCTION

Context-Free Grammar (CFG) is a foundational concept in formal language theory and theoretical computer science. It provides a systematic framework for describing the syntax of languages using a set of rules. These rules define how strings of symbols, comprised of terminals (basic units) and non-terminals (syntactic categories), can be generated. Each non-terminal can be replaced by a sequence of terminals and/or other non-terminals according to specified production rules. The process begins with a designated start symbol and proceeds through successive applications of these rules to generate all possible valid strings (sentences) in the language (Salomaa, 1969).

CFGs play a critical role in various domains such as compiler design, natural language processing, and computational linguistics. In compiler construction, they are used to formalize and verify the syntax of programming languages, aiding in parsing and syntax analysis. In natural language processing, CFGs are employed to model the syntactic structure of human languages, facilitating tasks such as parsing and grammar checking. The study of CFGs also underpins fundamental research in automata theory, parsing algorithms, and the theoretical limits of language recognition in computing (Postal & Langendoen, 1984).

Standard languages and limited automata are insufficient to handle languages of significant complexity due to their simplicity and limitations. The utilization of context-free grammar enables the creation of languages that are more captivating; a significant portion of the syntax of a language for high-level programming, for instance, can be delineated in this manner. This chapter begins by providing a precise description of context-free grammar and proceeds to examine several illustrative cases (Domaratzki et al., 2002). The subsequent section of the chapter delves into the examination of derivations inside a context-free grammar. The connection between a derivation and the basic structure of the string being generated is explored, as well as the potential presence of uncertainty in grammar, which can add complexity to this relationship. In addition, several methods are explored by which grammar might be streamlined to facilitate the process of addressing inquiries regarding the strings within the associated language (Chomsky & Schützenberger, 1959; Ehrenfeucht et al., 1985).

The chapter goes beyond the limitations of regular languages and finite automata to explore context-free grammars (CFGs). CFGs enable the generation of more complex languages, including those that describe the syntax of high-level programming languages (Schabe & Waters, 1995). CFGs will be formally defined and examined with the help of several examples, learning how to derive strings and address the issue of ambiguity. Simplifying grammar to facilitate easier analysis will also be discussed. This chapter provides the foundation for understanding how context-free grammar can be applied to real-world languages and computational problems (Walters, 1989).

4.1. USING GRAMMAR RULES TO DEFINE A LANGUAGE

In the context of the English language, the term "grammar" pertains to the set of rules that govern the construction of phrases and sentences. A grammar, in this context, refers to a collection of rules that are less complex than the rules of English. These rules are used to generate strings in a particular language. In the initial illustrations within this part, grammar serves as an alternative method for expressing the recursive definitions employed in Chapter 1 for language definition (Widodo, 2006).

- **Example 4.1: The language A^nB^n**

The derivation of strings in the language A^nB^n, defined as $\{a^nb^n \mid n \geq 0\}$, can be achieved using context-free grammar and the following recursive definition:

$\Lambda \in A^nB^n$ For every $S \in A^nB^n$, $aSb \in A^nB^n$

Consider S as a variable that represents any string in the language A^nB^n. Rule 1, denoted as $S \rightarrow \Lambda$, states that the random string can be represented as Λ, achieved by replacing the variable S with Λ. In order to generate any other string, one must initiate the process with rule 2, which is represented as $S \rightarrow aSb$. Substituting S with aSb is the first stage in the process of deriving the string. This is followed by the application of rules 1 and 2 to assign a value to the new S. The process of derivation will continue indefinitely so long as the string contains the variable S. For the purpose of this specific illustration (Hochmann et al., 2008), the final step will always consist of substituting the letter S with the empty string Λ.

If α comprises at least one instance of S, the notation:

$$\alpha \Rightarrow \beta$$

β is derived from α by replacing a single instance of S with either Λ or *aSb*. Employing this notation:

$$S \Rightarrow aSb \Rightarrow aaSbb \Rightarrow aaaSbbb \Rightarrow aaabbb$$

To delineate the series of actions (three instances of using rule 2, followed by one instance of applying rule 1) that was employed to obtain the string *aaabbb* from the language A^nB^n.

To further simplify the notation, rules 1 and 2 can be expressed as:

$$S \rightarrow \Lambda \mid aSb$$

And reading the symbol "|" as meaning "or". When formulating the rules of a language (Mees & Collins, 1982), assign more priority to concatenation than to the symbol "|".

- **Example 4.2 The Language Expr**

In this context, an in-depth examination of the language called *Expr* is carried out. This language is characterized by algebraic expressions that incorporate the binary operators + and ∗. Additionally, it includes both left and right parentheses, which help structure these expressions, as well as a single identifier *a*. The purpose of examining *Expr* is to understand how these components interact to form valid algebraic expressions (Aho et al., 1979).

To achieve this, employ a recursive definition, which provides a systematic way to describe the structure and formation of expressions within *Expr*. This recursive approach is essential because it allows to define complex expressions in terms of simpler ones, building up from basic elements (Schabes & Waters, 1995). The detailed recursive definition used to describe *r* is outlined as follows:

$$a \in Expr.$$

$$\text{For every } x \text{ and } y \text{ in } Expr, x + y \text{ and } x * y \text{ are in } Expr.$$

$$\text{For every } x \in Expr, (x) \in Expr.$$

Rule 2 pertains to the utilization of two distinct letters, *x*, and *y*, as the expressions being merged using either the addition (+) or multiplication (∗) operators may not be identical. Thus:

$$S \rightarrow a \mid S + S \mid S * S \mid (S)$$

To obtain the string *a + (a ∗ a)*, for instance, employ the following series of steps:

$$S \Rightarrow S + S \Rightarrow a + S \Rightarrow a + (S) \Rightarrow a + (S * S) \Rightarrow a + (a * S) \Rightarrow a + (a * a)$$

The concatenation of string *S* with itself, denoted as *S + S,* obtained in the initial phase of this derivation implies that the ultimate expression should be seen as the addition of two subordinate expressions. Although the sub-expressions obtained are not identical, they both belong to the set of expressions called *Expr* and may thus be derived from *S* (Sperber et al., 2009).

The explanation of an expression in *Expr* is contingent upon the interpretation selected, and there may exist multiple viable options (Droste & Vogler, 2014). The formula given by *a + (a ∗ a)* produces at least two possible derivations:

$$S \Rightarrow S + S \Rightarrow a + S \Rightarrow a + S * S \Rightarrow a + a * S \Rightarrow a + a * a$$

and

$$S \Rightarrow S * S \Rightarrow S + S * S \Rightarrow a + S * S \Rightarrow a + a * S \Rightarrow a + a * a$$

The initial derivation implies that the expression can be divided into two separate sub-expressions, while the subsequent derivation suggests that the expression can be obtained by multiplying two distinct sub-expressions (Jones & Liskov, 1978).

The standard principles of precedence for algebraic expressions dictate that multiplication takes precedence over addition. By implementing this precedence rule, the expression *a +(a∗a)* is evaluated by first calculating the product *a∗ a*. This ensures that the expression is interpreted as a sum, rather than a product (Reghizzi & San Pietro, 2019). Given the absence of any indications in the grammar rules favoring the first derivation over the second, a plausible inference is that it would be more advantageous to employ an alternative language wherein each string essentially has just one derivation.

This subject will be revisited in Section 4.4, where the concept of ambiguity in a language is explored (Tanaka et al., 2005).

The language *Expr* is simplified by imposing certain restrictions on the expressions.

To expand the range of operations beyond addition and multiplication, one can incorporate additional grammar rules. If one wishes to incorporate additional "atomic" expressions beyond the identifier *'a'*—such as more general identifiers or numeric literals like 16 and 1.3E^{-2}—one can introduce another variable, *'A'*, to achieve this.

This allows the expansion of the language to include a broader range of fundamental expressions, thereby enhancing the expressiveness and versatility of *Expr*. By defining *'A'* to represent these additional atomic expressions (Dowty, 1978), one can seamlessly integrate them into recursive definition, ensuring that the language remains robust and capable of handling a wider variety of algebraic expressions:

$$S \to A \mid S+S \mid S*S \mid (S)$$

The next step is to look for grammatical rules that begin with the letter *A* and would result in all of the subexpressions that are sought at this point.

For the sake of this illustration, a different language will be taken into consideration, which will be labeled as *L*, in which the grammar rules that generate *L* require the utilization of more than one variable (Currie, 2008).

- **Example 4.3: Palindromes and Nonpalindromes**

By utilizing the grammar principles mentioned above, it is possible to generate the language known as *Pal*, which is composed of palindromes over the alphabet *{a, b}:*

$$S \to \Lambda \mid a \mid b \mid aSa \mid bSb$$

What about its counterpart, *NonPal*? The final two grammatical rules in the explanation of *Pal* still apply effectively. If *x* is not a palindrome, then both *axa* and *bxb* are also not palindromes. However, creating a recursive definition for *NonPal* is not as straightforward as it is for *Pal*. This is because there is no finite set of strings, like *{Λ, a, b}*, that can serve as fundamental building blocks for the definition. The complexity of *NonPal* arises from the need to account for the infinite and varied ways in which strings can fail to be palindromes, making its recursive definition more intricate and challenging to construct (Bzymek & Lovett, 2001).

In order to identify the key characteristic of a nonpalindrome, it is necessary to make the assumption:

$$x = abbbbaaba$$

The string *x* is "*abyba*", where *y* is equal to "*bbbaa*". By examining the symbols on the left and right ends and progressing inward, one cannot determine if *x* is a palindrome until *y* is reached.

However, if one observes that *y* resembles *bza* for a certain string *z*, it becomes evident that *x* is a palindrome, even without examining any symbols of *z*. *NonPal* is a term that refers to something that is not palatable or enjoyable (Yang et al., 2017).

a. For all $A \in \{a,b\}^*$, aAb and bAa are the elements of NonPal;

b. For all S in $NonPal, aSa$ and bSb are in $NonPal$ (Mohri & Pereira, 1998).

To derive grammar rules that generate *NonPal*, a second variable *A* is introduced, which represents any member from the set *{a,b}**. The comprehensive set of regulations for *NonPal* is (Črepinšek et al., 2005).

$$S \rightarrow aSa \mid bSb \mid aAb \mid bAa$$

$$A \rightarrow Aa \mid Ab \mid \Lambda$$

abbbbaaba is derived as:

$$S \Rightarrow aSa \Rightarrow abSba \Rightarrow abbAaba$$

$$\Rightarrow abbAaaba \Rightarrow abbAbaaba \Rightarrow abbAbbaaba \Rightarrow abbbbaaba$$

Additionally, it is sometimes necessary to add a number of variables in order to construct a language *L* by utilizing the grammar. It is important to note that the start variable is distinct from the others, and the symbol *S* is typically used to indicate it (Robinson, 1996). Every variable that is left over can be thought of as a representation of a random string in an auxiliary language that is included in the definition of *L*. This language encompasses all of the strings that can be created from that variable. In addition to the inclusion of reciprocal recursion, the language can be interpreted as a recursive definition of the letter *L*. Multiple things are defined sequentially in terms of each other, as opposed to a single item being described in terms of itself in a sequential fashion (Dickins & Woods, 1988).

4.2. CONTEXT-FREE GRAMMARS DEFINITIONS

4.2.1. Definition of Context-Free Grammars (CFG)

It is a 4-tuple $G = (V, \Sigma, S, P)$, where V and P remain disjoint finite sets, $S \in V$, and P remains a finite set of formulas having the form $A \to \alpha$, where $A \in V$ *and* $\alpha \in (V \cup \Sigma)^*$. While the elements of V are known as variables or nonterminals, the members of Σ are referred to as terminal symbols, or simply terminals. Other terms for terminals include terminal symbols. On the other hand, the elements of P pertain to grammatical rules or products, whereas the letter S stands for the initial variable (Salomaa, 1969). The symbol $\to$ will be used to denote productions in grammar, while the symbol $\Rightarrow$ will be used to represent a step in a derivation (Nakamura & Matsumoto, 2002). The symbols or written representations are:

$$\alpha \Rightarrow^n \beta \, and \, \alpha \Rightarrow^* \beta$$

or,

$$\alpha \Rightarrow_G \beta \, or \, \alpha \Rightarrow^n \beta \, or \, \alpha \Rightarrow^* G \beta$$

If G (V, Σ, S, P), the first statement means that there are strings α_1, α_2, and γ in $(V \cup \Sigma)*$ and a production $A \to \gamma$ in P such that:

$$\alpha = \alpha_1 A \alpha_2$$

$$\beta = \alpha_1 \gamma \alpha_2$$

To clarify, β can be derived from α in a single step by implementing the A γ production rule. Subscript G shall be omitted whenever there is no possibility of ambiguity (Čulík, 1967).

- **Example: 4.4. The Language *AEqB***

For the language $AEqB = \{xe\{a,b\}^* \mid n_a(x) = n_b(x)\}$ that exclusively utilizes S. If x is a nonnull string in $AEqB$, then x can be expressed as either ay, where $y \in L_b = \{z \mid n_b(z) = n_a(z)+1\}$, or by, where $y \in La = \{z \mid n_a(z) = n_b(z)+1\}$. Currently, the suitable productions are:

$$S \to \Lambda | aB | bA$$

Productions that commence with the letters A and B are required (Della & Ghezzi, 1978).

If a string x in language L_a begins with the letter a, then the remaining substring is a member of the set *AEqB*. What if it commences with the letter '*b*'? Let x be equal to b_y, where y has two more occurrences of the letter '*a*' than occurrences of the letter '*b*'. It is important to note that any string y that has two more occurrences of the letter '*a*' than the letter '*b*' can be formed by combining two strings, y_1 *and* y_2, each having one more occurrence of the letter '*a*'. In order to observe this, consider the comparative quantities of the letters '*a*' and '*b*' in every first segment of the string '*y*'. More precisely (Sakakibara, 1992), examine each segment

'*z*', let $d(z)=na(z)-nb(z)$ (Uppström, 1968).

The prefix of y with the fewest characters is Λ, and the value of *d*(Λ) is *0*. The longest prefix is y itself, and according to the assumption (Xu, 2018), the value of *d*(*y*) *is 2*. Whenever a single symbol is added to a prefix, the d-value undergoes a change of exactly 1, either increasing or decreasing.

Did you know?

Context-free grammars (CFGs) were first introduced by Noam Chomsky in the 1950s to describe the syntax of natural languages.

If a quantity begins at 0, increments by 1 at each iteration, and ultimately reaches 2, it is inevitable that it will reach 1 at some stage. Hence, if there exists a string y_1 such that the Hamming distance of y_1 is equal to 1, and another string y_2, then the concatenation of y_1 and y_2, denoted as $y = y_1\ y_2$, would have a Hamming distance of 2. Therefore, the Hamming distance of y_2 must likewise be 1 (Fedorchenko & Baranov, 2015).

The argument applies identically to a string in L_a that starts with the letter "a". It can be inferred that *AEqB* is produced by Context-Free Grammar (CFG) using the given set of productions:

$$S \to \Lambda | aB | bA$$

$$A \to aS\ | bAA$$

$$B \to bS\ | aBB$$

An interesting characteristic of this context-free grammar (CFG) is that if one designates A as the initial variable instead of S, it still functions as a grammar that generates the language *La*. The same applies to B and *Lb* (Von & Lyer, 1985).

The following theorem provides several methods for generating additional examples of context-free languages by starting with existing CFLs and developing new ones (Chen, 1993).

ACTIVITY 4.1

Create a context-free grammar for a simple programming language that includes variables, assignment statements, and arithmetic expressions. Use the following components:

- Variables: represented by single lowercase letters (e.g., x, y, z)
- Assignment statements: in the form variable = expression
- Arithmetic expressions: consisting of variables, integers, and the operators +, -, *, /

Write the CFG rules and provide a derivation for the assignment statement x = y + 3 * (z - 1).

4.3. REGULAR LANGUAGES AND REGULAR GRAMMARS

Regular languages are a category of formal languages that may be represented using regular expressions. Regular languages, which are the most basic sort of languages in the Chomsky hierarchy, can be identified and processed by finite automata. Regular languages exhibit closure properties, meaning they remain regular when subjected to operations like union, concatenation, and Kleene star. This property enhances their versatility in accurately representing patterns and sequences. The regular languages over an alphabet Σ, defined as the languages consisting of individual symbols σ for every σ in Σ, are considered to be context-free languages (García et al., 1987).

- **Example 4.5 A CFG Corresponding to a Regular Expression**

Let L ⊆ $\{a,b\}^*$ be the language:

$$bba(ab)^*+(ab+ba^*b)^*ba$$

The implementation of the structures would be a challenging task if it were to be precise: the expression *ab* + *ba*∗*b* alone encompasses all three ways, including three instances of concatenation. To decrease the total number of variables in the grammar, it is not necessary to create distinct variables for the languages *{a}* and *{b}*. Additionally, there are extra shortcuts that can be applied to accomplish this (Sheng & Li, 2006).

(It is essential to keep in mind that exactly adhering to the structures has the potential to facilitate the prevention of errors)

In order to commence, begin by presenting the productions $S \rightarrow S_1 \mid S_2$, as the language is a combination of two languages (Manna et al., 2011), namely L_1 and L_2. Thus:

$$S_1 \rightarrow S_1 ab \mid bba$$

Introducing an additional variable:

$$S_2 \rightarrow T\, S_2 \mid ba$$

Will subsequently attend to *L2*. Ultimately, the productions (Akama & Nantajeewarawat, 2012):

$$T \rightarrow ab \mid bUbU \rightarrow aU \mid \Lambda$$

The context-free grammar (CFG) for language L consists of five variables and their corresponding products:

$$S \to S_1 | S_2 S_1 \to S_1 ab | bba S_2 \to T S_1 \ | ba$$

$$T \to ab | bUbU \to aU | \Lambda$$

This automaton is capable of accepting the language composed of any combination of 'a' and 'b' characters, followed by the sequence (Dassow et al., 2012) *'ba'*. (Figure 4.1).

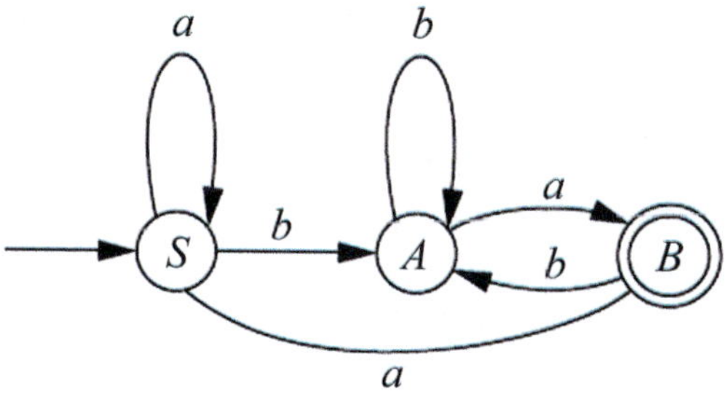

Figure 4.1. *Illustration of an FA accepting* $\{\boldsymbol{a}, \boldsymbol{b}\}^*$ *{ba}.*

Source: John C Martin, Creative Commons License.

The concept underlying the corresponding Context-Free language (CFG) is that the states in the Finite Automaton (FA) are equivalent to the variables in the language (Demri, 2001). Additionally, each transition in the FA corresponds to a specific element in the CFG:

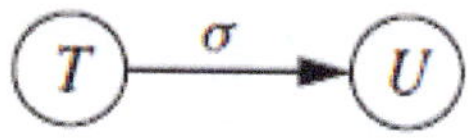

The grammar will contain a production of the form *T σU*. The six transitions depicted in the image correspond to the six productions (Yu et al., 1994):

$$S \to aS | bAA \to bA | aBB \to bA \ | aS$$

The grammar will only include Λ-productions, where the right side is Λ. The progression of changes (Hong et al., 2007):

$$S \xrightarrow{b} A \xrightarrow{b} A \xrightarrow{a} B \xrightarrow{a} S \xrightarrow{b} A \xrightarrow{a} B$$

Corresponds to the sequence of steps

$$S \Rightarrow bA \Rightarrow bbA \Rightarrow bbaB \Rightarrow bbaaS \Rightarrow bbaabA \Rightarrow bbaabaB$$

The relationship between states and variables in an FA becomes clearer now. A state represents the FA's ability to respond to the next input symbol, while the variable at the end of the current string represents the state of the derivation. This state of the derivation determines how to generate the correct portion of the string for each possible terminal symbol (Andrei et al., 2004).

4.4. DERIVATION TREES AND AMBIGUITY

Right up to this point, the primary emphasis has been on identifying the collection of strings that can be produced by a grammar that is not dependent on context. As demonstrated by Example 4.2, it is beneficial to take into consideration the procedure that a context-free grammar (CFG) uses to generate a string. In situations where a string has numerous potential derivations, one of those derivations may be more appropriate than the others. A derivation can provide insights into the structure of a string (Wich, 2005).

A tree diagram (Figure 4.2) can be used to display the derivation of a string, which helps in visualizing the process of the derivation as well as the structure of the string that is associated with it. This is similar to how diagramming a phrase can illustrate the grammatical structure of the phrase (D'Alessandro et al., 2020). In a derivation tree, the starting variable S is equivalent to the root node of the representation. A production $A \rightarrow \alpha$ that is utilized in the derivation is represented by each internal node N in the tree, together with its offspring within the tree.

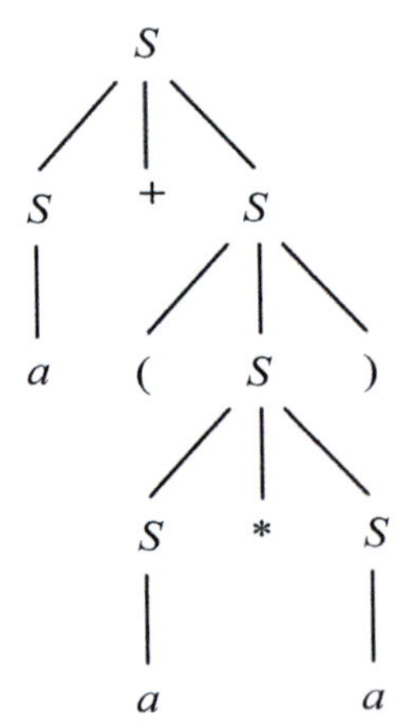

Figure 4.2. *Illustration of A derivation tree for a(a*a) in example 4.2.*

Source: S.P Eguane, Creative Commons License.

Whereas the symbol N is used to represent the variable A, the symbols of α are represented by the children in the order of left to right. If the production is $A \rightarrow \Lambda$, then the node N will only have one child that represents the empty string Λ. This is because the production is a linear transformation. In the tree, each leaf node symbolizes either a terminal symbol or the empty string Λ according to the context. The string that is being generated is produced by reading the leaf nodes in the opposite direction, from left to right (Brabrand et al., 2010).

In order to refer to a particular instance of a variable, the phrase "*variable-occurrence*" will be introduced. Take, for example, the case where S and A are variables; the string $S + (A * S)$ is made up of three instances of the variables (Weischedel et al., 1993). In this particular setting, one can indicate that a step in a derivation is defined by the current string, a particular instance of a variable that is contained within the string, and the production that has to be applied to that particular instance of the variable (Giegerich & Zu Siederdissen, 2010).

The fact that there is only one derivation tree for every derivation in a Context-Free Grammar (CFG) should not come as a surprise to anyone. When the derivation begins, the starting sign S, which represents the root node of the tree, is used to indicate the beginning of the process. Based on the initial production that takes place during the derivation, a choice is made for the children of this node. *A* production is carried out at each subsequent iteration of the process (Koechlin, 2022). There is a variable occurrence that is associated with this production, and it correlates to a certain node N in the tree. By going through this procedure, the precise region of the tree that is home to N and its progeny can be determined. In order to illustrate the point, the derivation is as follows:

Remember

Ambiguity in a grammar occurs when a single string can be generated in multiple ways, leading to different parse trees.

$$S \Rightarrow S+S \Rightarrow a+S \Rightarrow a+(S) \Rightarrow a+(S*S) \Rightarrow a+(a*S) \Rightarrow a+(a*a)$$

Each example of the string $a + (a * a)$ must start:

$$S \Rightarrow S+S$$

Currently, there are two viable options to move on, as the subsequent step could pertain to either of the two instances of S. If the rightmost option is selected in order to get *S+(S),* one would still have two alternatives for the subsequent phase (Dekkers et al., 1992).

When it was mentioned before that "if a string contains multiple possible derivations, one may be more suitable than another," it was specifically about derivations that correspond to various derivation trees, rather than derivations that differ in other ways. Within the derivations associated with the derivation tree in Figure 4.2, there are no significant distinctions, simply variations based on the selection of the next step involving the occurrence of S (Carpi et al., 2021).

4.5. SIMPLIFIED FORMS AND NORMAL FORMS

Concerning the strings that are generated by a language that does not take context into account, in many cases, questions are easier to handle when one has prior knowledge regarding the structure of the productions (Ge & Xu, 2010). On occasion, this entails acknowledging that some kinds of inventions are never present, while on other occasions, it entails acknowledging that every production adheres to a structure that is really straightforward. For example, take into consideration the scenario in which one has to find out whether or not *G* is responsible for producing a string *x*. Investigate all of the potential derivations in a methodical manner, beginning with the first step, then moving on to the second step, and eventually arriving at the answer (Waswa & Redkar, 2020).

There is either no change in the amount *t,* which represents the number of terminals in the current string of a derivation or there is an increase when each step is performed. In the event that G does not possess any Λ-productions, which are productions of the form $A \rightarrow \Lambda$, it is impossible for the length (l) of the current string to decrease (Wang et al., 2019). Therefore, the sum of t and l, which is denoted by *t+l*, cannot decrease either. Assuming that G does not possess any "unit productions", it is inevitable that the sum will increase. A derivation of x starts with S, where *l+t =1*, and ends with x, where *l+t =2x*. As a result, it is possible to draw the conclusion that no derivation has more than two steps that are equal to one (Loveland, 1969). One can draw the conclusion that x is not a member of the language that is formed by G if an exhaustive attempt is made to identify all potential derivations within a particular number of steps or less. This section will demonstrate the process of modifying an arbitrary Context-Free Grammar (CFG) G in such a way that the final grammar does not contain any productions of the types that have been stated. Despite this, it continues to generate the language *L(G),* with the exception of the empty string Λ, which may or may not be generated. In conclusion, the procedure of altering G is presented in order to get rid of both kinds of products as the first stage in the process (Pietruszczak et al., 2020).

An example that serves, as an illustration, will be used to show the concept of the algorithm that is used to remove Λ *productions*. Assume that one of the productions in G is such that Λ can be derived from both variables B and C, either in one or more steps, along with other strings of terminals that are not null (Yano et al., 1994).

$$A \rightarrow BCDCB$$

After applying the procedure, the possibility of replacing B and C with Λ will be eliminated. However, it is still necessary to ensure that any non-null strings that could have been obtained from A using these steps can still be obtained (Andrews, 1983).

- **Definition**

i. Every A with a production A→ Λ is nullable.

ii. If A_1, A_2, . . . , A_k are nullable variables, and

- $B \rightarrow A_1,\ A_2, \ldots.. A_k$.

The methodology employed to eradicate unit products from context-free grammar is quite analogous. The following rules are taken into account:

i. If $A \rightarrow B$ is a production and B is not identical to A, then B can be derived from A.

ii. If C is derivable from A, $C \rightarrow B$ is a production, and B is not equivalent to A, then B is also derivable from A.

iii. There are no other variables that can be derived from A (Arkoudas, 2005).

- **Example: 4.6 Converting a CFG to Chomsky Normal Form**

The purpose of this example is to illustrate all of the techniques that are discussed in this section. These techniques include the identification of nullable variables, the removal of Λ-productions, the identification of A-derivable variables for each A, the removal of unit productions, and the conversion to Chomsky normal form techniques (Messchendorp, 2022). When it comes to products, it is important to take into consideration the context-free grammar G:

$$S \rightarrow TU \mid V$$

$$U \rightarrow cU \mid \Lambda V \rightarrow aVc \mid W W \rightarrow bW \mid \Lambda$$

i. **Determining Which Variables are Nullable:** Considering their participation in Λ-productions, the variables T, U, and W are considered to be nullable factors. As a result of the production V → W, the variable V is negligible. S is also nullable, either because of the production S → TU or because of S → V. Both of these interpretations are valid. There is a presence of all the factors (Nelson, 1953).

2. **Removing Lambda-Productions:** Prior to the elimination of the Λ-productions, the following productions are included:

$$S \rightarrow TS \rightarrow UT \rightarrow abU \rightarrow cV \rightarrow acW \rightarrow b$$

After eliminating Λ-productions,

$$S \rightarrow TU \mid T \mid U \mid V \quad T \rightarrow aTb \mid ab$$

$$U \rightarrow cU \mid cV \rightarrow aVc \mid ac \mid WW \rightarrow bW \mid b$$

3. **Determining Variables that Can Be Derived from A, for Each A:** The S-derivable variables are T, U, V, and W, with W being included due to the production V → W. The variable that can be derived from V is W (Goldberg et al., 1982).

4. **Adding the Productions:**

$$S \rightarrow aTb \mid ab \mid cU \mid c \mid aVc \mid ac \mid bW \mid bV \rightarrow bW \mid b$$

At this stage;

$$S \rightarrow TU \mid aTb \mid ab \mid cU \mid c \mid aVc \mid ac \mid bW \mid b$$

$$T \rightarrow aTb \mid ab$$

$$U \rightarrow cU \mid c$$

$$V \rightarrow aVc \mid ac \mid bW \mid bW \rightarrow bW \mid b$$

To convert to Chomsky's normal form:

$$S \rightarrow TU \mid XaTXb \mid XaXb \mid XcU \mid c \mid XaVXc \mid XaXc \mid XbW \mid b$$

$$T \rightarrow XaTXb \mid XaXb$$

$U \rightarrow XcU \mid c$

$V \rightarrow XaV\ Xc \mid Xa\ Xc \mid XbW \mid bW \rightarrow XbW \mid b$

The reason why this grammar does not conform to Chomsky's normal form is only due to the productions $S \rightarrow X_a\ T\ X_b, S \rightarrow X_b V\ X_c, T \rightarrow X_a T\ X_b$, and V → XaV Xc. The above instructions lead to (Alamirew, 2017):

$S \rightarrow TU \mid XaY1 \mid XaXb \mid XcU \mid c \mid XaY2 \mid Xa\ Xc \mid XbW \mid bY1 \rightarrow T\ Xb$

$Y2 \rightarrow V\ Xc$

$T \rightarrow XaY3 \mid XaXbY3 \rightarrow T\ Xb$

$U \rightarrow XcU \mid c$

$V \rightarrow XaY4 \mid XaXc \mid XbW \mid bY4 \rightarrow V\ Xc$

$W \rightarrow XbW \mid b$

(It is evident that having both *Y1* and *Y3*, as well as both *Y2* and *Y4*, is unnecessary. Therefore, one can reduce *G1*.) (Crossley 2007).

SUMMARY

- The context-free grammars (CFGs) and their applications in defining more complicated languages than those handled by regular languages and finite automata are the topics that are discussed in this chapter. Beginning with a formal description of a context-free grammar (CFG), it then goes on to present a number of examples that illustrate how context-free grammars can be used to build languages. A few examples of this include the languages A^nB^n, algebraic expressions, palindromes, and non-palindromes. Another topic that is covered in this chapter is the derivation of strings in a CFG, as well as the problem of ambiguity, which refers to the fact that a single string might have numerous sources of origin.
- CFGs have the ability to explain the syntax of high-level programming languages, and they can also simplify grammars in order to reduce complexity. These are two of the most important points. Additionally, an introduction to the notation and rules for CFGs is provided in this chapter. Specialized languages, such as Expr and palindromes, are discussed. In addition, the chapter discusses ambiguity and derivation trees, emphasizing the significance of having distinct derivations for every string in order to prevent ambiguity.

REVIEW QUESTIONS

1. Define a context-free grammar (CFG) and explain its components.
2. How does a CFG differ from a regular grammar?
3. Provide an example of a language generated by a CFG and explain the derivation process.
4. What is ambiguity in a CFG, and why is it problematic?
5. Describe the process of simplifying a context-free grammar.
6. How can derivation trees be used to represent the structure of strings generated by a CFG?
7. Explain the importance of unique derivations in context-free grammars.
8. Discuss how context-free grammars can be used to describe the syntax of high-level programming languages.

MULTIPLE CHOICE QUESTIONS

1. What is a context-free grammar (CFG)?

a. A grammar that is free of context

b. A 4-tuple consisting of variables, terminal symbols, a start variable, and production rules

c. A type of grammar that generates regular languages

d. A grammar that cannot generate complex languages

2. **Which of the following is an example of a language generated by a context-free grammar?**
    a. A language where the number of 'a's equals the number of 'b's
    b. A language with an arbitrary number of 'a's followed by 'b's
    c. A language where the number of '0's equals the number of '1's and '2's
    d. A language with 'a's, 'b's, and 'c's in any order
3. What does the notation S → Λ | aSb represent?
    a. S can be replaced by Λ or aSb
    b. S can only be replaced by Λ
    c. S can only be replaced by aSb
    d. S can be replaced by any string
4. In the derivation of a string, what does the notation $\alpha \Rightarrow \beta$ mean?
    a. α is derived from β
    b. β is derived from α
    c. α and β are equivalent
    d. α and β are both terminal strings
5. **What is the primary concern when a grammar is ambiguous?**
    a. The grammar cannot generate any strings
    b. The grammar generates strings that are not in the language
    c. A single string can have multiple derivations
    d. The grammar generates only regular languages
6. **Which of the following languages can be generated by a CFG with productions**

    $S \rightarrow \Lambda | aB | bA, A \rightarrow aS | bAA, and\ B \rightarrow bS | aBB$?
    a. The language of palindromes
    b. The language of non-palindromes
    c. A language where the number of 'a's equals the number of 'b's
    d. The language of algebraic expressions

Answers to Multiple Questions

1. (b); 2. (a); 3. (a); 4. (b); 5. (c); 6. (c)

REFERENCES

1. Aho, A. V., Kernighan, B. W., & Weinberger, P. J. (1979). Awk—A pattern scanning and processing language. *Software: Practice and Experience, 9*(4), 267–279.
2. Akama, K., & Nantajeewarawat, E. (2012). Simplifying query-answering problems by unfolding. In *Fourth International Conference on Machine Vision (ICMV 2011):*

Computer Vision and Image Analysis; Pattern Recognition and Basic Technologies (Vol. 8350, pp. 675–679).

3. Alamirew, L. A. (2017). Alternative method to check ambiguity in context free grammars. *Journal of Engineering and Technology (JET), 8*(2), 71–80.
4. Andrei, S., Chin, W. N., & Cavadini, S. V. (2004). Self-embedded context-free grammars with regular counterparts. *Acta Informatica, 40*(5), 349–365.
5. Andrews, P. B. (1983). On simplifying the matrix of a WFF. In *Automation of Reasoning: 2: Classical Papers on Computational Logic 1967–1970* (pp. 102–116).
6. Arkoudas, K. (2005). Simplifying proofs in Fitch-style natural deduction systems. *Journal of Automated Reasoning, 34*, 239–294.
7. Brabrand, C., Giegerich, R., & Møller, A. (2010). Analyzing ambiguity of context-free grammars. *Science of Computer Programming, 75*(3), 176–191.
8. Bzymek, M., & Lovett, S. T. (2001). Evidence for two mechanisms of palindrome-stimulated deletion in Escherichia coli: Single-strand annealing and replication slipped mispairing. *Genetics, 158*(2), 527–540.
9. Carpi, A., D'Alessandro, F., Ibarra, O. H., & McQuillan, I. (2021). Relationships between bounded languages, counter machines, finite-index grammars, ambiguity, and commutative regularity. *Theoretical Computer Science, 862*, 97–118.
10. Chen, W. Y. (1993). Context-free grammars, differential operators and formal power series. *Theoretical Computer Science, 117*(1–2), 113–129.
11. Chomsky, N., & Schützenberger, M. P. (1959). The algebraic theory of context-free languages. In *Studies in Logic and the Foundations of Mathematics* (Vol. 26, pp. 118–161).
12. Črepinšek, M., Mernik, M., Bryant, B. R., Javed, F., & Sprague, A. (2005). Inferring context-free grammars for domain-specific languages. *Electronic Notes in Theoretical Computer Science, 141*(4), 99–116.
13. Crossley, S. A., Louwerse, M. M., McCarthy, P. M., & McNamara, D. S. (2007). A linguistic analysis of simplified and authentic texts. *The Modern Language Journal, 91*(1), 15–30.
14. Čulík, K. (1967). On some transformations in context-free grammars and languages. *Czechoslovak Mathematical Journal, 17*(2), 278–311.
15. Currie, J. D. (2008). Palindrome positions in ternary square-free words. *Theoretical Computer Science, 396*(1–3), 254–257.
16. D'Alessandro, F., Carpi, A., Ibarra, O., & McQuillan, I. (2020). Relationships between bounded languages, counter machines, finite-index grammars, ambiguity, and commutative equivalence. *Theoretical Computer Science, 862*, 97–118.
17. Dassow, J., Manea, F., & Truthe, B. (2012). On external contextual grammars with subregular selection languages. *Theoretical Computer Science, 449*, 64–73.
18. Dekkers, C., Nederhof, M. J., & Sarbo, J. J. (1992). Coping with ambiguity in decorated parse forests. In *Coping with Linguistic Ambiguity in Typed Feature Formalisms, Proceedings of a Workshop held at ECAI* (pp. 11–19).

19. Della Vigna, P., & Ghezzi, C. (1978). Context-free graph grammars. *Information and Control, 37*(2), 207–233.

20. Demri, S. (2001). The complexity of regularity in grammar logics and related modal logics. *Journal of Logic and Computation, 11*(6), 933–960.

21. Dickins, P. M. R., & Woods, E. G. (1988). Some criteria for the development of communicative grammar tasks. *TESOL Quarterly, 22*(4), 623–646.

22. Domaratzki, M., Pighizzini, G., & Shallit, J. (2002). Simulating finite automata with context-free grammars. *Information Processing Letters, 84*(6), 339–344.

23. Dowty, D. R. (1978). Governed transformations as lexical rules in a Montague Grammar. *Linguistic Inquiry, 9*(3), 393–426.

24. Droste, M., & Vogler, H. (2014). The Chomsky-Schützenberger theorem for quantitative context-free languages. *International Journal of Foundations of Computer Science, 25*(8), 955–969.

25. Ehrenfeucht, A., Kleijn, H. C. M., & Rozenberg, G. (1985). Adding global forbidding context to context-free grammars. *Theoretical Computer Science, 37*, 337–360.

26. Fedorchenko, L., & Baranov, S. (2015). Equivalent transformations and regularization in context-free grammars. *Cybernetics and Information Technologies, 14*(4), 29–44.

27. García, P., Vidal, E., & Casacuberta, F. (1987). Local languages, the successor method, and a step towards a general methodology for the inference of regular grammars. *IEEE Transactions on Pattern Analysis and Machine Intelligence, 9*(6), 841–845.

28. Ge, J., & Xu, J. (2010). Fold-Hopf bifurcation in a simplified four-neuron BAM (bidirectional associative memory) neural network with two delays. *Science China Technological Sciences, 53*, 633–644.

29. Giegerich, R., & zu Siederdissen, C. H. (2010). Semantics and ambiguity of stochastic RNA family models. *IEEE/ACM Transactions on Computational Biology and Bioinformatics, 8*(2), 499–516.

30. Goldberg, A., Purdom, P., & Brown, C. (1982). Average time analysis of simplified Davis-Putnam procedures. *Information Processing Letters, 15*(2), 72–75.

31. Hochmann, J. R., Azadpour, M., & Mehler, J. (2008). Do humans really learn A^nB^n artificial grammars from exemplars? *Cognitive Science, 32*(6), 1021–1036.

32. Hong, M., Soderstrom, T., & Zheng, W. X. (2007). A simplified form of the bias-eliminating least squares method for errors-in-variables identification. *IEEE Transactions on Automatic Control, 52*(9), 1754–1756.

33. Jones, A. K., & Liskov, B. H. (1978). A language extension for expressing constraints on data access. *Communications of the ACM, 21*(5), 358–367.

34. Koechlin, F. (2022). New analytic techniques for proving the inherent ambiguity of context-free languages. In *Foundations of Software Technology and Theoretical Computer Science (FSTTCS)* (Vol. 250, pp. 10–4230).

35. Loveland, D. W. (1969). A simplified format for the model elimination theorem-proving procedure. *Journal of the ACM (JACM), 16*(3), 349–363.

36. Manna, M., Scarcello, F., & Leone, N. (2011). On the complexity of regular-grammars with integer attributes. *Journal of Computer and System Sciences, 77*(2), 393–421.

37. Mees, I., & Collins, B. (1982). A phonetic description of the consonant system of Standard Dutch (ABN). *Journal of the International Phonetic Association, 12*(1), 2–12.

38. Messchendorp, E. B. (2022). Short traditional and long simplified: The paradox of contemporary traditional Taiwanese characters that consist of fewer strokes than their equivalent simplified forms. *Journal of Chinese Writing Systems, 6*(4), 297–317.

39. Mohri, M., & Pereira, F. C. (1998). Dynamic compilation of weighted context-free grammars. In *36th Annual Meeting of the Association for Computational Linguistics and 17th International Conference on Computational Linguistics* (Vol. 2, pp. 891–897).

40. Nakamura, K., & Matsumoto, M. (2002). Incremental learning of context-free grammars. In *Grammatical Inference: Algorithms and Applications: 6th International Colloquium, ICGI 2002 Amsterdam, The Netherlands, September 23–25, 2002 Proceedings* (Vol. 6, pp. 174–184).

41. Nelson, R. J. (1953). WV Quine. The problem of simplifying truth functions. *The Journal of Symbolic Logic, 18*(3), 280–282. [Offprint 1952, on sale by the Mathematical Association of America.]

42. Pietruszczak, A., Klonowski, M., & Petrukhin, Y. (2020). Simplified Kripke-style semantics for some normal modal logics. *Studia Logica, 108*(3), 451–476.

43. Postal, P. M., & Langendoen, D. T. (1984). English and the class of context-free languages. *Computational Linguistics, 10*(3–4), 177–181.

44. Reghizzi, S. C., & San Pietro, P. (2019). Non-erasing Chomsky-Schützenberger theorem with grammar-independent alphabet. *Information and Computation, 269*, 104442.

45. Robinson, P. (1996). Learning simple and complex second language rules under implicit, incidental, rule-search, and instructed conditions. *Studies in Second Language Acquisition, 18*(1), 27–67.

46. Sakakibara, Y. (1992). Efficient learning of context-free grammars from positive structural examples. *Information and Computation, 97*(1), 23–60.

47. Salomaa, A. (1969). On the index of a context-free grammar and language. *Information and Control, 14*(5), 474–477.

48. Schabes, Y., & Waters, R. C. (1995). Tree insertion grammar: A cubic-time, parsable formalism that lexicalizes context-free grammar without changing the trees produced. *Computational Linguistics, 21*(4), 479–513.

49. Sheng, L., & Li, Y. (2006). Regular grammars with truth values in lattice-ordered monoid and their languages. *Soft Computing, 10*, 79–86.

50. Sperber, M., Dybvig, R. K., Flatt, M., Van Straaten, A., Findler, R., & Matthews, J. (2009). Revised6 report on the algorithmic language Scheme. *Journal of Functional Programming, 19*(S1), 1–301.

51. Tanaka, H., Bergstrom, D. A., Yao, M. C., & Tapscott, S. J. (2005). Widespread and nonrandom distribution of DNA palindromes in cancer cells provides a structural platform for subsequent gene amplification. *Nature Genetics, 37*(3), 320–327.

52. Uppström, L. R. (1968). A modified method for determination of boron with curcumin and a simplified water elimination procedure. *Analytica Chimica Acta, 43*, 475–486.

53. Von Lavante, E., & Lyer, V. S. V. (1985). Simplified implicit block-bidiagonal finite difference method for solving the Navier-Stokes equations. *AIAA Journal, 23*(7), 1130–1132.

54. Walters, R. F. (1989). A note on context-free languages. *Journal of Pure and Applied Algebra, 62*(2), 199–203.

55. Wang, T., Cheng, Z., Bu, R., & Ma, R. (2019). Stability and Hopf bifurcation analysis of a simplified six-neuron tridiagonal two-layer neural network model with delays. *Neurocomputing, 332*, 203–214.

56. Waswa, P., & Redkar, S. (2020). A direct approach for simplifying nonlinear systems with external periodic excitation using normal forms. *Nonlinear Dynamics, 99*(2), 1065–1088.

57. Weischedel, R., Meteer, M., Schwartz, R., Ramshaw, L., & Palmucci, J. (1993). Coping with ambiguity and unknown words through probabilistic models. *Computational Linguistics, 19*(2), 359–382.

58. Wich, K. (2005). Sublogarithmic ambiguity. *Theoretical Computer Science, 345*(2, 3), 473–504.

59. Widodo, H. P. (2006). Approaches and procedures for teaching grammar. *English Teaching: Practice and Critique, 5*(1), 122–141.

60. Xu, C. (2018). Local and global Hopf bifurcation analysis on simplified bidirectional associative memory neural networks with multiple delays. *Mathematics and Computers in Simulation, 149*, 69–90.

61. Yang, C., Crain, S., Berwick, R. C., Chomsky, N., & Bolhuis, J. J. (2017). The growth of language: Universal Grammar, experience, and principles of computation. *Neuroscience & Biobehavioral Reviews, 81*, 103–119.

62. Yano, Y., Long, M. H., & Ross, S. (1994). The effects of simplified and elaborated texts on foreign language reading comprehension. *Language Learning, 44*(2), 189–219.

63. Yu, S., Zhuang, Q., & Salomaa, K. (1994). The state complexities of some basic operations on regular languages. *Theoretical Computer Science, 125*(2), 315–328.

CHAPTER 5

Pushdown Automata

LEARNING OBJECTIVES

After studying this chapter, you will be able to:

- Define and describe the structure and functioning of pushdown automata (PDA).
- Differentiate between deterministic and nondeterministic pushdown automata.
- Explain how pushdown automata can be used to recognize context-free languages.
- Illustrate the process of designing a PDA for a given language.
- Understand the relationship between context-free grammars (CFG) and pushdown automata.
- Apply the concept of stack operations in PDAs.
- Analyze the limitations and capabilities of PDAs compared to finite automata and Turing machines.

Construct pushdown automata for specific context-free languages.

KEY TERMS FROM THIS CHAPTER

Acceptance by empty stack
Deterministic pushdown automaton (DPDA)
Nondeterministic pushdown automaton (NPDA)
Stack alphabet
Context-free grammar (CFG)
Input alphabet
Pushdown automaton (PDA)
Transition function

UNIT INTRODUCTION

On the concept of computation, a field of theoretical computing science, there exists a specific kind of automaton which utilizes a stack. This automaton is known as a pushdown automaton (PDA) (Muller & Schupp, 1985).

Pushdown automata play a crucial role in the study of computing power. They have a greater degree of abilities compared to finite-state machines, although get fall short of the capacity offered by Turing machines. Pushdown automata come in two kinds: deterministic and nondeterministic. Deterministic can identify all deterministic context-free languages, whereas nondeterministic may identify all languages that have no context (Ginsburg & Spanier, 1966). Deterministic are often employed in the design of parsers (Okhotin & Salomaa, 2014).

The concept of "pushdown" in this context shows the analogy of the stack behaving such as a tray dispenser in a cafeteria, where operations exclusively focus on the topmost element. In contrast, a stack automaton permits access to and manipulation of elements further down the stack. Stack automata can identify a set of languages that is strictly larger than the set recognized by pushdown automata. A nested stack automaton offers complete access and the ability to stack values as entire sub-stacks, instead of just individual finite symbols (Kutrib & Malcher, 2012) (Figure 5.1).

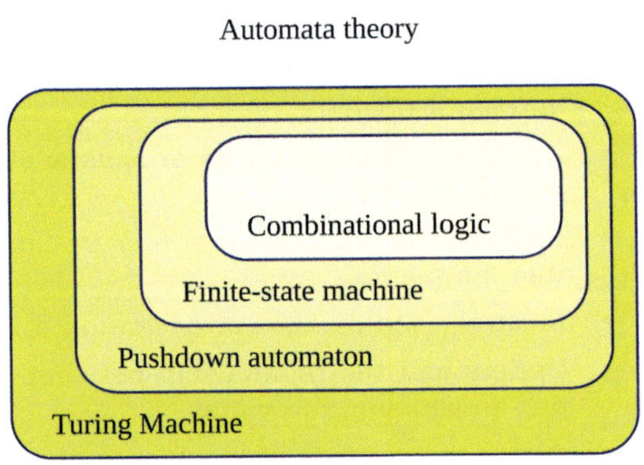

Figure 5.1. *Illustration of the classes of automata.*

Source: John E Hopercoft, Creative Commons License.

In the concept of computation, the pushdown automaton (PDA) seems a type of automaton which utilizes a stack to enhance its memory capabilities beyond what a finite-state machine can offer. PDAs are a handy tool when it comes to recognizing context-free languages (Abdulla et al., 2013). These languages fall somewhere in between regular languages and the more complex ones that Turing machines can handle. In this section, one delves into the structure, functioning, and applications of PDAs. It also distinguishes between deterministic and nondeterministic versions, showcasing their utility in knowing context-free languages. These languages play a vital role in the design and analysis of programming languages (Janoušek & Melichar, 2009).

5.1. INFORMAL DESCRIPTION

Similar to standard expressions having a corresponding automaton called the finite automaton, context-free grammar additionally possesses a specific machine counterpart known to be the pushdown automaton. Here, the equivalence is a bit short in satisfaction because the pushdown automaton operates in a nondeterministic manner, along with the deterministic version will accept a subset of all context-free languages (Heizmann et al., 2017). Luckily, this subset covers the syntax of many programming languages. A pushdown automaton operates similarly to a finite automaton, but with the added capability of controlling an input tape along with a stack, which functions as a "first in-last out" list. Symbols can only be entered or eliminated at the highest point of the list (Abbott, 1983). When a symbol is entered at the top, the symbol previously at the top becomes second from the top, the symbol previously second from the top becomes third, and so on. Similarly, when a symbol is removed from the top of the list, the symbol previously second from the top becomes the top symbol, the symbol previously third from the top becomes second, and so on. A familiar example of a stack is the stack of plates on a spring that one sees in cafeterias (Miriyala & Harandi, 1991). There is a spring below the plates with just enough strength so that exactly one plate appears above the level of the counter. When that top plate is removed, the load on the spring is lightened, and the plate directly below appears above the level of the counter. If a plate is then put on top of the stack, the pile is pushed down, and only the new plate appears above the counter. For our purposes, one assume that the spring is arbitrarily long, so we may add as many plates as we desire (Nelson et al., 2007).

Such a stack of plates, coupled with a finite control, can be used to recognize a +. The set is a context-free language, generated by the grammar S-0S0. It is not hard to show that l cannot be accepted by any finite automaton. To accept l, we shall make use of a finite control with two states, and , and a stack on which we place blue, green, and red plates. The device will operate by the following rules (Fikes, 1982).

i. The machine begins with a single red plate upon the stack and its finite control set to state .
ii. When an input to a device is 0 along with the device entering state , the blue plates is set on the stack. When the input for the device remains 1 and a device remains in state , a green plate gets added to the stack. In both scenarios, the finite control stays in state .
iii. When the input is 'c' along with the device remaining in state , it smoothly transitions to state without any plates being added or removed (Nasr et al., 2017).

iv. When the input value is 0 along with the device having reached state featuring a blue plate on the top of a stack representing 0, the plate is simply removed. When the input is 1 along with the device being in state that has a green plate on top of its stack, the plate can simply be removed. In both scenarios, the finite control stays in state .

v. In every other instance, the device is unable to make any move (Balzer et al., 1977).

The device stated above takes an input string when, upon processing the final symbol within the string, the row of plates is left empty. It is important to keep in mind that once the stack becomes empty, there are no more possible moves. Basically, the device functions in the following manner. While in state q u, the device creates a visual representation of its data by adding a blue plate to the stack for every 0 encountered, and a green plate for every 1 encountered (Duris & Galil, 1982). When the input is 'c', the device transitions to state . Afterward, the rest of the input is contrasted with the stack by removing a plate at the top of the stack whenever the input symbol matches certain criteria. If the top plate is not the correct color, the device will come to a stop and will not be able to continue processing the input. Once all the plates align with the inputs, the red plate situated at the bottom of each stack will eventually become visible (Carayol & Wöhrle, 2003). The red plate is promptly removed and also the device is considered acceptable as the input string. Only if the string that appears after the "c" in the device is the opposite of what came before it, the entire plates can be removed (Allauzen et al., 2014).

5.2. PUSHDOWN AUTOMATA

Look at finite automata that recognize the language

$$L_1(M) = \{a^m b^n \mid m, n \geq 1\}.$$

It is observed that M transitions from to when *a's* are encountered. When encountering the letter '*b*', *M* transitions from state to and remains in state as more '*b's* are received (Qiu, 2007).

Assume that the input string is given by:

$a^m b^n$,

Then the resulting state is final state and so M accepts .

Let's take a look at the language (M), which consists of strings that have an equal number of *a's* and *b's*, represented as {|. The finite automaton constructed for language is different from the one constructed for language (XU et al., 1996).

Considering the language (M) = {{| there is not necessity to remember the number of *a's*. The following have to be remembered.

i. Whether the first symbol is '*b*' (to reject the string)
ii. Whether '*a*' follows '*b*' (to reject the string)
iii. Whether '*a*' follows '*a*' and '*b*' follows '*b*' (to accept the string) (Bednárová et al., 2014).

We know that FA has only a finite number of states, M cannot remember the number of *a's* in where '*n*' is larger than the number of states of M.

The FA does not accept the sets of the form ||. This is taken care by a "PUSHDOWN AUTOMATA".

Now demonstrate a model of a Pushdown Automata (PDA) (Chrétien et al., 2015).

5.2.1. Nondeterministic PDA (Definition)

An NPDA is defined by the 7-tuple

$$M = (Q, \Sigma, \Gamma, \delta, q_0, Z, F)$$

Remember

Remember, a pushdown automaton (PDA) uses a stack as its additional memory structure, which allows it to handle a broader class of languages, specifically context-free languages. This makes PDAs more powerful than finite automata but less powerful than Turing machines.

Whereas; Q is the Finite set of internal states of the control unit; Σ is the Input alphabet; Γ = Finite set of symbols called "Stack alphabet"; δ: Q × (Σ ∪ {l}) × Γ ⊠ finite subsets of Q × Γ* is the transition function; = Initial state of the control unit Q; Z = Stack start symbol; and $F \subseteq Q$ = Set of Final states. The arguments of are the current state of the control unit, the current input symbol, and the current symbol on the top of the stack.

The result is a set of pairs (q, x)

Where; q = next state of the control unit (Salomaa & Yu, 1994); x = string that is put on top of the stack in place of the single symbol there before.

The 'stack' is an additional component available as part of PDA. The 'stack' increases its memory. With respect to {|, we can store *a's* in the stack. When the symbol '*b*' is encountered, an '*a*' from the stack can be removed. If the stack becomes empty on the completion of processing a given string, then the PDA accepts the string (Coquidé et al., 1991) (Figure 5.2)

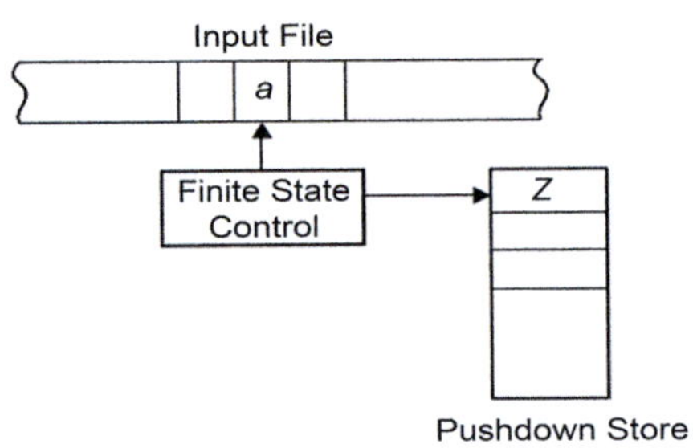

Figure 5.2. *Illustration of Model of Pushdown Automaton (PDA).*

Source: Jeffry D Ulleman, Creative Commons License

5.2.2. Transition Functions for NPDA

The transition function for an NPDA has the form

$$\delta: Q \times (\Sigma \cup \{\lambda\}) \times \Gamma \rightarrow \textit{Finite subsets of } Q \times \overline{\Gamma}$$

Now, δ has three arguments instead of the previous number. The initial two arguments remain unchanged (Zhang & Vyazovkin, 2006).

i. State

ii. Either , or a symbol to the set of input characters.

The symbol on the top of the stack is the third argument.

Like how an input symbol was "consumed" during the function application, the stack symbol also gets "consumed" and removed from the stack. It is important to note that although the second argument , can be empty, it cannot be an input symbol from the alphabet, meaning no data symbol is consumed. However, this option is not available for the third argument (Namikawa & Hashimoto, 2004).

The transition function always uses a symbol that is in the stack, and no shift is possible if its contents is empty.

In addition, there is a possibility of a -transition where the second one is λ, indicating the potential for a move that requires no consuming of an input symbol. There are no available moves when the stack is empty (Reddy et al., 2013).

- **Example:** Consider the set of transition rules of an NPDA given by

$$\delta\left(q_1,a,b\right)=\left\{\left(q_2,cd\right),\left(q_3,\lambda\right)\right\}$$

When the control unit reaches state , along with an input symbol read represents '*a*', while the symbol upon the top of the stack represents '*b*', there are two possible scenarios that can unfold.

i. In the process, the control unit typically transitions to a specific state, while the string '*cd*' takes the place of '*b*' at the top of the stack.
ii. The control unit enters a new state, , as it removes the symbol *b* via the highest point of the stack (Hopkins et al., 2011).

While the function applies within the deterministic case, the automaton shifts to another state q Q and adds a new string for symbols x Γ^* onto the stack. When working on a nondeterministic pushdown automaton, the outcome of applying is a finite collection of (*q*, *x*) pairs (Pighizzini, 2009).

5.2.3. Drawing NPDAs

Diagrams for NPDAs are typically not included. However, by making some minor extensions, one can easily illustrate an NPDA in which illustrates an NFA (Amsden, 2003).

Instead of assigning an element to an arc, one had the option to mark arcs with

$a \mid x,\ y$ where $a \in \Sigma$, $x \in \Gamma$ and $y \in \Gamma^*$.

Now, look at the NPDA provided.

$$(Q=\{q_0, q_1, q_2, q_3\}, \Sigma=\{a,b\}, \Gamma=\{0,1\}, \delta, q_0, Z=0, F=\{q_3\})$$

$$\delta(q_0, a, 0)=\{(q_1, 10), (q_3, \lambda)\}$$
$$\delta(q_0, \lambda, 0)=\{(q_3, \lambda)\}$$
$$\delta(q_1, a, 1)=\{(q_1, 11)\}$$
$$\delta(q_1, b, 1)=\{(q_2, \lambda)\}$$
$$\delta(q_1, b, 1)=\{(q_2, \lambda)\}$$
$$\delta(q_1, \lambda, 0)=\{(q_3, \lambda)\}$$

This NPDA is drawn as follows.

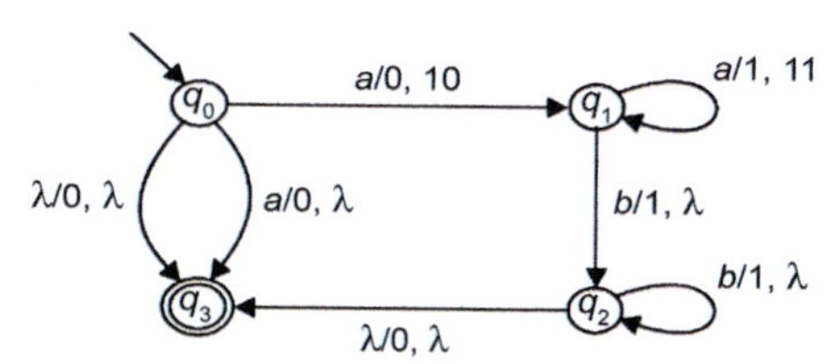

It is important to keep in mind that the stack's top is thought to be on the left side (Goldstine et al., 2005). For instance, when one encounters an '*a*' at the very beginning, the stack transitions from '0' to '10'.

5.2.4. Execution of NPDA

Imagine a scenario where someone happens to be navigating through a string using a DFA, and one is required to step in and complete the task. Two important concepts need to be understood

i. Determining the current state within the DFA, and
ii. Identifying the rest of the input (Dreyfus et al., 2014).

However, in the case of an NPDA, an additional piece of information needs to consider is the contents within the stack (Ibarra & Tran, 2012).

5.2.4.1. Instantaneous Description of a PDA

The PDA's instantaneous overview consists of three components: *q*, *w*, and *u*.

Whereas current state of the automaton (*q*); unread part of the input string (*w*); and stack contents (*u*) expressed as a string, (the symbol positioned at the top of each stack is the one on the leftmost side) (Bednárová et al., 2014).

5.2.4.2. Transitioning of a PDA

If the symbol "|–" represents a move within the NPDA, and if one assumes that (q_1, a, x) is the current state and {(q_2 , y),...}, is the new state, then it is possible to conclude the following.

$$(q_1, aW, xz) \mid - (q_2, W, yz)$$

In this context, *W* represents the remaining part of the string after '*a*', while *Z* represents the remaining contents of the stack below '*x*'.

The given notation describes the transition from state into state . It indicates that an '*a*' is taken of the input string, *aW*, along with the *x* on the top (left) within the stack *xZ* is substituted with *y*, resulting in *yZ* remaining on the stack (Goldstine et al., 2005).

5.2.4.3. Acceptance

Assume that you have the NPDA given by

$$M = (Q, \Sigma, \Gamma, \delta, q_0, Z, F).$$

To recognize string *w*, begin with the instantaneous assumption

$$(q_0, W, z)$$

Where; is the start state; *w* is the entire string to be processed, and *z* is the start stack symbol (Takahashi & Ito, 2023). Starting with this instantaneous description, make zero or more moves, just as is done with an NFA. There are two kinds of moves that can be made:

i. λ-Transitions: If you are in state *q1*, *x* is the top (leftmost) symbol in the stack, and

$$\delta(q_1, \lambda, x) = \{(q_1, W_2), \cdots\cdots\}$$

Subsequently, the symbol *x* can be substituted using the string w_2 with the transition to state q_2 can be made (Kutrib et al., 2017).

ii. Nonempty transitions: In the scenario where, one finds oneself in state *q1*, with '*a*' as the next unused input symbol and *x* as the most recent (leftmost) symbol across the stack,

$$\delta(q_1, a, x) = \{(q_2, W_2), \cdots\cdots\}$$

After eliminating the letter '*a*' about the input string, substituting the symbol *x* via the string w_2, or transitioning to state q_2

If you are in the final state when you reach the end of the string (and may be make some λ-transition after reaching the end), then the string is accepted by the NPDA. It does not matter what is on the stack (Meduna, 2003).

5.2.6. An Example of NPDA Execution

Consider the NPDA represented by

$$\delta(q_0, a, 0) = \{(q_1, 10), (q_3, \lambda)\}$$
$$\delta(q_0, \lambda, 0) = \{(q_3, \lambda)\}$$
$$\delta(q_1, a, 1) = \{(q_1, 11)\}$$
$$\delta(q_1, b, 1) = \{(q_2, \lambda)\}$$
$$\delta(q_2, b, 1) = \{(q_2, \lambda)\}$$
$$\delta(q_1, \lambda, 0) = \{(q_3, \lambda)\}$$

Recognizing the string "aaabbb" can be achieved by following a particular order of moves (Blom & Bloem, 2000).

$$(q_0, aaabbb, 0) \quad (q_1, aabbb, 10)$$
$$(q_1, abbb, 110)$$
$$(q_1, bbb, 1110)$$
$$(q_2, bb, 110)$$
$$(q_2, b, 10)$$
$$(q_2, \lambda, 0)$$

5.2.7. Accepting Strings with NPDA (Formal Version)

The notation "|–" is used to indicate a single move of an NPDA.

- "*"is used to indicate a sequence of zero or more moves.
- +"is used to indicate a sequence of one or more moves (Dreyfus et al., 2014).

If $M = (Q, \Sigma, \Gamma, \delta, q_0, Z, F)$ is an NPDA, then the language accepted by M, L(M), is given by

$$L(M) = \left\{ w \in \Sigma^* : (q_0, w, z) \overset{*}{\vdash} (p, \lambda, u), p \in F, u \in \Gamma^* \right\}.$$

- **Example 5.1:** Construct a Pushdown Automata (PDA) accepting $\{a^n b^m a^n \mid m, n \geq 1\}$ by null store.
- **Solution**

The PDA which will accept

$$\{a^n b^m a^n \mid m, n \geq 1\}$$

is given below

$$PDA = (\{q_0, q_1\}, \{a, b\}, \{a, z_0\}, \delta, q_0, z_0, \phi)$$

Where; δ is given by (Tran, 2006).

$$(1)\, \delta(q_0, a, z_0) = \{(q_0, a z_0)\}$$
$$(2)\, \delta(q_0, a, a) = \{(q_0, aa)\}$$
$$(3)\, \delta(q_0, b, a) = \{(q_1, a)\}$$
$$(4)\, \delta(q_1, b, a) = \{(q_1, a)\}$$
$$(5)\, \delta(q_1, a, a) = \{(q_1, \lambda)\}$$
$$(6)\, \delta(q_1, \lambda, z_0) = \{(q_1, \lambda)\}$$

Thus, it is evident that the process of storing '*a's* begins until the occurrence of '*b*' ((1) and (2)). When the present input symbol seems *b*, a state transition occurs, but there is no modification to the Pushdown Automata structure ((3)). After the *b's* within the input string have completed their action at position ((4)), the other *a's* are removed ((5)).

Utilizing (6), z_0 is erased (Matthes & Uustalu, 2004).

Hence one had

$$(q_0, a^n b^m a^n, z_0) \overset{*}{\vdash} (q_1, \lambda, z_0) \vdash (q_1, \lambda, \lambda)$$

Thus, one sees that $a^n b^m a^n \in N(PDA)$

- **Example 5.2:** Construct a PDA accepting $\{a^n b^{2n} \mid n \geq 1\}$ by empty store.
- **Solution**

The PDA that will accept $\{a^n b^{2n} \mid n \geq 1\}$ is given by (Makkai & Pitts, 1987).

$$PDA = (\{q_0, q_1, q_2\}, \{a, b\}, \{a, z_0\}, \delta, q_0, z_0, \phi)$$

where δ is given by

$$\delta(q_0, a, z_0) = \{(q_1, a z_0)\}$$
$$\delta(q_1, a, a) = \{(q_1, aa)\}$$
$$\delta(q_1, b, a) = \{(q_2, a)\}$$
$$\delta(q_2, b, a) = \{(q_1, \lambda)\}$$
$$\delta(q_1, \lambda, z_0) = \{(q_1, \lambda)\}$$

ACTIVITY 5.1

Objective: To design a pushdown automaton (PDA) for a given context-free language without using mathematical expressions.

Activity:

The chosen language for this PDA design is the set of strings containing equal numbers of '*a's* and '*b's*. Begin by identifying the components of the PDA, including states such as Start, Processing, and Accepting; input symbols '*a*' and '*b*'; stack symbols where 'X' is used to match pairs; the initial state, which is Start; the stack start symbol 'Z' marking the bottom of the stack; and the accepting state, which is Accepting. Next, draw a state diagram with circles representing the states and arrows showing transitions between these states. Label each arrow with the input symbol and the stack operation (push or pop). For instance, an '*a*' input from the Start state pushes 'X' onto the stack and moves to the Processing state. In the Processing state, each '*a*' input pushes another 'X' onto the stack, while each '*b*' input pops an 'X' from the stack. The PDA transitions to the Accepting state when the input is finished, and the stack is empty. Test the PDA with example strings, such as "*aabb*," to ensure it processes each input correctly and modifies the stack appropriately. Finally, provide an explanation of the PDA design, detailing how it manages the chosen language and how the stack operations enable the recognition of valid strings.

5.3. RELATIONSHIP BETWEEN PDA AND CONTEXT FREE LANGUAGES

5.3.1. Simplifying CFGs

The productions of context-free grammars can be coerced into a variety of forms without affecting the expressive power of the grammar (Weir, 1992).

5.3.1.1. Empty Production Removal

If the empty string does not belong to a language, then there is no way to eliminate production of the form $A \to \lambda$ from the grammar (Fresse et al., 2018). If the empty string belongs to a language, then we can eliminate λ from all productions, and the same for the single productions $S \to \lambda$. In this case we can eliminate any occurrences of S from the right-hand-side of productions (van Heerdt et al., 2019).

5.3.1.2. Unit Production Removal

We can eliminate productions of the form A → B from a CFG.

5.3.1.3. Left Recursion Removal

A variable A is left-recursive if it occurs in a production of the form

$$A \to Ax$$

for any $x \in (V \cup T)^*$. A grammar is left-recursive if it contains at least one left-recursive variable. Every CFL can be represented by a grammar that is not left-recursive (Ahrens et al., 2015).

5.3.2. Normal Forms of Context-Free Grammars

5.3.2.1. Chomsky Normal Form

A grammar is in Chomsky Normal form if all productions are of the form

$$A \rightarrow BC$$

$$A \rightarrow a$$

Where; A, B and C are variables and 'a' is a terminal. Any context-free grammar that does not contain λ can be put into Chomsky Normal Form (Rosenkrantz, 1967).

5.3.3. Greibach Normal Form (GNF)

All creations in grammar belong to the Greibach Normal Forms if they are of a specific form.

$$A \rightarrow ax$$

Where 'a' is a terminal having $x \in V^*$.

Grammars within the Greibach Normal Form tend to be significantly longer compared to the context-free grammars from which these were derived. GNF is a valuable tool in demonstrating the equivalence between NPDA and CFG. Therefore, GNF proves to be valuable when transforming a CFG into an NPDA (Urbanek, 1986).

5.3.4. CFG to NPDA

Constructing a comparable (NPDA) using any context-free grammar within GNF is a simple process. Any string of a context-free language has a leftmost derivation. We set up the NPDA so that the stack contents "corresponds" to this sentential form: every move of the NPDA represents one derivation step (Morita et al., 1997).

The sentential form is:

$$(\text{The characters already read}) + (\text{symbols on the stack}) - (\text{Final } z(\text{initial stack symbol}))$$

In the NPDA, we will construct, the states that are not of much importance. All the real work is done on the stack. We will use only the following three states, irrespective of the complexity of the grammar.

i. The start state, q_0, serves as an initial point for initializing the process. The transition via q_0 to q_1 is utilized to place the initial symbol of the grammar onto the stack.

$$\delta(q_0, \lambda, Z) \rightarrow \{(q_1, S_Z)\}$$

ii. The primary responsibility lies with state q_1. Each derivation step is depicted as a transition from q_0 to q_1.

iii. The acceptance of the string is determined by the transition via q_1 to q_f (Hossain et al., 2021).

$$\delta(q_1, \lambda, z) \rightarrow \{(q_f, z)\}$$

Example: Consider the grammar

$$P = \{S \rightarrow a, S \rightarrow aAB, A \rightarrow aA, A \rightarrow a, B \rightarrow bB, B \rightarrow b\}$$

The parts of these creations can be rearranged to transform them into transition functions.

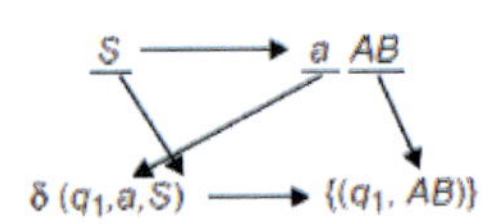

Thus, one obtains this table:

$(Start)$	$\delta(q_0, \lambda, z) \rightarrow \{(q_1, Sz)\}$
$S \rightarrow a$	$\delta(q_1, a, S) \rightarrow \{(q_1, \lambda)\}$
$S \rightarrow aAB$	$\delta(q_1, a, S) \rightarrow \{(q_1, AB)\}$
$A \rightarrow aA$	$\delta(q_1, a, A) \rightarrow \{(q_1, A)\}$
$A \rightarrow a$	$\delta(q_1, a, A) \rightarrow \{(q_1, \lambda)\}$
$B \rightarrow bB$	$\delta(q_1, b, B) \rightarrow \{(q_1, B)\}$
$B \rightarrow b$	$\delta(q_1, b, B) \rightarrow \{(q_1, \lambda)\}$
$(finish)$	$\delta(q_1, \lambda, z) \rightarrow \{(q_f, z)\}$

For instance, the derivation

$$S \Rightarrow aAB \Rightarrow aaB \Rightarrow aabB \Rightarrow aabb$$

$$S \Rightarrow aAB \Rightarrow aaB \Rightarrow aabB \Rightarrow aabb$$

Maps into the sequence of moves

$$\begin{aligned} (q_0, aabb, z) \quad & (q_1, aabb, Sz) \\ & (q_1, abb, ABz) \\ & (q_1, bb, Bz) \\ & (q_1, b, Bz) \\ & (q_1, \lambda, z) \\ & (q_2, \lambda, \lambda) \end{aligned}$$

5.3.5. NPDA to CFG

It has been demonstrated that an equivalent NPDA may be gained for any CFG. Furthermore, it can be demonstrated that any NPDA can be transformed into an equivalent CFG. It is now explained the equivalence between Context-Free Grammars (CFGs) and Non-deterministic Finite Automata (NFDAs) (Clark, 2015). It is commonly accepted, albeit unproven, that any NPDA may be converted into a comparable NPDA that adheres to the following structure:

i. Firstly, it is important to note that the NPDA possesses a solitary final state that it exclusively transitions to when the stack is devoid of any elements.
ii. All transitions have the form

$$\delta(q, a, A) = \{c_1, c_2, c_3, \cdots\cdots\}$$

Where; each c_i has one of the two forms

$$(q_j, \lambda)$$

$$(q_j, BC)$$

When we write a grammar, we can use any variable names we choose. Within programming languages, it is a common practice to use descriptive variable names (Pentus, 1997). When translating an NPDA to CFG, the names of variables are utilized to encode data about the current state of the NPDA along the stack content. These variable names are structured in a specific form.

$$[q_i, Aq_j],$$

Where; q_i and q_j are states and A shows the variable.

The interpretation for the variable [q_i q_j] represents the NPDA transition from one state to another, i.e. q_i along with Ax upon the stack to state q_j or x on stack.

Every transition form δ (q_i , a, A) = (q_j , λ) can be associated with a grammar rule.

$$\delta(q_i, a, A) = (q_j, BC)$$

The outcome of this process is a vast array of grammar rules, with each rule corresponding to a specific pair for states qx along with qy in the NPDA (Kasangian et al., 1983).

5.3.6. Deterministic Pushdown Automata

There are two key distinctions between a non-deterministic finite acceptance and a deterministic finite acceptor:

i. The change in the transition function δ is generally deterministic for a DFA, but non-deterministic for an NFA.

ii. A non-deterministic finite automaton can include lambda transitions (Valiant, 1975).

There are certain differences between a non-deterministic pushdown automaton and a pushdown automaton:

i. The transition function seems single-valued for a deterministic pushdown automaton (DPDA) and multi-valued for a non-deterministic pushdown automaton (NPDA).

ii. Both Non-deterministic Pushdown Automaton and Deterministic Pushdown Automaton can have lambda (λ) transitions. However, a DPDA can only have a lambda transition if there are no other potential transitions available (Linna, 1979).

A deterministic CFL is a language that can be recognized by a DPDA. The deterministic context-free languages are a proper subset of the context-free languages.

5.4. PROPERTIES OF CONTEXT FREE LANGUAGES

5.4.1. Pumping Lemma for CFG

The "Pumping Lemma" is a powerful theorem that demonstrates the relationship between certain strings within a language. It reveals that if certain strings are part of the language, then there are other strings with certain properties which must also be included. The concept of the Pumping Lemma for Context-Free Languages is explained next. Assume L constitutes a free of context language, afterwards strings for L that have a length of at least '*m*' symbols can be expanded to generate more characters in L. The value of '*m*' is determined by the specific language (Ewert et al., 2002).

Let L be an infinite context-free language. Then there is some positive integer 'm' such that, if S is a string of L of Length at least '*m*', then

i. $S = uvwxy$ (for some u, v, w, x, y)

ii. $|vwx| \leq m$

iii. $|vx|$ $^{3}1$

iv. $uv^{i}wx^{i}y \in L$.

It should be understood that

i. If the text S is long enough, it will contain two substrings, v along with x, at some point. There are elements (u) preceding v, elements (w) among v or x, and elements (y) following x.

ii. The content among v and x will not be extensive since the length of | vwx cannot exceed m.

iii. Both substrings v and x will not be empty, although either one of them could be.

iv. If one replicates substring v a certain number of times (i), and replicates x the same amount of times, the resulting string is going to be in the language (Gazdag et al., 2019).

- **Definitions here**

A variable is valuable when it appears during the derivation for a certain string. Some important properties of the variables are:

i. The variable can be found in a sentential form that is reachable from the start symbol,

ii. A string for terminals may be obtained via the sentential development (the variable does not lead to a dead end).

iii. A variable is considered "recursive" if it can generate a string that includes itself. For instance, the following expression indicates A is recursive for u along with y,

$$S \overset{*}{\Rightarrow} uAy$$

There are multiple possibilities for A (Ramos et al., 2019). The two types of recursions are:

i. Directly recursive, means that the production occurs without any intermediary steps.

$$A \rightarrow x_1 A x_2$$

ii. Variable calls another variable that eventually leads back to the original variable *xi* means indirectly recursive.

$$A \rightarrow X_1 \cdots$$

$$X_1 \rightarrow \cdots X_2 \cdots$$

$$X_2 \rightarrow \cdots X_3 \cdots$$

$$X_N \rightarrow \cdots A \cdots$$

5.4.2. Proof of Pumping Lemma

Let's consider a context-free language represented by L. Then there exists the context-free grammar G which generates language L. Say,

i. The language L contains an infinite number of strings, so there is no limit to the length for strings that belong to L (Hsieh, 2018).

ii. The language does not include the ë .

iii. G does not have any productions or lambda-productions.

There is a limited number of variables within a grammar, along with the productions over every variable possess finite lengths. For a grammar to generate strings of any length, at least one variable must be beneficial and recursive. Assuming there are no recursive variables (Fetaji et al., 2021).

Given that the initial symbol remains non-recursive, it should only be defined using terminals along with other variables. Then, since these variables are now non-recursive, they must be characterized about terminals along with additional variables, and so forth. Eventually, one exhausts all available variables before the generated string reaches its end. Thus, there exists a limit on the number of characters of the string that can be produced from the initial symbol. This statement challenges the previous assertion that a language is finite (Jung et al., 2009).

Therefore, it seems that our initial assumption of there being no recursive variables may be incorrect. Let's take a string X that belongs to L.

If X is long enough, then the derivation for X must have included the recursive utilization of a variable. Given that A was utilized in the derivation (Boonyavatana & Slutzki, 1988), it can be inferred that the derivation must have commenced as:

$$S \overset{*}{\Rightarrow} uAy$$

For certain values for u along with y. Since the letter A was used repeatedly, the derivation needs to have continued as

$$S \overset{*}{\Rightarrow} uAy \overset{*}{\Rightarrow} uvAxy$$

Ultimately, the derivation should have removed all variables until it reaches a string

X that belongs to the language (Ehrenfeucht et al., 1986).

$$S \overset{*}{\Rightarrow} uAy \overset{*}{\Rightarrow} uvAxy \overset{*}{\Rightarrow} uvxxy = x$$

This indicates that there are steps in the derivation process.

$$A \overset{*}{\Rightarrow} vAx$$

$$A \overset{*}{\Rightarrow} w$$

Possibilities exist. Therefore, the derivation

$$A \overset{*}{\Rightarrow} vwx$$

Should be possible.

It should be noted here that the above does not imply that *a* was used recursively only once (Finkel et al., 1997). The * of ⇒* could cover many uses of A, as well as other recursive variables. The potential applications of this concept could encompass various uses of A, along with other recursive variables.

There must be a final recursive step. Let's explore the longest strings that may be derived over *v*, *w*, and *x* without resorting to recursion. Following that there exists a certain number '*m*' that ensures the absolute value of $|vwx| < m$. Given that the grammar lacks all λ-productions and unit productions, each step of the calculation either introduced a terminal or extends the length regarding the sentential form. Given the derivation A ⇒* vAx, one can conclude that the length of $|vx| > 0$.

Finally, given that *uvwx* occurs during the calculation and both A �* and A �* w are possible, it can be concluded that uv^iwx^i also relates to L. The proof for all parts associated with the lemma is now complete (Maletti, 2005).

SUMMARY

- Pushdown automata (PDA) are an essential concept in the theory of computation, providing a bridge between finite automata and Turing machines. PDAs extend the capabilities of finite automata by incorporating a stack, which allows them to recognize context-free languages. These languages are significant in computer science, particularly in the parsing and interpretation of programming languages.
- The chapter begins with an introduction to the basic structure and operation of PDAs, emphasizing the role of the stack in memory management. It then distinguishes between deterministic and nondeterministic PDAs, explaining that while deterministic PDAs are limited to recognizing deterministic context-free languages, nondeterministic PDAs can recognize all context-free languages. Practical examples illustrate the construction and functioning of PDAs, highlighting their ability to process nested structures and balanced parentheses, common in programming language syntax.
- Further, the chapter delves into the relationship between context-free grammars (CFGs) and PDAs, demonstrating the equivalence between the two and the method of converting a CFG into a PDA. This understanding is fundamental for compiler design and syntax analysis. The chapter concludes with advanced topics such as simplifying CFGs, removing left recursion, and transforming PDAs into their deterministic counterparts, providing a comprehensive understanding of the computational power and limitations of pushdown automata.

REVIEW QUESTIONS

1. Describe the structure and components of a pushdown automaton.
2. Explain the difference between deterministic and nondeterministic pushdown automata.
3. How does a pushdown automaton recognize a context-free language?
4. Provide an example of a language that can be recognized by a PDA but not by a finite automaton.
5. Discuss the relationship between context-free grammars and pushdown automata.
6. What are the limitations of deterministic pushdown automata compared to nondeterministic ones?
7. How can a context-free grammar be converted into an equivalent pushdown automaton?
8. Describe the stack operations in a pushdown automaton with an example.

MULTIPLE CHOICE QUESTIONS

1. **What is the main difference between a finite automaton and a pushdown automaton?**
   a. Finite automata use a tape for memory, while pushdown automata use a stack.
   b. Pushdown automata can recognize context-free languages.
   c. Finite automata can recognize more complex languages than pushdown automata.
   d. Both a and b
2. **Which of the following is true about deterministic pushdown automata (DPDA)?**
   a. They can recognize all context-free languages.
   b. They have a multi-valued transition function.
   c. They can have λ-transitions only if no other transition is possible.
   d. They can recognize a larger set of languages than nondeterministic pushdown automata.
3. **What does the stack in a pushdown automaton allow it to do?**
   a. Remember the number of occurrences of a symbol.
   b. Recognize nested structures.
   c. Perform arithmetic operations.
   d. Both a and b
4. **In a nondeterministic pushdown automaton (NPDA), what does the transition function return?**
   a. A single next state and stack string.
   b. A set of possible next states and stack strings.
   c. A single next state only.
   d. A set of possible input symbols.
5. **Which of the following languages can be recognized by a pushdown automaton?**
   a. Regular languages
   b. Context-free languages
   c. Context-sensitive languages
   d. Both a and b
6. **What is the purpose of the stack start symbol in a pushdown automaton?**
   a. To indicate the initial state of the PDA.
   b. To mark the bottom of the stack.
   c. To determine the input alphabet.
   d. To define the set of final states.

Answers to Multiple Questions

1. (d) 2. (c) 3. (d) 4. (b) 5. (d) 6. (b)

REFERENCES

1. Abbott, R. J. (1983). Program design by informal English descriptions. Communications of the ACM, 26(11), 882-894.
2. Abdulla, P. A., Atig, M. F., Delzanno, G., & Podelski, A. (2013). Push-down automata with gap-order constraints. In Fundamentals of Software Engineering: 5th International Conference, FSEN 2013, Tehran, Iran, April 24-26, 2013, Revised Selected Papers .5 , (pp. 199-216).
3. Ahrens, B., Kapulkin, K., & Shulman, M. (2015). Univalent categories and the Rezk completion. Mathematical Structures in Computer Science, 25(5), 1010-1039.
4. Allauzen, C., Byrne, B., de Gispert, A., Iglesias, G., & Riley, M. (2014). Pushdown automata in statistical machine translation. Computational Linguistics, 40(3), 687-723.
5. Amsden, B. S. (2003). The evolution of parliamentary debate: a content analysis of NPDA judging philosophies 1999-2002. Parliamentary Debate, 8(1), 92-100.
6. Balzer, R., Goldman, N., & Wile, D. (1977). On the use of programming knowledge to understand informal process descriptions. ACM SIGART Bulletin, (63), 72-75.
7. Bednárová, Z., Geffert, V., Mereghetti, C., & Palano, B. (2014). Removing nondeterminism in constant height pushdown automata. Information and Computation, 237, 257-267.
8. Blom, H. A., & Bloem, E. A. (2000). Probabilistic data association avoiding track coalescence. IEEE Transactions on Automatic Control, 45(2), 247-259.
9. Boonyavatana, R., & Slutzki, G. (1988). The interchange or pump (di) lemmas for context-free languages. Theoretical computer science, 56(3), 321-338.
10. Carayol, A., & Wöhrle, S. (2003). The Caucal hierarchy of infinite graphs in terms of logic and higher-order pushdown automata. In FST TCS 2003: Foundations of Software Technology and Theoretical Computer Science: 23rd Conference, Mumbai, India, December 15-17, 2003. Proceedings .23 , (pp. 112-123).
11. Chrétien, R., Cortier, V., & Delaune, S. (2015). From security protocols to pushdown automata. ACM Transactions on Computational Logic (TOCL), 17(1), 1-45.
12. Clark, A. (2015). The syntactic concept lattice: Another algebraic theory of the context-free languages?. Journal of Logic and Computation, 25(5), 1203-1229.
13. Coquidé, J. L., Dauchet, M., Gilleron, R., & Vágvölgyi, S. (1991). Bottom-up tree pushdown automata and rewrite systems. In Rewriting Techniques and Applications: 4th International Conference, RTA-91 Como, Italy, April 10–12, 1991 Proceedings . 4, (pp. 287-298).
14. Dreyfus, A., Héam, P. C., Kouchnarenko, O., & Masson, C. (2014). A random testing approach using pushdown automata. Software Testing, Verification and Reliability, 24(8), 656-683.
15. Duris, P., & Galil, Z. (1982). On reversal-bounded counter machines and on pushdown automata with a bound on the size of the pushdown store. Information and Control, 54(3), 217-227.

16. Ehrenfeucht, A., Hoogeboom, H. J., & Rozenberg, G. (1986). Coordinated pair systems; part I: Dyck works and classical pumping. RAIRO-Theoretical Informatics and Applications, 20(4), 405-424.

17. Ewert, S., & van der Walt, A. (2002). A pumping lemma for random permitting context languages. Theoretical Computer Science, 270(1-2), 959-967.

18. Fetaji, M., Fetaji, B., & Asilkan, Ö. (2021). Analyses of the case studies for the efficiency of pumping lemma for the context-free languages. CRJ, (1), 9-15.

19. Fikes, R. E. (1982). A commitment-based framework for describing informal cooperative work. Cognitive Science, 6(4), 331-347.

20. Finkel, A., Willems, B., & Wolper, P. (1997). A direct symbolic approach to model checking pushdown systems. Electronic Notes in Theoretical Computer Science, 9, 27-37.

21. Fresse, B., Turchin, V., & Willwacher, T. (2018). The homotopy theory of operad subcategories. Journal of Homotopy and Related Structures, 13(4), 689-702.

22. Gazdag, Z., Tichler, K., & Csuhaj-Varjú, E. (2019). A pumping lemma for permitting semi-conditional languages. International Journal of Foundations of Computer Science, 30(01), 73-92.

23. Ginsburg, S., & Spanier, E. H. (1966). Finite-turn pushdown automata. SIAM Journal on Control, 4(3), 429-453.

24. Goldstine, J., Leung, H., & Wotschke, D. (2005). Measuring nondeterminism in pushdown automata. Journal of Computer and System Sciences, 71(4), 440-466.

25. Heizmann, M., Schilling, C., & Tischner, D. (2017). Minimization of visibly pushdown automata using partial Max-SAT. In Tools and Algorithms for the Construction and Analysis of Systems: 23rd International Conference, TACAS 2017, Held as Part of the European Joint Conferences on Theory and Practice of Software, ETAPS 2017, Uppsala, Sweden, April 22-29, 2017, Proceedings, Part I 23 (pp. 461-478).

26. Herzog, C. (1997). Pushdown automata with bounded nondeterminism and bounded ambiguity. Theoretical Computer Science, 181(1), 141-157.

27. Hopkins, D., Murawski, A. S., & Ong, C. H. L. (2011). A fragment of ML decidable by visibly pushdown automata. In Automata, Languages and Programming: 38th International Colloquium, ICALP 2011, Zurich, Switzerland, July 4-8, 2011, Proceedings, Part II .38 , (pp. 149-161).

28. Hossain, N., Islam, S., & Huda, M. N. (2021). Development of bangla spell and grammar checkers: Resource creation and evaluation. IEEE Access, 9, 141079-141097.

29. Hsieh, S. C. (2018). To pump or not to pump when proving non-regularity. Journal of Computing Sciences in Colleges, 33(5), 199-205.

30. Ibarra, O. H., & Tran, N. Q. (2012). On synchronized multi-tape and multi-head automata. Theoretical Computer Science, 449, 74-84.

31. Janoušek, J., & Melichar, B. (2009). On regular tree languages and deterministic pushdown automata. Acta Informatica, 46(7), 533-547.

32. Jung, H., Min, K., & Park, S. (2009). Development of a Web-based Adaptive System for Learning Pumping Lemma. The Journal of Korean Association of Computer Education, 12(5), 87-94.

33. Kasangian, S., Kelly, G. M., & Rossi, F. (1983). Cofibrations and the realization of non-deterministic automata. Cahiers de topologie et géométrie différentielle, 24(1), 23-46.

34. Kutrib, M., & Malcher, A. (2012). Reversible pushdown automata. Journal of Computer and System Sciences, 78(6), 1814-1827.

35. Kutrib, M., Malcher, A., & Wendlandt, M. (2017). Tinput-driven pushdown, counter, and stack automata. Fundamenta Informaticae, 155(1-2), 59-88.

36. Linna, M. (1979). Two decidability results for deterministic pushdown automata. Journal of Computer and System Sciences, 18(1), 92-107.

37. Makkai, M., & Pitts, A. M. (1987). Some results on locally finitely presentable categories. Transactions of the American Mathematical Society, 299(2), 473-496.

38. Maletti, A. (2005). Relating tree series transducers and weighted tree automata. International Journal of Foundations of Computer Science, 16(04), 723-741.

39. Matthes, R., & Uustalu, T. (2004). Substitution in non-wellfounded syntax with variable binding. Theoretical Computer Science, 327(1-2), 155-174.

40. Meduna, A. (2003). Simultaneously one-turn two-pushdown automata. International Journal of Computer Mathematics, 80(6), 679-687.

41. Miriyala, K., & Harandi, M. T. (1991). Automatic derivation of formal software specifications from informal descriptions. IEEE transactions on Software Engineering, 17(10), 1126.

42. Morita, K., Nishihara, N., Yamamoto, Y., & Zhang, Z. (1997). A hierarchy of uniquely parsable grammar classes and deterministic acceptors. Acta Informatica, 34, 389-410.

43. Muller, D. E., & Schupp, P. E. (1985). The theory of ends, pushdown automata, and second-order logic. Theoretical Computer Science, 37, 51-75.

44. Namikawa, J., & Hashimoto, T. (2004). Dynamics and computation in functional shifts. Nonlinearity, 17(4), 1317.

45. Nasr, S. B., Bécan, G., Acher, M., Ferreira Filho, J. B., Sannier, N., Baudry, B., & Davril, J. M. (2017). Automated extraction of product comparison matrices from informal product descriptions. Journal of Systems and Software, 124, 82-103.

46. Nelson, M. A. V., Alencar, P. S., & Cowan, D. D. (2007). Informal description and analysis of geographic requirements: an approach based on problems. Software & Systems Modeling, 6, 223-245.

47. Okhotin, A., & Salomaa, K. (2014). Complexity of input-driven pushdown automata. ACM SIGACT News, 45(2), 47-67.

48. Pentus, M. (1997). Product-free Lambek calculus and context-free grammars. The Journal of Symbolic Logic, 62(2), 648-660.

49. Pighizzini, G. (2009). Deterministic pushdown automata and unary languages. International Journal of Foundations of Computer Science, 20(04), 629-645.

50. Pighizzini, G., & Pisoni, A. (2015). Limited automata and context-free languages. Fundamenta Informaticae, 136(1-2), 157-176.

51. Plátek, M., Mráz, F., Pardubská, D., & Průša, D. (2022). On pumping RP-automata controlled by complete LRG (¢, $)-grammars. In Proceedings of the 22nd Conference Information Technologies–Ap plications and Theory (ITAT 2022) . Vol. 3226, (pp. 111-121).

52. Qiu, D. (2007). Automata theory based on quantum logic: reversibilities and pushdown automata. Theoretical Computer Science, 386(1-2), 38-56.

53. Ramos, M. V., Almeida, J. C. B., Moreira, N., & de Queiroz, R. J. (2019). Some applications of the formalization of the pumping lemma for context-free languages. Electronic Notes in Theoretical Computer Science, 344, 151-167.

54. Reddy, S. T., Tarafdar, P. K., Kamlekar, R. K., & Swamy, M. J. (2013). Structure and thermotropic phase behavior of a homologous series of bioactive N-acyldopamines. The Journal of Physical Chemistry B, 117(29), 8747-8757.

55. Rosenkrantz, D. J. (1967). Matrix equations and normal forms for context-free grammars. Journal of the ACM (JACM), 14(3), 501-507.

56. Salomaa, K., & Yu, S. (1994). Measures of nondeterminism for pushdown automata. Journal of Computer and System Sciences, 49(2), 362-374.

57. Takahashi, Y., & Ito, A. (2023). On the Unmixedness Problems of Colored Pushdown Automata. IEICE TRANSACTIONS on Information and Systems, 106(3), 303-308.

58. Tran, Q. N. (2006). Interactive computer algebra software for teaching and helping students to study foundations of computer science.

59. Urbanek, F. J. (1986). On Greibach normal form construction. Theoretical computer science, 44, 229-236.

60. Valiant, L. G. (1975). Regularity and related problems for deterministic pushdown automata. Journal of the ACM (JACM), 22(1), 1-10.

61. van Heerdt, G., Moerman, J., Sammartino, M., & Silva, A. (2019). A (co) algebraic theory of succinct automata. Journal of Logical and Algebraic Methods in Programming, 105, 112-125.

62. Weir, D. J. (1992). A geometric hierarchy beyond context-free languages. Theoretical Computer Science, 104(2), 235-261.

63. XU, J., INOUE, K., WANG, Y., & ITO, A. (1996). A note on alternating pushdown automata with sublogarithmic space. IEICE TRANSACTIONS on Information and Systems, 79(4), 259-270.

64. Zhang, Y., & Vyazovkin, S. (2006). Comparative cure behavior of DGEBA and DGEBP with 4-nitro-1, 2-phenylenediamine. Polymer, 47(19), 6659-6663.

CHAPTER 6

Decidability

LEARNING OBJECTIVES

After studying this chapter, you will be able to:

- Differentiate between decidable and undecidable problems.
- Describe the concept of decidability in the context of automata and formal languages.
- Explain the proofs of decidability for various problems related to finite automata and context-free grammars.
- Understand the undecidability of certain computational problems.
- Apply the concepts of decidability and undecidability to solve problems in theoretical computer science.

KEY TERMS FROM THIS CHAPTER

Algorithm
Decidability
Diagonalization
Turing machine (TM)
Undecidability
Context-free grammar (CFG)
Deterministic finite automaton (DFA)
Non-deterministic finite automaton (NFA)
Turing-recognizable
Universal turing machine

UNIT INTRODUCTION

In this chapter, one delves into the realm of algorithms and their ability to tackle various problems. It presents a comprehensive analysis of issues that can be resolved algorithmically and those that are beyond the reach of algorithms. The main goal is to investigate the boundaries of algorithmic solvability (Immerman et al., 2004) and have a well understanding of the concept of solvability by algorithms, as a significant portion of computer science revolves around problem-solving. It may be unexpected to discover that certain problems cannot be solved (Baget et al., 2011).

What is the importance of studying insolvability? Ultimately, demonstrating the impossibility of solving a problem may seem futile when faced with the task of finding a solution. There are two compelling reasons why it is crucial to delve into this phenomenon (Galatos & Jipsen, 2013). Understanding the point at which a problem becomes algorithmically unsolvable is valuable as it prompts the recognition that the problem needs to be simplified or modified to arrive at an algorithmic solution. Just like any tool, it is important to be aware of the features and limitations of computers to use them effectively. Another factor to consider is the cultural aspect. Engaging with problems that have clear solutions can be intellectually stimulating, but exploring the realm of unsolvable problems can provide an invaluable viewpoint on computation and start imagination (Rabin, 1969).

6.1. DECIDABLE LANGUAGES

This section provides a few instances of languages that can be determined by algorithms. Our primary focus is on languages related to automaton and grammar. As an illustration, one introduces an algorithm that examines whether a given string belongs to a context-free language (CFL). There are various reasons why these languages are intriguing. Firstly, certain issues of this nature are connected to practical applications. Furthermore, there are additional challenges related to automata and grammar that cannot be resolved through algorithms. Beginning with instances where determinability is achievable allows for a better understanding of the instances where determinability is not possible (Kierstead & Remmel, 1983).

6.1.1. Decidable Problems Concerning Regular Languages

Starting by examining some computational problems related to finite automata. Algorithms are provided to determine when a finite automaton processes a string and the language that it recognizes is empty, one can determine if pair finite automatons tend to be equivalent (Dudakov & Karlov, 2021).

It is worth noting that different computational issues are represented through languages. It is advantageous to do this since one has already established a framework for addressing languages. As an illustration, the accepting problem for DFAs involves determining whether a specific predictable finite automaton takes a string. Suppose Testing how a DFA *B* takes an input *w* is equivalent to determining if ⟨B,w⟩ belongs to the language ADFA. In a similar vein, one can express various computational problems by examining whether they belong to a specific language. Demonstrating which language is decidable is equivalent to demonstrating that a computational issue is decidable (Karhumäki & Maon, 1986). Within the theorem, one demonstrates the decidability of ADFA. Therefore, this theorem demonstrates that it is possible to determine if a specific finite automaton takes a given string.

6.1.1.1. Theorem 6.1 ADFA is a Decidable Language

- **Proof Idea:** It is sufficient to provide a TM *M* which can determine the acceptance of ADFA. Given an input *M* = "On input ⟨B, ⟩, in which *B* represents a DFA and ⊠ acts as a string,
  i. Execute *B* on the given input ⊠
  ii. If the simulation concludes within an acceptable state, it should be accepted. If the final state is not accepted, the input should be rejected.

- **Proof:** Specific implementation of this proof will be briefly discussed. If one had experience in creating programs within any common language for programming, envision how one might create a program to execute the simulation (Wolf, 2022).

First, take a closer look at the input ⟨B, ⟩. This is a depiction of a DFA *B* alongside a string w. An appropriate way to represent *B* is by using a list that includes five of its elements: Q, Σ, δ, , and F. Upon receiving its input, *M* begins by assessing the validity of DFA *B* along with string *w*. If not, *M* declines.

Then *M* does the simulation right away. The system keeps a record of *B's* present state or position relative to the input *w* from documenting this data on its tape. At the beginning, *B* starts in state q_0, and its input position is set to be the leftmost sign of *w*. After *M* completes evaluating the final symbol of , *M* will either accept or reject the input based on the state of *B*. If *B* allows, *M* will accept the input. Conversely, if *B* is operating in a non-accepting state, *M* will reject it (Salomaa, 1975).

A comparable theorem can be proven for nondeterministic finite automata. Suppose

6.1.1.2. Theorem 6.2 ANFA is a Decidable Language

- **Proof:** Start with a Turing Machine *N* that can determine the solution for ANFA. One can create N to function similarly to M by modeling an NFA rather than a DFA. An approach given from a different angle to showcase a fresh concept of this proof: Utilize N to incorporate M into a subroutine. Since M is specifically designed to operate with DFAs, N takes the NFA it is given as input and converts it into a DFA before sending it to M (Jones & Thomas, 2018).

N = "On input ⟨B, ⟩, whereas B shows NFA or is a string:

i. Transform NFA B into a comparable DFA C.
ii. Perform TM M to Theorem 4.1 with input ⟨C, w⟩
iii. when M accepts, accept, if not reject

When incorporating TM M into stage 2, involves integrating M toward the design for N to serve as sub procedure. Similarly, one can ascertain if a regular expression produces a given string. Consider the set AREX = which consists of pairs {⟨R, w⟩| where R is an expression with regularity that produces string w.

6.1.1.3. Theorem 6.3 is a Decidable Language

- **Proof:** A Turing machine P can determine the solution for .

First, given an input ⟨R, ⟩, the algorithm checks it is a regular expression.

i. Next, transform the regular expression R into an equivalent NFA A.
ii. Perform TM N with input ⟨A, ⟩.
iii. When N accepts, accept, whether N rejects, reject (Wilke, 1993).

Theorems explain that it is equally valid to provide a Turing machine via a DFA, an NFA, as well as a regular expression over the reason of decidability. This is due to the machine's ability to seamlessly convert between different forms of encoding (Demri, 2001).

Next, we will explore a distinct type of problem-related to finite automata:

determining if the language about a finite automaton is empty. One needs to establish whether a finite automaton takes any strings or not. Suppose

6.1.1.4. Theorem 6.4 is a Decidable Language

- **Evidence:** it is known that a Deterministic Finite Automaton (DFA) accepts a string if and only if it is possible to get to an accepted state via its initial state by following the directions of the DFA (Straubing et al., 1995).

T = "On input ⟨A⟩, whereas A shows a DFA:

i. First, identify the initial state of A.
ii. Continue the process until all states have been marked.
iii. Identify any state that receives a transition from a previously marked state and mark it accordingly.
iv. If there are no marked accept states, the input is accepted. Otherwise, it is rejected (Maon, 1986).

Based on the following theorem, it is possible to determine if two DFAs know a similar language. Allow

6.1.1.5. Theorem 6.5 is a Decidable Language

- **Proof:** To establish the validity of this theorem, One creates a novel DFA C by combining A and B. C will accept strings that are authorized by both A or B, yet not both. Therefore, if both A and B know a similar language, C cannot take anything (Bertoni et al., 2003). C is known for its language

$$L(C)=\left(L(A)\cap\overline{L(B)}\right)\cup\left(\overline{L(A)}\cap L(B)\right)$$

This expression is also known as the symmetrical difference between L(A) and L(B) and is depicted in the accompanying figure. Here, the complement for L(A) is represented as The symmetric distinction is applicable in this case because the condition L(C) = iff L(A) = L(B). By utilizing the constructions over proving the closure of the class of standard languages within complementation, union, and intersection one can create C from A and B (Karhumäki et al., 2005).

These constructions are step-by-step procedures that can be executed by Turing machines. After constructing C, one can ~~utilize Theorem 4.4 to~~ determine if L(C) is empty. If the sets A and B are both empty, then they must be equal (Chockler & Kupferman, 2004; Jeż, 2008).

F = "On input ⟨A, B⟩, whereas A and B are DFAs:

i. Create DFA C as instructed
ii. Execute TM T ~~via Theorem 4.4~~ with input ⟨C⟩
iii. If T is accepted, then accept. If T does not accept, then reject (Brüggemann & Wood, 1998).

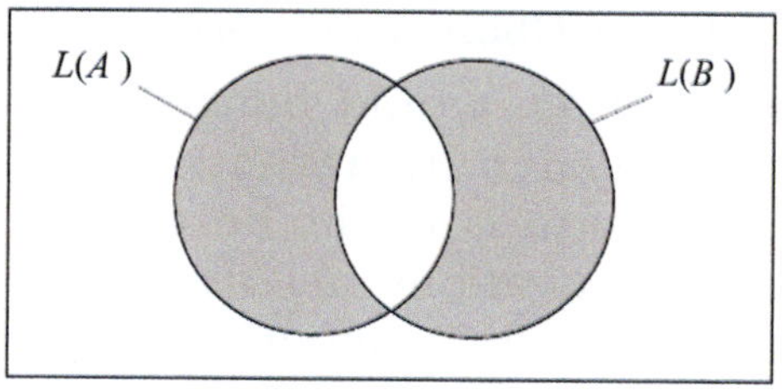

Figure 6.1. *Illustration of The symmetric difference between the languages L (A) and L (B).*

Source: Michel Sipser, Creative Commons License.

6.1.2. Decidable Problems Concerning Context-Free Languages

In this description, one discusses algorithms that can be used to ascertain if a Context-Free Grammar (CFG) is capable of generating a specific string, as well as algorithms to Figure 6.1 out if the language within the CFG is vacant (Hopcroft, 1969). Allow

6.1.2.1. Theorem 6.6 A_{CFG} is a Decidable Language

- **Proof Idea:** the concept is that it is needed to determine if a given context-free grammar *G* can generate a specific string *w*. One approach is to utilize *G* to systematically analyze all derivations and ascertain if any of them correspond to ω. If *G* fails to produce w, this algorithm will never stop. This concept presents a Turing machine that serves as a recognizer for A_{CFG} but falls short of being a decider (Niemi, 1984).

To transform this Turing machine to a decider, it must be certain how the algorithm attempts a finite number of derivations.

It has been demonstrated that if G were to be in Chomsky's normal form, all derivation of ω would consist of $2n-1$ steps, in which n represents the length of *w*. Therefore, it might be sufficient to check just derivations in *2n+1* actions to Figure 6.1 out if *G* generates *w*. There is a limited number of these derivations (Hartmanis, 1967).

- **Proof:** Here is the Turing machine S for ACFG:

S = "On input ⟨G, w⟩, whereas G is a CFG, where w is a string:

i. Transform G into an equivalent grammar within Chomsky's normal form.
ii. Provide a comprehensive list of derivations, considering the length of *w*. When *n* = *0*, only include derivations about one step.
iii. Consider ù if any of those derivations produce it; otherwise, reject (Raz, 1997).

The algorithm within TM S is not optimized for practical use, but it is straightforward to explain, and efficiency is not our focus in this context. In Part Three of this book, one delves into the intricacies surrounding the efficiency of algorithms in terms of their running time and memory usage. There is potential for achieving even higher efficiency in knowing deterministic context-free languages. Therefore, all the statements made regarding the solvability of problems related to Context-Free Grammars are equally applicable to Pushdown Automata.

Now, shift our focus to the issue of evaluation emptiness for a language used by CFG. Like the approach with DFAs, it is possible to demonstrate that the issue of determining if a CFG produces strings of any kind is solvable (Ehrenfeucht et al., 1983). Consider

$$E_{CFG} = \{◆G◆|G \text{ is a } CFG \text{ and } L(G)=\varnothing\}.$$

6.1.2.2. Theorem 6.7 E_{CFG} is a Decidable Language

- **Proof:** One possible approach to finding an algorithm over this issue is to consider using TM S to Theorem 6.5. It is stated that one could assess whether Context-Free Grammar can produce a specific string ω. To Figure 6.2 out if L (G) $=\theta$, an algorithm can attempt to iterate through every possibility *w's*, one by one. However, there is an endless number of ω's to experiment with, so this approach may continue indefinitely. One should consider adopting an alternative strategy (Clark & Eyraud, 2007). For to ascertain if the language for grammar does not exist, it is necessary to examine if the start variable can produce a string for terminals. It assesses the ability of each variable to produce a string for terminals. Once the algorithm has established that a variable can generate a string of terminals, it maintains this information by marking that variable. If the algorithm discovers a rule that allows for the replacement of a variable with a string of symbols, each of those has been marked. The algorithm proceeds in this manner until it is unable to label any more variables (Smikun, 1976). This algorithm is implemented by TM R.

- **Proof:** R = "On input ⟨G⟩, whereas G is a CFG:

i. Identify every terminal symbol within G.

ii. Continue the process until no additional variables are noted.

iii. Identify any variable A in cases where G contains a rule. A → U_1U_2 • • • U_k along with every symbol U_1 • • • U_k have already been marked.

iv. when the starting variable is unmarked, accept; contrary, reject (Vyalyi & Rubtsov, 2015).

Now, delve into the issue of determining how two context-free grammars produce identical language. Consider

$$EQ_{CFG} = \{\blacklozenge G, H\blacklozenge | G \text{ and } H \text{ are } CFGs \text{ and } L(G) = L(H)\}.$$

Theorem 6.5 provided an algorithm that can determine the corresponding language EQ_{DFA} over finite automata. One utilized the decision process for E_{DFA} to establish the decidability of EQ_{DFA}. Given that ECFG is also decidable, one might assume that a similar approach can be employed to establish the decidability of EQ_{CFG}. However, there seems to be an issue regarding this idea! Complementation of intersection does not preserve the class for context-free language (Finkel, 2009).

Now one demonstrates that Turing machines can determine the decidability of languages without context.

6.1.2.3. Theorem 6.8 Every Context-Free Language is Decidable

- **Proof Idea:** Assume that A is a context-free language. This proof aims to show the decidability of A. An ill-conceived idea would directly transform a Pushdown Automaton (PDA) into a Turing Machine (TM). Simulating a stack using the Turing Machine's highly adaptable tape is a simple task. The PDA for language A may exhibit nondeterminism, but this is acceptable since it may be transformed into a nondeterministic Turing Machine (TM). It is known that any nondeterministic TM might be turned towards an equivalent deterministic TM. Certain branches within a PDA's computation have the potential to go on indefinitely, constantly manipulating the stack despite ever coming to a stop. The simulated Turing Machine would likewise exhibit non halting branching in its computation, rendering it incapable of making a definitive decision. An alternative concept is required (Eremondi et al., 2018). Alternatively, one demonstrates the validity of this theorem using the Turing Machine S, which one specifically constructed it ~~Theorem 4.5~~ to decide ${}_{CFG}$.

- **Proof:** Consider a context-free grammar G that represents language A. Now, we need to design a Turing machine TM M_G that can decide if a given input falls to A or not. One creates a duplicate of G and names its MG. Below is how it works

M_G = "On input ω:

i. Execute TM S on the given input ⟨G, ù ⟩.

ii. when the device accepts, accept; when it rejects, reject

Theorem 6.8 serves as the crucial connection between the four primary categories of languages one has discussed thus far: regular, context-free, decidable, and Turing-recognizable. Figure 6.2 illustrates this connection (Průša & Reinhardt, 2017).

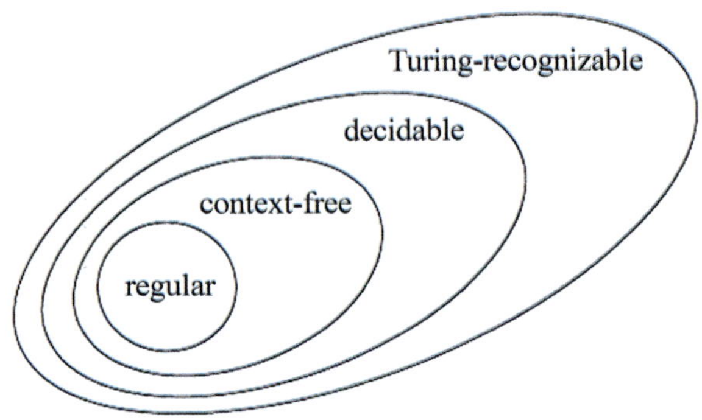

Figure 6.2. *Illustration of the relationship among classes of languages.*

Source: ADLEMAN, L, Creative Commons License.

6.2. UNDECIDABILITY

In this part, one will demonstrate a few of the most significant theorems in the concept of computation, which hold great philosophical significance. There exists a particular issue that cannot be solved through algorithms. It may seem that computers possess such immense power that one might assume they can solve any problem eventually. The theorem provided here highlights an essential limitation of computers (Koellner, 2006). What types of problems cannot be solved by computers? Do they exist only in the realm of the intellectual elite? It is not completely true! It's surprising how certain everyday problems humans encounter can be incredibly difficult to solve computationally. There is a particular type of issue which cannot be solved, where one is provided with a computer program along with a clear specification of what the program should accomplish (such as sorting a list of numbers). One must ensure that the program functions according to the specified requirements. Given the precise nature of each program along with the specification, one aims to streamline the verification procedure by utilizing a properly programmed computer. Unfortunately, one will be let down. Software verification poses a challenge that cannot be overcome by computer technology alone (Moore, 1990). In this section along with Chapter 5, one may come across several problems that cannot be solved computationally. The main goal is to assist one in gaining an understanding of the kinds of issues that cannot be solved and to provide you with methods of proving their unsolvability (Norval, 2004).

Now focus on our first theorem which proves the impossibility of solving a particular language problem: deciding if a Turing machine takes a specific input string. One refers to it as A_{TM}, drawing a parallel in $-A_{\text{DFA}}$ or A_{CFG}. However, while

Let ADFA or ACFG be proven to be decidable, while A_{TM} is believed to be undecidable. Consider

$$A_{TM} = \{\text{◆}M, \omega\text{◆} | M \text{ is a } TM \text{ and } M \text{ accepts } \omega\}.$$

- **Theorem 6.9** A_{TM} *is Undecidable*

Now, before one delf into the proof, it's worth noting the fact $-\text{A}_{\text{TM}}$ is Turing-recognizable. Therefore, this theorem proves that recognizers possess more skills than deciders. Applying a condition where a Turing Machine must stop on every possible input limits the range of languages it is capable of recognize (Ramalingam, 1994). What follows, Turing machine U can decide whether a given input relates to the language recognized by A_{TM}.

U = "On input ⟨M, w⟩, Given that M is a Turing Machine and w has a string:

i. Run M upon input *w*

ii. If M ever enters its accept state, accept; if M ever enters its reject state, reject."

It's important to understand that this machine will keep running upon input M,ω when M keeps running on w. This is the reason why such machine cannot figure out the membership of M,ω to A_TM. When the algorithm had a means of determining that M does not halt on *w*, it might be rejected in this scenario. Nevertheless, it is impossible for an algorithm to make this choice, as one will soon discover (Laufer, 1997).

The Turing machine U is fascinating in its way. This is an illustration of the universal Turing machine that was initially suggested by Alan Turing in 1936. This machine is referred to as universal since it can simulate every other Turing machine based on its description. The universal Turing device performed a crucial role in the early stages of developing stored-program computers.

6.2.1. The Diagonalization Method

The uncertainty of A_{TM} is proven using a technique known as diagonalization, which was initially identified by mathematical expert Georg Cantor in 1873. Cantor was interested in exploring the issue of quantifying the magnitudes of infinite sets. When faced with two infinite sets, determining their relative sizes or if they are equal can be quite a challenge. Responding to these questions over finite sets is straightforward. One can determine the size of a finite set by counting its elements. However, attempting to tally the elements for an infinite set remains an endless endeavor! It is not possible to utilize the counting procedure to ascertain the proportions of sets that are infinite (Saad et al., 2006).

Consider, for instance, the set for even integers along with the set that includes every string over {0,1}. Both sets are infinite or therefore surpass any finite set in size. However, can one determine if either of both sets is larger compared to the other? How can we determine the relative sizes of different objects? Consider, for instance, the set for even integers along with the set that includes all strings across {0,1} ss. Both sets were infinite and therefore surpassed any finite set in size (Tsallis, 1978; Rogers et al., 1987). However, is there a distinction in size between the two? What is the method for comparing the relative sizes of objects?

Cantor presented an elegant answer to that issue. It was noted that when the elements for one set may be paired with the elements of another set, the two finite sets had the same size. This approach evaluates the magnitudes without relying on enumeration. One can further expand upon this concept to encompass infinite sets. Here is an extra precise explanation. Another way to refer to these kinds of functions is by using different terms. For example, one can use "injective" to describe a one-to-one function, "surjective" to describe a onto function, along "bijective" to describe a function that is both one-to-one and onto (Leininger et al., 2001).

6.2.1.1. Example 6.1

Consider N as the set for natural numbers $\{1, 2, 3\}$ along with Ɛ as the set for even natural numbers $\{2, 4, 6\}$. By applying Cantor's definition of size, it becomes apparent that it possess equal magnitudes. The function f maps to another value by simply doubling the input, $f(n)=2n$. A table can greatly assist in visualizing f more clearly (Schenk et al., 2008) as follows:

N (Natural Number)	f(n) (Even Natural Number)
1	2
2	4
3	6
4	8
5	10
6	12
7	14
8	16
9	18
10	20

Certainly, this example appears quite unusual. It is worth noting that appears to be smaller than $\mathcal{N}$ because seems a proper subset for $\mathcal{N}$. However, it is possible to match each member for $\mathcal{N}$ with its corresponding member of $\mathcal{E}$. Therefore, one may conclude that these two sets are the same size (Mandelshtam, 2000).

6.2.1.2. Example 6.2

Now one delves into a particularly peculiar example. If one considers the set $Q=\left\{\frac{m}{n}|m,n\in\mathcal{N}\right\}$, which consists of positive numbers that are rational, it appears to be significantly larger than another set. However, both sets are of equal size based on our definition. One establishes an association with $\mathcal{N}$ to demonstrate that Q was countable. An efficient approach is to enumerate all the parts of Q. Next, one matches the initial item on the list using the value 1 from $\mathcal{N}$, the subsequent item on the list via the value 2 via $\mathcal{N}$, and so forth. It is imperative to ensure that each member is listed only once (Vollgraf & Obermayer, 2006). To obtain the above list, an infinite matrix is constructed, which includes each of the positive rational numbers. This is illustrated in Figure 6.3. The *ith* row includes all numbers using numerator i along with the *jth* column includes all numbers alongside denominator j. Therefore, the value $\frac{i}{j}$ can be found in the corresponding position of the *ith* row along with the *jth* column (Liang & Pang, 1994).

Next, one will convert this matrix onto a list. An ineffective approach would involve starting the list by including all the parts in the initial row. That approach may not be ideal as the first row was infinite, which would prevent the list from progressing through the second row. Rather, the elements of the diagonals are listed, superimposed upon the diagram, beginning at the corner. The first diagonal consists of a single element, while the second diagonal is made up of two elements (So & Liu, 2000).

The initial three items on the list have $\frac{1}{1}$, $\frac{2}{1}$, and $\frac{1}{2}$. A complication develops within the third diagonal. It includes fractions such as $\frac{3}{1},\frac{2}{2}$, and $\frac{1}{3}$. If one to include these in the list, the result would be 3. It is interesting to note that 1 = 2 12, and this equation is repeated twice (Mouawad & Perahia, 1993). One prevents this by omitting an element that would result in duplication. So one includes just the two additional elements $\frac{3}{1}$ and $\frac{1}{3}$. Building upon this, one can generate a comprehensive list of every one of the elements in Q.

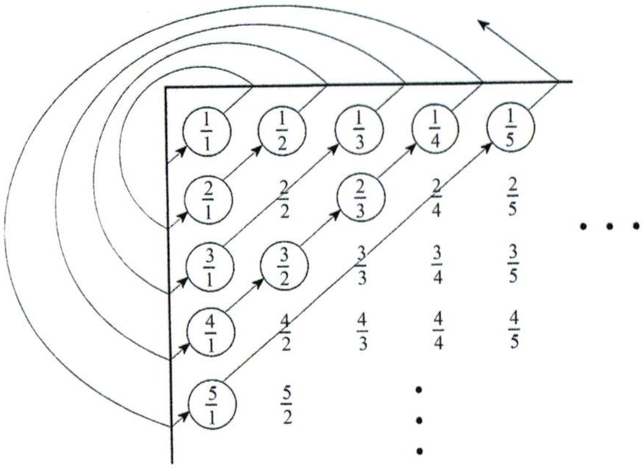

Figure 6.3. *Illustration of A correspondence of $\mathcal{N}$ and $\mathcal{Q}$. .*

Source: Alon, N., Creative Commons License.

Upon observing the correspondence between N and Q, one might be inclined to believe that it is possible to demonstrate that both infinite sets possess equal cardinality. Ultimately, it is sufficient to establish a connection, and this example serves as evidence that unexpected connections can indeed be found. Nevertheless, certain infinite sets lack any connection. These sets are quite large. These sets are referred to as uncountable (Epperly et al., 2022).

An uncountable set is exemplified by the set for real numbers. A real number can be defined as a number that can be represented with a decimal. Some instances of real numbers include $\pi = 3.1415926$ and $\sqrt{2} = 1.4142135$. Consider the set for real numbers. Cantor's proof demonstrated that the set in question is uncountable. As part of his work, he broughforth the diagonalization method (Blaha et al., 2010).

6.2.1.3. Theorem 6.10 R is Uncountable

- **Proof:** To demonstrate that $\mathcal{R}$ is uncountable, one can establish the absence of any correspondence between $\mathcal{N}$ and $\mathcal{R}$. The proof follows a contradictory approach. Now consider the relationship f among $\mathcal{N}$ and $\mathcal{R}$. Our task is to demonstrate that f does not function as intended. For it to qualify as an association, f must pair every element of one set with every element of another set. However, one can discover an x that is not matched with items in $\mathcal{N}$, leading to a contradiction (Neuhauser, 1994).

One can determine the value of x by actively constructing it. One selects each digit for x to ensure that x is distinct from any of the real numbers related to an element. Ultimately, one can confidently conclude that x is distinct from any actual number that it is paired with (Kaveh & Nikbakht, 2007).

Now demonstrate this concept by providing an example. If the relationship between e and f exists. For the sake of illustration, assign some arbitrary values to the function f. One can start with f (1) = 3.14159 . . ., f (2) = 55.55555 . . ., f (3) = . . ., or so on. Next, f associates the number 1 with 3.14159 . . ., and number 2 with 55.55555 . . ., and furthermore. Here is a table displaying some values for a hypothetical connection between N and R two sets (Afsari, 2008).

n	$f(n)$
1	3.14159...
2	55.55555...
3	0.12345...
4	0.50000...
⋮	⋮

One can create the desired x with its decimal depiction. This number falls within the range of 0 and 1, meaning that all its important digits have fractional digits located after the decimal point. The objective is to guarantee that x is not equal to $f(n)$ for any value of n. To establish that $x \neq f(n)$ for any n, one can choose any digit other than 1 for the initial digit of x, which is different from the first a fraction digit 1 for $f(1)=3.14159$. Now assume it is 4 without any specific reason (Schenk et al., 2006).

To guarantee that $x \neq f(2)$, one assigns any value to the second digit for x that is distinct as the second fraction digit 5 for $f(2)=55.555555$.Without any specific reason, we assign the value of 6. The third decimal place of the function $f(3)=0.12345$ is 3. Therefore, one assigns a value of 4 to the variable x, which is distinct from the previous value. By proceeding down, the diagonal for the table of, one may derive all the digits for x, as illustrated in the subsequent table, x cannot be equal to $f(n)$ for any value of n, as it deviates from $f(n)$ in the *nth* decimal place. (An issue occurs because certain integers, like 0.1999 and 0.2000, are considered equal while having differing decimal forms.) To circumvent this issue, one ensures that the digits 0 and 9 are never included when constructing x (Mizusaki et al., 2010).

n	$f(n)$
1	3.<u>1</u>4159...
2	55.5<u>5</u>555...
3	0.12<u>3</u>45...
4	0.500<u>0</u>0...
⋮	⋮

$x = 0.4641\ldots$

The previous theorem has a significant application in the field of computation theory. Certain languages cannot be determined or recognized by Turing machines since there is an infinite number of languages, while the number of Turing machines is finite. Due to the nature of Turing machines along with the vast number of languages that exist, inevitably, certain languages will not be noticed by any Turing machine. These languages cannot be recognized by a Turing machine, as one mentions in the next corollary (Handy & Carter, 2004).

6.2.2. An Undecidable Language

Now one can proceed with the proof of Theorem 6.9, which establishes the inability to determine the language.

$$A_{TM} = \{◆M, w◆ | M \text{ is a } TM \text{ and } M \text{ accepts } w\}.$$

- **Evidence:** Assuming the decidability of ATM, one can derive a contradiction. Consider the scenario where H acts as a decider over ATM. When given the input M,ω, consisting of a Turing Machine M and a string ω, H will halt and accept if M also accepts ω. In addition, H will halt and reject if M does not accept w (Myasnikov & Rybalov, 2008). Put simply, one assumes that the H is a Turing Machine, were

$$H(\langle M, w\rangle) = \begin{cases} accept & \text{if } M \text{ accepts } w \\ reject & \text{if } M \text{ does not accept } w. \end{cases}$$

Now, one will create a new Turing machine, referred to as D, which will utilize H as its subroutine. This new Turing machine asks H to figure out the behavior of M when it is given its overview as input. Once D has established this information, it proceeds to do the opposite. Essentially, it disregards if M takes along with accepts if M fails to accept. Here is a brief overview of **D**.

D = "On input ⟨M ⟩, whereas M is a TM:

i. First, one executes *H* on the given input ⟨M, ⟨M ⟩⟩.

ii. Output the inverse of *H's* output. Essentially, if *H* accepts, then reject; or if *H* rejects, then accept (Karhumäki & Maon, 1986).

Do not let yourself get confused by the concept of a machine operating upon its definition! It is not uncommon for programs to be run with themselves as input, which can happen in real-world scenarios. Take, for instance, a compiler, which is a program responsible for translating other programs. It is logical to run a Python program upon itself since a compiler over the language Python can be written in Python (Miller & Shore, 2004). To summarize

$$D(\langle M\rangle) = \begin{cases} accept & \text{if } M \text{ does not accept } \langle M\rangle \\ reject & \text{if } M \text{ accepts } \langle M\rangle. \end{cases}$$

Have you ever wondered about the outcome when running *D* via its language *D* to be input? As a result, one obtains

$$D(\langle D\rangle) = \begin{cases} accept & \text{if } D \text{ does not accept } \langle D\rangle \\ reject & \text{if } D \text{ accepts } \langle D\rangle. \end{cases}$$

Regardless of *D's* actions, it is compelled to take the opposite course, leading to an evident contradiction. Therefore, TM D or TM H can't exist.

Let's go over the steps for this proof. Assume that a Turing machine *H* can decide the language A_{TM}. Construct a Turing machine *D* using *H*, which will accept the input *M* only if *M* refuses to accept the input of *M*. Lastly, execute *D* on itself. Therefore, the machines perform the subsequent actions, with the final line resulting in a contradiction (Jafari, 2024).

i. When considering M, ω the acceptance of ù by *M* determines whether H accepts it or not.

ii. *D* dismisses ⟨M ⟩ precisely if *M* takes ⟨M ⟩

iii. *D* rejects ⟨D⟩ if and only if *D* accepts ⟨D⟩ (Hillebrand et al., 1995).

Where can I find the diagonalization within the proof for Theorem 6.9 It becomes clear when one analyzes tables for behavior over TMs H or D. These tables contain a comprehensive list of Turing Machines, with each machine's corresponding descriptions arranged in rows and columns M_1, M_2 ,. The entries indicate if the device in a particular row accepts what is entered in a specific column M_1, M_2. Whether the machine embraces the input or gets stuck in a loop, the entry will be marked as either accept or blank, respectively. One fabricated the entries within the following find to exemplify the concept (Goldblatt & Jackson, 2012).

	$\langle M_1\rangle$	$\langle M_2\rangle$	$\langle M_3\rangle$	$\langle M_4\rangle$	⋯
M_1	*accept*		*accept*		
M_2	*accept*	*accept*	*accept*	*accept*	
M_3					⋯
M_4	*accept*	*accept*			
⋮		⋮			

Figure 6.4. *Illustration of entry i, j is accept if* ***I*** *accepts* $\boldsymbol{M_j}$.

Source: Babai, L., Creative Commons License.

The values shown in the Figure 6.4 represent the outcomes of executing *H* on inputs related to Figure 6.4. If M_3 refuses to take input ⟨M_2⟩, then the record for row M_3 while column ⟨M_2⟩ ⟩ is marked as reject since *H* rejects data ⟨M_3, ⟨M_2⟩⟩ (Hartmanis & Hopcroft, 1970).

	(M_1)	(M_2)	(M_3)	(M_4)	...
M_1	*accept*	*reject*	*accept*	*reject*	
M_2	*accept*	*accept*	*accept*	*accept*	...
M_3	*reject*	*reject*	*reject*	*reject*	
M_4	*accept*	*accept*	*reject*	*reject*	
⋮		⋮			

Figure 6.5. *Illustration of the value for H upon input ⟨Mi, ⟨Mj⟩⟩ is represented by entry i, j.*

Source: Ichel Sipser, Creative Commons License.

In Figure 6.5 it is included D. Based on the assumption that both H and D are Turing Machines, it must appear upon the list M_1, M_2 ,, among all Turing Machines. It is worth noting that D calculates the inverse for the diagonal entries. There is a contradiction that arises at the location of the question mark, where the content must be the reverse of itself (Hartmanis & Hopcroft, 1967).

	(M_1)	(M_2)	(M_3)	(M_4)	...	(D)	...
M_1	*accept*	*reject*	*accept*	*reject*		*accept*	
M_2	*accept*	*accept*	*accept*	*accept*	...	*accept*	...
M_3	*reject*	*reject*	*reject*	*reject*		*reject*	
M_4	*accept*	*accept*	*reject*	*reject*		*accept*	
⋮		⋮			⋱		
D	*reject*	*reject*	*accept*	*accept*		?	
⋮		⋮					⋱

Figure 6.6. *Illustration of If D is present within the illustration, a contradiction arises at what point. "?".*

Source: Blum,M, Creative Commons License.

ACTIVITY 6.1

Objective: The objective of this activity is to enhance students' understanding of decidable and undecidable problems, to develop their skills in algorithmic thinking, and to encourage collaborative learning and critical analysis.

Activity Description: In this activity, students will work in small groups to classify a set of given problems as either decidable or undecidable. They will outline an algorithm for a decidable problem and explain why an undecidable problem cannot be solved by any algorithm, using concepts like the diagonalization method or the halting problem. Each group will present their findings to the class, discussing the key reasons for their classifications and the implications for computational theory. This activity aims to help students grasp the practical and theoretical boundaries of computation while fostering collaborative learning and critical thinking skills.

6.3. A TURING-UNRECOGNIZABLE LANGUAGE

In the previous section, we demonstrated a language called A_{TM} that is not decidable. Now one presents a language that is not even recognizable by a Turing machine. It is important to note that A_{TM} is not suitable for this purpose, as we have demonstrated which A_{TM} is Turing is recognizable. According to the theorem presented, if a language along with its complement are equally Turing-recognizable, then the language can be determined (Ristin & Gullberg, 2014).

Therefore, for every language that cannot be decided by a Turing machine, both the language itself and its complement cannot be recognized by a Turing machine. The complement for the language is defined as the set of all strings which are not part of the language. A language is considered co-Turing-recognizable when it is the opposite of a Turing-recognizable language (Daly et al., 2023).

Theorem 6.11 a Language is Decidable if it is Turing-Recognizable and Co-Turing-Recognizable

Put simply, a language is considered decidable only if both the language itself and its complement can be recognized by a Turing machine.

- **Proof:** There are two hypotheses to demonstrate. If A is decidable, it is evident that each of A and the opposite of A are Turing-recognizable. A decidable language is always Turing-recognizable, therefore the complement for a decidable language is additionally decidable (Effendi et al., 2021).

In the opposite scenario, where both A and $\overline{A}$ were Turing-recognizable, one assigns M_1 as the recognizer with A and M_2 be the recognizer for A. The following Turing machine M is a decider for A.

As the recognizer for A. Hereinafter the Turing machine M can determine if a given input belongs to set A (Schneiderman, 1986).

M = "On input w:

i. Simultaneously execute both machines M_1 and M_2 on input w.

ii. When M_1 agrees to, accept; when M_2 accepts, reject (Swaminathan et al., 2013).

By running both machines in parallel, M is equipped with two tapes - one over simulating M_1 and another for simulating M_2 In this scenario, M goes through the process of simulating each stage for every machine, and this keeps going until any of them accepts (Perley, 2012).

Now one demonstrates that M determines A. Each string w belongs either part of set A or its complement, denoted as $\overline{A}$. Consequently, whether M_1 or M_2 is obliged to accept the input ω. Since M halts anytime M_1 or M_2 agrees to, M always stops and hence qualifies as a decider. Moreover, it processes every character in A and discards all strings that are not in A. Given that M serves as the decider for A, it follows that A is decidable (Kwan & Hirose, 1996).

SUMMARY

- This chapter delves into the concepts of decidability and undecidability, illustrating the power and limits of algorithms in solving problems. It begins by introducing decidable languages, providing examples and proofs of decidability for various problems related to finite automata and context-free grammars. The chapter discusses how computational problems can be represented by languages, and proving the decidability of these languages equates to proving the decidability of the corresponding problems.
- The chapter then transitions to the concept of undecidability, presenting problems that cannot be solved algorithmically. One of the most significant results discussed is the undecidability of the language A_{TM}, which relates to determining whether a given Turing machine accepts a given input. Through this discussion, readers gain an understanding of the fundamental limitations of computation and the philosophical implications of these results.

REVIEW QUESTIONS

1. Define decidability and explain its importance in the theory of computation.
2. What is the difference between decidable and undecidable problems? Provide examples.
3. Describe the method used to determine whether a given deterministic finite automaton (DFA) accepts a particular string.
4. Explain the concept of the universal Turing machine and its significance.
5. Discuss the diagonalization method and its role in proving undecidability.
6. What are Turing-recognizable languages? Provide an example to illustrate.
7. Explain why the problem of determining whether a Turing machine accepts a given input is undecidable.

MULTIPLE CHOICE QUESTIONS

1. Which of the following is a decidable problem?

a. Determining if a Turing machine accepts a given input.

b. Determining if a context-free grammar generates any strings.

c. Determining if two context-free grammars are equivalent.

d. Determining if a Turing machine halts on all inputs.

2. The problem of testing whether a given deterministic finite automaton (DFA) accepts a given string is:

a. Undecidable

b. Turing-recognizable

c. Decidable

d. None of the above

3. Which concept demonstrates the undecidability of the problem of determining whether a Turing machine accepts a given input?

a. Pumping lemma

b. Diagonalization method

c. Pigeonhole principle

d. Regular expressions

4. Who introduced the concept of diagonalization in the context of undecidability?

a. Alan Turing

b. Georg Cantor

c. Kurt Gödel

d. Alonzo Church

5. The universal Turing machine is capable of:

a. Solving all computational problems

b. Simulating any other Turing machine

c. Deciding all languages

d. Recognizing all languages

6. Which of the following is not a representation used for regular languages?

a. Deterministic finite automaton (DFA)

b. Non-deterministic finite automaton (NFA)

c. Context-Free Grammar (CFG)

d. Regular expression

Answers to Multiple Questions

1. (b); 2. (c); 3. (b); 4. (b); 5. (b); 6. (c)

REFERENCES

1. Afsari, B. (2008). Sensitivity analysis for the problem of matrix joint diagonalization. *SIAM Journal on Matrix Analysis and Applications, 30*(3), 1148–1171.
2. Baget, J. F., Leclère, M., Mugnier, M. L., & Salvat, E. (2011). On rules with existential variables: Walking the decidability line. *Artificial Intelligence, 175*(9, 10), 1620–1654.
3. Bertoni, A., Choffrut, C., Goldwurm, M., & Lonati, V. (2003). On the number of occurrences of a symbol in words of regular languages. *Theoretical Computer Science, 302*(1–3), 431–456.

4. Blaha, P., Hofstätter, H., Koch, O., Laskowski, R., & Schwarz, K. (2010). Iterative diagonalization in augmented plane wave-based methods in electronic structure calculations. *Journal of Computational Physics, 229*(2), 453–460.

5. Brüggemann-Klein, A., & Wood, D. (1998). One-unambiguous regular languages. *Information and Computation, 140*(2), 229–253.

6. Chockler, H., & Kupferman, O. (2004). ⊠-regular languages are testable with a constant number of queries. *Theoretical Computer Science, 329*(1–3), 71–92.

7. Clark, A., & Eyraud, R. (2007). Polynomial identification in the limit of context-free substitutable languages. *Journal of Machine Learning Research, 8*, 1725–1745.

8. Daly, K., Carter, E., & Sabates, R. (2023). Silenced by an unknown language? Exploring language matching during transitions from complementary education to government schools in Ghana. *Compare: A Journal of Comparative and International Education, 53*(4), 585–602.

9. Demri, S. (2001). The complexity of regularity in grammar logics and related modal logics. *Journal of Logic and Computation, 11*(6), 933–960.

10. Dudakov, S., & Karlov, B. (2021). On decidability of theories of regular languages. *Theory of Computing Systems, 65*(3), 462–478.

11. Effendi, J., Sakti, S., & Nakamura, S. (2021). End-to-end image-to-speech generation for untranscribed unknown languages. *IEEE Access, 9*, 55144–55154.

12. Ehrenfeucht, A., Haussler, D., & Rozenberg, G. (1983). On regularity of context-free languages. *Theoretical Computer Science, 27*(3), 311–332.

13. Epperly, E. N., Lin, L., & Nakatsukasa, Y. (2022). A theory of quantum subspace diagonalization. *SIAM Journal on Matrix Analysis and Applications, 43*(3), 1263–1290.

14. Eremondi, J., Ibarra, O. H., & McQuillan, I. (2018). On the density of context-free and counter languages. *International Journal of Foundations of Computer Science, 29*(2), 233–250.

15. Finkel, O. (2009). Highly undecidable problems for infinite computations. *RAIRO-Theoretical Informatics and Applications, 43*(2), 339–364.

16. Galatos, N., & Jipsen, P. (2013). Residuated frames with applications to decidability. *Transactions of the American Mathematical Society, 365*(3), 1219–1249.

17. Goldblatt, R., & Jackson, M. (2012). Well-structured program equivalence is highly undecidable. *ACM Transactions on Computational Logic (TOCL), 13*(3), 1–8.

18. Handy, N. C., & Carter, S. (2004). Large vibrational variational calculations using 'multimode' and an iterative diagonalization technique. *Molecular Physics, 102*(21, 22), 2201–2205.

19. Hartmanis, J. (1967). Context-free languages and Turing machine computations. In *Proceedings of Symposia in Applied Mathematics* (Vol. 19, pp. 42–51).

20. Hartmanis, J., & Hopcroft, J. E. (1970). What makes some language theory problems undecidable. *Journal of Computer and System Sciences, 4*(4), 368–376.

21. Hillebrand, G. G., Kanellakis, P. C., Mairson, H. G., & Vardi, M. Y. (1995). Undecidable boundedness problems for data log programs. *The Journal of Logic Programming, 25*(2), 163–190.

22. Hopcroft, J. E. (1969). On the equivalence and containment problems for context-free languages. *Mathematical Systems Theory, 3*(2), 119–124.

23. Immerman, N., Rabinovich, A., Reps, T., Sagiv, M., & Yorsh, G. (2004). The boundary between decidability and undecidability for transitive-closure logics. In *Computer Science Logic: 18th International Workshop, CSL 2004, 13th Annual Conference of the EACSL, Karpacz, Poland, September 20–24, 2004. Proceedings* (Vol. 18, pp. 160–174).

24. Jafari, J. (2024). Easy ontology and undecidable sentences. *Metaphysica, 25*(1), 163–173.

25. Je⊠, A. (2008). Conjunctive grammars generate non-regular unary languages. *International Journal of Foundations of Computer Science, 19*(03), 597–615.

26. Jones, S. A., & Thomas, R. M. (2018). Word problems of groups: Formal languages, characterizations and decidability. *Theoretical Computer Science, 750*, 2–23.

27. Karhumäki, J., & Maon, Y. (1986). A simple undecidable problem: Existential agreement of inverses of two morphisms on a regular language. *Journal of Computer and System Sciences, 32*(3), 315–322.

28. Karhumäki, J., Plandowski, W., & Rytter, W. (2005). On the complexity of decidable cases of the commutation problem of languages. *Theoretical Computer Science, 337*(1–3), 105–118.

29. Kaveh, A., & Nikbakht, M. (2007). Block diagonalization of Laplacian matrices of symmetric graphs via group theory. *International Journal for Numerical Methods in Engineering, 69*(5), 908–947.

30. Kierstead, H. A., & Remmel, J. B. (1983). Indiscernibles and decidable models. *The Journal of Symbolic Logic, 48*(1), 21–32.

31. Koellner, P. (2006). On the question of absolute undecidability. *Philosophia Mathematica, 14*(2), 153–188.

32. Kwan, H., & Hirose, K. (1996). Unknown language rejection in language identification system. In *Proceedings of Fourth International Conference on Spoken Language Processing (ICSLP'96)* (Vol. 3, pp. 1776–1779).

33. Laufer, B. (1997). The lexical plight in second language reading: Words you don't know, words you think you know, and words you can't guess. In *Second Language Vocabulary Acquisition: A Rationale for Pedagogy* (Vol. 1, pp. 20–34).

34. Leininger, M. L., Sherrill, C. D., Allen, W. D., & Schaefer III, H. F. (2001). Systematic study of selected diagonalization methods for configuration interaction matrices. *Journal of Computational Chemistry, 22*(13), 1574–1589.

35. Liang, S., & Pang, H. (1994). Approximate diagonalization using the density matrix renormalization-group method: A two-dimensional-systems perspective. *Physical Review B, 49*(13), 9214.

36. Mandelshtam, V. A. (2000). The multidimensional filter diagonalization method: I. Theory and numerical implementation. *Journal of Magnetic Resonance, 144*(2), 343–356.

37. Maon, Y. (1986). On the equivalence of some transductions involving letter to letter morphisms on regular languages. *Acta Informatica, 23*, 585–596.

38. Miller, R., Nies, A., & Shore, R. (2004). The⊠⊠-theory of R (≤, ⊠, ⊠) is undecidable. *Transactions of the American Mathematical Society, 356*(8), 3025–3067.

39. Mizusaki, T., Kaneko, K., Honma, M., & Sakurai, T. (2010). Filter diagonalization of shell-model calculations. *Physical Review C—Nuclear Physics, 82*(2), 024310.

40. Moore, C. (1990). Unpredictability and undecidability in dynamical systems. *Physical Review Letters, 64*(20), 2354.

41. Mouawad, L., & Perahia, D. (1993). Diagonalization in a mixed basis: A method to compute low-frequency normal modes for large macromolecules. *Biopolymers: Original Research on Biomolecules, 33*(4), 599–611.

42. Myasnikov, A. G., & Rybalov, A. N. (2008). Generic complexity of undecidable problems. *The Journal of Symbolic Logic, 73*(2), 656–673.

43. Neuhauser, D. (1994). Circumventing the Heisenberg principle: A rigorous demonstration of filter-diagonalization on a LiCN model. *The Journal of Chemical Physics, 100*(7), 5076–5079.

44. Niemi, V. (1984). The undecidability of form equivalence for context-free and E0L forms. *Theoretical Computer Science, 32*(3), 261–277.

45. Norval, A. J. (2004). Hegemony after deconstruction: The consequences of undecidability. *Journal of Political Ideologies, 9*(2), 139–157.

46. Perley, N. (2012). The language of an unknown country: Intratextuality in Proust's in search of lost time. *19th-Century Music, 36*(2), 136–145.

47. Pr⊠ša, D., & Reinhardt, K. (2017). Undecidability of the emptiness problem for context-free picture languages. *Theoretical Computer Science, 679*, 118–125.

48. Rabin, M. O. (1969). Decidability of second-order theories and automata on infinite trees. *Transactions of the American Mathematical Society, 141*, 1–35.

49. Ramalingam, G. (1994). The undecidability of aliasing. *ACM Transactions on Programming Languages and Systems (TOPLAS), 16*(5), 1467–1471.

50. Raz, D. (1997). Length considerations in context-free languages. *Theoretical Computer Science, 183*(1), 21–32.

51. Ristin-Kaufmann, N., & Gullberg, M. (2014). The effects of first exposure to an unknown language at different ages. *Bulletin Suisse de Linguistique Appliquée, 99*, 17–29.

52. Rogers, S. E., Chang, J. L., & Kwak, D. (1987). A diagonal algorithm for the method of pseudo compressibility. *Journal of Computational Physics, 73*(2), 364–379.

53. Saad, Y., Zhou, Y., Bekas, C., Tiago, M. L., & Chelikowsky, J. (2006). Diagonalization methods in PARSEC. *Physica Status Solidi (b), 243*(9), 2188–2197.

54. Salomaa, A. (1975). On some decidability problems concerning developmental languages. In *Studies in Logic and the Foundations of Mathematics* (Vol. 82, pp. 144–153).

55. Schenk, O., Bollhöfer, M., & Römer, R. A. (2006). On large-scale diagonalization techniques for the Anderson model of localization. *SIAM Journal on Scientific Computing, 28*(3), 963–983.

56. Schenk, O., Bollhöfer, M., & Römer, R. A. (2008). On large-scale diagonalization techniques for the Anderson model of localization. *SIAM Review, 50*(1), 91–112.

57. Schneiderman, E. (1986). Using the known to teach the unknown. *American Annals of the Deaf, 131*(1), 51–52.

58. Smikun, L. B. (1976). Connection between context-free groups and groups with decidable problems of automata equivalence. *Cybernetics, 12*(5), 687–691.

59. So, F., & Liu, K. L. (2000). A study of the Fokker–Planck equation of bistable systems by the method of state-dependent diagonalization. *Physica A: Statistical Mechanics and its Applications, 277*(3, 4), 335–348.

60. Straubing, H., Thérien, D., & Thomas, W. (1995). Regular languages defined with generalized quantifiers. *Information and Computation, 118*(2), 289–301.

61. Swaminathan, S., MacSweeney, M., Boyles, R., Waters, D., Watkins, K. E., & Möttönen, R. (2013). Motor excitability during visual perception of known and unknown spoken languages. *Brain and Language, 126*(1), 1–7.

62. Tsallis, C. (1978). Diagonalization methods for the general bilinear Hamiltonian of an assembly of bosons. *Journal of Mathematical Physics, 19*(1), 277–286.

63. Vollgraf, R., & Obermayer, K. (2006). Quadratic optimization for simultaneous matrix diagonalization. *IEEE Transactions on Signal Processing, 54*(9), 3270–3278.

64. Vyalyi, M. N., & Rubtsov, A. A. (2015). On regular realizability problems for context-free languages. *Problems of Information Transmission, 51*(4), 349–360.

65. Wilke, T. (1993). An algebraic theory for regular languages of finite and infinite words. *International Journal of Algebra and Computation, 3*(4), 447–489.

66. Wolf, P. (2022). From decidability to undecidability by considering regular sets of instances. *Theoretical Computer Science, 899*, 25–38.

67. Zhang, H., & Ying, M. (2010). Decidable fragments of first-order language under stable model semantics and circumscription. In *Proceedings of the AAAI Conference on Artificial Intelligence* (Vol. 24, No. 1, pp. 375–380).

CHAPTER

7 Turing Machines

LEARNING OBJECTIVES

After studying this chapter, you will be able to:

- Define a Turing machine and explain its components.
- Distinguish between deterministic and non-deterministic Turing machines.
- Describe the transition function, instantaneous description, and moves of a Turing machine.
- Program a Turing machine to solve specific computational problems.
- Explain the concept of Turing machines as acceptors and transducers.
- Understand the equivalence of various Turing machine modifications.
- Explain the Church-Turing thesis and its implications.
- Discuss recursive and recursively enumerable languages.
- Identify the significance of the halting problem and its implications for computation.

KEY TERMS FROM THIS CHAPTER

Church-Turing thesis
Halting problem
Non-deterministic Turing machine
Recursively enumerable language
Turing machine
Deterministic Turing machine
Instantaneous description
Recursive language
Transition function
Universal Turing machine

UNIT INTRODUCTION

The concept of an algorithm and effective process has been developed multiple times. In Chapter 3, one presented a practical method to ascertain whether the collection accepted from finite automation had no elements, possessed a limited number of elements, or was boundless. It may be tempting to believe that regarding any class for languages alongside finite details, there is an easy way to answer such inquiries. Unfortunately, that is not true. As an illustration, it is impossible to determine how the complement for a context-free language is empty, but one can determine if the language itself is empty. One is seeking a specific method that addresses the question in the context of a particular context-free language (Goldin et al., 2004). Instead, one is looking for a universal procedure that can accurately answer the question across all context-free languages. It is evident that if one only has to know if a certain context-free language has a vacant complement, then there exists an algorithm that answers this question. There exists an algorithm that provides a positive response and another that provides a negative response, regardless of the inputs. There must be one correct option among these. Clearly, determining which of the two algorithms provides the correct response may not be immediately apparent. In the early 1900s, mathematician David Hilbert embarked on a mission to discover a method to determine the validity of any mathematical statement (Wegner & Goldin, 2003). Specifically, he sought a method to ascertain the truth of any given formula within first-order predication calculus when applied to integers. Since the first-order predicate calculus is powerful enough to express the statement that the language generated by a context-free grammar is £*, had Hilbert been successful, our problem of deciding whether the complement of acfl is empty would be solved. However, in 1931, Kurt Gödel published his famous incompleteness theorem, which proved that no such effective procedure could exist. He developed a formula using predicate calculus utilized for integers, which was defined in such a way that it was impossible to either confirm or refute in such a logical system (Rogozhin, 1996). The formalization along with subsequent explanation of this theory, along with the refinement of our intuitive understanding of an effective procedure, stands as a remarkable intellectual accomplishment of time. After formalizing the concept of an effective process, it became evident that numerous specific functions could not be computed using such a procedure. Indeed, the existence of these functions can be readily observed through a counting argument. Examine the set of functions that map nonnegative integers to {0, 1}. Such functions may be mapped to real numbers. Assuming that effective processes can be described finitely, it is possible to establish a one-to-one correspondence between the class for all effective processes and the integers (Shannon, 1956).

Given the absence of direct mapping within integers and real numbers, it follows that certain functions exist which cannot be computed through effective methods. There is an overwhelming abundance of functions, an infinite number, and a finite number of procedures. Therefore, the presence of non-computable functions should come as no surprise. It is quite remarkable that specific issues and functions of great importance in the fields of mathematics, computer science, and various other fields cannot be computed. In contemporary academia, the Turing machine has emerged as the widely recognized regulation of an effective process (Hjelmfelt et al., 1991). It is not possible to definitively establish the equivalence between the Turing machines model and our intuitive understanding of a computer. However, there are strong arguments supporting this equivalence, commonly referred to as the Church's hypothesis. The Turing Machine has been said to be on par with modern digital computers and encompasses the broadest mathematical concepts of computation (Zylberberg et al., 2011).

A Turing machine seems a conceptual representation of computation that involves the manipulation of symbols based on predefined rules. Even with its straightforward design, this model has the ability to execute any computer algorithm (Benioff, 1980). A model of a Turing machine that is implemented in a physical form. An abstract device able to manipulate symbols upon a tape based on a set of rules is an essential model of computation. Although it is simple, it has the capability to replicate any computer algorithm. This chapter examines the constituents, operational capabilities, and diversities of Turing machines, how they are important in delineating computing procedures, and their theoretical ramifications (Böhm & Jacopini, 1966).

7.1. TURING MACHINE MODEL

7.1.1. What is a Turing Machine?

The Turing Machine is analogous to a kind of Pushdown Automaton. Both systems have a finite-state machine for a primary component and include a supplementary storage (Žák, 1983). A Pushdown Automaton utilizes a "stack" for storage, while a Turing Machine utilizes a "tape" that is infinitely extendable in both directions. The tape is composed of a sequence of "squares", with each square capable of containing only one symbol. The tape head, also known as the read-write head, has the ability to read a symbol stored on the tape, create a symbol onto the tape, and shift one square in any direction (Malekmohamadi et al., 2020).

There are two types of Turing Machine that are currently accessible.

i. Deterministic Turing Machine.

ii. Non-deterministic Turing Machine.

One shall only be discussing Deterministic Machines. Contrary to other automata, a Turing Machine lacks an "input". Instead, there are typically symbols on the tape prior to the Turing Machine's operation, which it may or may not read. If wanted, the initial tape can be considered as "input".

"Acceptors only yield a binary output, either accepting or rejecting. Transducers can generate more intricate outcomes. Besides acceptors, a Turing Machine further decides whether it accepts its input. The output of the computation can be considered as the results left upon the tape after the Turing Machine finishes (Jack & Shagrir, 2011). Thus, a Turing Machine can be described as a "transducer."

7.1.2. Definition of Turing Machines

The structure of a Turing Machine M consists of seven components

$(Q, \Sigma, \Gamma, \delta, q_0, \#, F)$

Whereas Q shows set of states

The set of symbols, denoted by Σ, is finite and represents the input alphabet. Γ is a finite collection of symbols known as the "tape alphabet". The symbol "δ" represents the partial transition function (Benioff, 1980). The symbol 'blank' is denoted by # Î*T*, the initial state is q_0 which belongs to the set of states Q. The set $F \subseteq Q$, which consists of final states, is an essential component. To ensure that the Turing machine can locate its input and determine when it has completed processing all of it, certain requirements must be met:

i. At first, the tape is blank, with every symbol represented by a #, except for a possible finite order of symbols that may be present.

ii. When there are originally nonblank symbols within the tape head is first positioned over one of them (Hernández et al., 2012).

This highlights the fact about the term "input," which refers to the non-blank symbols found on the tape, lacks the symbol #.

7.1.3. Transition Function, Instantaneous Description and Moves

The Turing Device's "Transition Function" is defined as follows:

$$\delta: Q \times \Gamma \rightarrow Q \times \Gamma \times \{L, R\}$$

Whenever the machine reaches a specific state (*Q*) and reads a particular symbol (*a*) found on the tape, it substitutes the symbol in the tape with another symbol (*b*), transitions to another state (*Q*), and shifts the tape heads a square either to the left (*L*) or towards the right (*R*) (Sherry, 1986). A Turing device's "Instantaneous Description" and "Configuration" necessitates.

1. The current state of the machine
2. The information stored on the tape
3. The location for the tape head onto the tape

This is expressed in a string format.

$$x_i \ \ldots\ldots \ x_j \ q_m x_k \ \ldots\ldots \ x_l$$

In which the *x*'s represent the symbols that make up the tape, q_m denotes the current state, along with the tape head positioned on the square that includes x_k (the sign next to q_m). The "*Move*" for a Turing machine may be represented as a pair of immediate descriptions, with a symbol "|–" separating them (Kamarianakis & Gao, 2010).

For instance, if

$$\delta(q_5, b) = (q_8, c, R)$$

One potential option is to

$$abbabq_5\ babb \ \ \vdash abbabcq_8\ abb$$

7.1.4. Programming a Turing Machine

Just like grammar has its control theme within the form of "productions," a Turing machine revolves around the concept of "transitions." The transitions are provided in the form of S-tuples, which can be a table or a list. Every tuple includes the current state, symbol written, symbol read, direction, and next state. Developing a list of instructions is referred to as "programming" a Turing machine (Asperti & Ricciotti, 2015). The initial position for the read head within a Turing machine's controller is typically over the initial input symbol on the left. It is not essential to do so, as it is straightforward to reach the initial input symbol when the machine starts anyplace on the nonblank part of the tape (Ogheneovo, 2014).

With the input $\Sigma = \{a, b\}$, this program split accomplishes the task and transitions to state q_1.

(q_0, a, a, L, q_0)

(q_0, b, b, L, q_0)

$(q_0, \#, \#, R, q_1)$

7.1.5. Turing Machines as Acceptors

A Turing machine stops when it exhausts all possible actions. When the process comes to a finalized state, it acknowledges the input; otherwise, it dismisses the input (Bedregal& Figueira, 2008).

The Turing machine defined as $T = (Q, \Sigma, \Gamma, \delta, q_0, \#, F)$ is capable of accepting a language L(M). Whereas: $q_0\ w \vdash xi\ q_f\ xj$ represents a transition during computation of the Turing Machine to a final state q_f

Assuming the Turing machine begins by placing its tape head attached to the leftmost symbol. An input is accepted by a Turing Machine if it comes to a halt within a final state. There are two possible scenarios where this could not occur:

1. The Turing machine may come to a prevent in a state that is not final (Marion, 1994).
2. The Turing machine may continue indefinitely, entering what is referred to as a "infinite loop."

7.1.6. How to Recognize a Language

This machine is capable of matching strings of a specific form

$\{a^n b^n: n \geq 0\}$

There is only one state that is considered the "final state," which is *q1*. State q_4, in this case, functions as a "error state" where no moves are possible (Kleinschmidt & Jaeger, 2015).

Current state	Symbol read	Symbol written	Direction	Next state
Find the left end of the input				
q_0	a	a	L	q_0
q_0	b	b	L	q_0
q_0	#	#	R	q_1
If leftmost symbol is "a". erase it. if "b" fail				
q_1	a	#	R	q_2
q_1	b	#	R	q_4
Find the right end of the input				
q_2	a	a	R	q_2
q_2	b	b	R	q_2
q_2	#	#	L	q_3
Erase the "b" at the left end of the input				
q_3	b	#	L	q_0

This machine operates through a repetitive loop:

q_0: move all the way to the left

q_1: erase on '*a*'

q_2: move all the way to the right

q_3: Erase a '*b*' Repeat

If the string does not conform to the pattern $\{a^n b^n: n \geq 0\}$, the result will be ultimately

a. Either observe an '*a*' in a nonfinal state q_3 while stopping,
b. observe a '*b*' within a final state q_1, transition towards nonfinal state q_4, and stop.

7.1.7. Turing Machines as Transducers

When utilizing a Turing machine as its transducer, its input is derived from the complete nonblank section of the initial tape, while the output is derived from the complete nonblank section of the tape if the machine halts.

A Turing machine specifies a function $y = f(x)$ on strings x, $y \in \Sigma^*$ in the set of all possible strings if

$$q_0 x \overset{*}{\vdash} q_f y$$

Where q_f represents the concluding state. The function index is considered "Turing computable" when it is a Turing computer capable of performing the task described above (Caucal, 2003).

7.2. COMPLETE LANGUAGES AND FUNCTIONS

A Turing machine possesses an output function that produces the contents if the tape that was input following the processing consequently, then the resulting input string may be regarded as the outcome of the computation. Thus, the Turing machine is viewed as a computational device that operates on functions mapping integers to integers (Hudak, 1989).

7.3. MODIFICATION OF TURING MACHINES

Two automata are considered equivalent when they both agree to an identical language. Two transducers are considered equivalent when they perform the same computation.

Two classes of automata, such as Standard Turing machines along nondeterministic Turing machines, are considered comparable if every transducer within one class has an equivalent counterpart in the other class. During each step of the process, the tape head has the option to move in either direction. One may improve this by including a "Stay option", meaning one will include "don't move" in the set $\{L, R\}$.

There is an equivalence between Turing machines that have a stay option along with Standard Turing Machines (Zenil, 2013).

7.3.1. N-Track Turing Machine

A Turing Machine with N tracks is characterized by the property that for every square within the tape contains a logical n-tuple of symbols corresponding to the tape alphabet. One way to conceptualize this would be a Turing machine that has several tape heads, each of which moves simultaneously (Gustafsson & Sternad, 2016).

There is an equivalence between N-Track Turing machines or standard Turing machines."

7.3.2. Semi-Infinite Tape/Offline/Multitape/ND Turing Machines

a. A Turing machine can possess a "semi-infinite tape" where the nonblank feedback is located at the far-left end of that tape. There is an equivalence between Turing machines using semi-infinite tape as well as Standard Turing machines (Hooper, 1966).

b. The "Offline Turing Machine" is equipped with two tapes. There are two tapes involved in the process. The first tape was read-only and held the input, while the second tape was read-write and started empty. Offline Turing machines or Standard Turing machines were equivalent.".

c. A multi-tape Turing Machine is equipped with an infinite number of tapes, each having its own separately regulated tape head, Multi-tape (Inoue et al., 2004).

d. Turing Machines were similar to Standard Turing Machines.

e. A "Nondetermin*istic Turing Machine*" is a type of Turing Machine where the Deterministic Finite Automaton that controls the tape is substituted with a *Non-deterministic Finite Automaton* (Ibarra, 1971).

"Nondeterministic Turing computers are essentially identical to Conventional Turing computers."

7.3.3. Multidimensional/Two-state Turing Machine

- **A "Multidimensional Turing Machine"** is a type of Turing Machine that operates on a Multidimensional "tape". For instance, a two-dimensional Turing Machine could store and retrieve information on an infinite plane that is divided into squares, like a checkerboard. The potential movements of the tape head can be denoted as {*N*, *E*, *S*, *W*}. A three-dimensional Turing computer might potentially have directions such as {*N*, *E*, *S*, *W*, *V*, *D*}. Multidimensional Turing Machines remain similar to Standard Turing Machines (Shore, 2014).
- **The Binary Turing Machine** is characterized by a tape alphabet that is limited to only two symbols. Binary Turing machines along with Standard Turing Machines have been deemed equivalent. A "Two-state Turing Machine" constitutes a Turing Machine that is limited to only two states. It has been established that two-state Turing machines have been the same as Standard Turing Machines (Dash & Nayak, 2012).

7.4. CHURCH–TURING'S THESIS

Alan Turing's groundbreaking work involved the formalization of the concept of an "effective producer," now commonly referred to as an algorithm. His definition of Turing machines played a crucial role in this endeavor. At the same time, mathematicians were independently tackling the identical problem (Arrighi & Dowek, 2012).

Emil Post	Production Systems
Alonzo Church	Lambda Calculus
Noam Chomsky	Unrestricted Grammars Stephen
Kleene	Recursive function Theory
Raymond Smullyn	Formal Systems.

All the mentioned formalisms have been proven to be equivalent to each other. As a result.

1. **Turing's Thesis (Weak Form):** Turing machines have the remarkable ability to compute any task that can be accomplished by a versatile digital computer.
    i. **Turing's Thesis (Strong Form):** Turing machines can compute any computable function. Proving the strong version of Turing's Thesis is a challenging task as it attempts to establish a connection between abstract mathematical concepts along tangible reality (De Benedetto, 2021).

7.4.1. Counting

For two sets to be placed into one-to-one correspondence, it is necessary and sufficient for them to have an equal number of elements (Aspnes et al., 1994).

- **For Example:**

  {red, yellow, green, blue}

  I I I I

  {apple, banana, cucumber, plum}

A method for establishing a direct relationship with a subset for natural numbers is as follows:

{red,	yellow,	green,	blue}
–	–	–	–
{1,	2,	3,	4}

7.4.2. Recursive and Recursively Enumerable Language

Conducting a Turing machine across a given input can result in three possible outcomes.

1. It is possible that the Turing machine Halt and accept the input.
2. Halt and reject the input; and
3. Never halt.

A language is considered "*recursive*" if it has a Turing machine that can accept all the strings belonging to the language and reject any string that does not belong to it, using the same alphabet.

When considering the recursion of a language L, it is important to note that its complement, L, ought to have the same property (Jain et al., 2001).

In the realm of theoretical computer science, a language is considered "*recursively enumerable*" if it can be recognized by a Turing machine which accepts all valid strings in the language while rejecting any strings that do not belong to it. Strings that do not belong to the language can result in rejection or lead to the Turing machine getting stuck in an infinite loop (Culik, 1979).

It is worth noting that all recursively enumerable languages are also recursive. However, it remains uncertain whether every language that can be recognized by a Turing machine is also decidable.

Turing Machines do not exhibit a recursive nature. The terminology is derived from recursive operate theory (Ambos & Lerman, 1986).

Remember

The Church-Turing thesis suggests that every function that may be computed through a successful approach can also be computed using a particular type of machine.

7.4.3. Enumerating Strings in a Language

Enumerating a set involves establishing a one-to-one relationship between each component of the set and the natural numbers. The collection of every one of strings over a given alphabet can be counted. Assuming a string represents a number using the |S| -ary number mechanism (Peterfreund, 2023). The strings within a language come from a specific subset of all possible strings Σ. However, is it feasible to list every string in each language?

If a language is recursive, the result is a Turing machine that will stop for it. To ensure that each finite string is generated, we can arrange the strings for Σ^* in the shortest-first order. One can evaluate each string using a specific machine, and once the machine takes the string, one can assign it to the following natural number. Additionally, one can list the repeatedly enumerated languages. One possesses a machine that is capable of halting and accepting any given string that falls within the language. The key lies in preventing the machine from becoming trapped in an endless loop when encountering certain strings (Hickey & Cohen, 1983). This is achieved using "Time-sharing". Now, prove this.

```
w:= Ø; N:= 0;
for i:= 1 to c0 do {
add the next string in Σ* to set W;
initialize a Turing machine for this new string; for each string in set W do {
let the Turing machine for it make one more; if the Turing machine halts {
accept or reject the string as appropriate; if the string is accepted {
N: = N + 1;
let this be string N of the language;
}
remove the string from set W;
}
```

7.4.4. Non-recursively Enumerable Languages

A language seems a subset of $\Sigma^*$the set of all possible strings. A language is simply a subset of symbols Σ^*.

One has demonstrated the enumerability of a certain type of machine. Given that recursively enumerable languages consist of strings agreed to by a Turing machine, it follows that the set of repeatedly enumerable languages can also be enumerated.

The power for an infinite set will not be countable, meaning it has an uncountable number of subsets c_0. Each one of these subsets represents a language.

Therefore, it is possible for there to exist languages that cannot be computed by a certain type of machine (Carpi et al., 2021).

Based on the Turing Thesis, it is believed that any effective process can be computed by a particular type of machine.

As a result, there exist languages that cannot be described by any efficient method. There is a way to discover a language *X* that cannot be enumerated recursively, and this process is known as "diagonalization" (Kapoutsis, 2005).

7.5. UNDECIDABILITY

7.5.1. Halting Problem

A Turing machine accepts a string to be its input. Strings can act as Turing machines. With their versatility as input for various machines, like strings had a vast array of practical uses. A "Universal Turing machine" can take an account of any Turing machine, along with an input, and applying that input to the specified machine (Manin, 2012). This paired input is denoted as $M + w$. The output generated is identical to that of M. The expression can be represented as a Universal Turing Machine $(M + w) = M\ w$.

It is entirely feasible to provide a Turing machine just like input to itself, such as M (M), since a Turing machine may be referred to using a string. It is not uncommon to engage in such unconventional practices. For instance, imagine writing a C prettyprinter to C and then utilizing the Prettyprinter upon itself. Another frequent application involves bootstrapping, where programmers utilize convenient spoken languages to create a basic compiler for the first time. This minimal compiler then serves to develop an enhanced compiler for the same language. Whenever a fresh addition is made to language L, one can recompile and utilize this latest addition in the subsequent version within the compiler. There are instances when Turing machines come to a stop, while in other cases, they continue indefinitely. Some input strings may cause a Turing machine to halt, while others can lead it into an endless loop (Prokopenko et al., 2019).

Can one determine, in general, if a particular machine will stop for a given input? That's the question posed by the halting problem. If it is indeed possible, there exists a practical method to examine a particular machine along with its input to ascertain whether the device will eventually stop with that input. If this is a feasible process, then one can construct a machine to carry it out (Devienne, 1990).

Consider a Turing machine called "Will Halt" that, presented with an input string $M + w$, may either halt or accept the string when Turing machine M halts upon input w, or halt and dismiss the string if Turing's machine M fails to stop on input w. When regarded as a Boolean function, "Will Halt *(M, w)*" stops and outputs "TRUE" in the first scenario, and stops and outputs "FALSE" in the second (Sayama, 2008).

7.5.2. Implications of Halting Problem

7.5.2.1. Programming

According to the "Halting Problem" theorem, it is not possible to figure out whether any program will halt on a given input.

In many cases, it is often necessary to remove infinite loops to programs for practical purposes. Occasionally, a "meta-program" is employed to examine another program for possible infinite loops, to ensure guaranteeing the meta-program's functionality in most cases (Findler et al., 2002). It is proven that the creation of a meta-program that consistently functions is an unattainable goal. This finding can also be utilized to showcase the infeasibility of certain other programs. Here is a general outline:

i. Firstly, if problem X were to be successfully resolved, it would lead to the resolution of the Halting problem.
ii. The Halting Problem remains unsolvable.
iii. Hence, problem X remains unsolvable (Burnett & McIntyre, 1995).

7.5.2.2. Artificial Intelligence (AI)

Attempts have been made to utilize the Halting Problem as a counterpoint to the feasibility of intelligent computers. Here is the argument:

i. There are limitations to what computers are capable of.
ii. However, one could accomplish those tasks.
iii. Hence, it is imperative that one surpass computers (Haleem et al., 2019).

The first premise provided is indeed true. One way to demonstrate the second premise is by presenting a program that successfully solves a specific part of the Halting Problem. Additionally, one can discuss a clever technique that is not included in the program but allows us to solve a slightly larger portion of the problem. There are indeed valid arguments that question the feasibility of AI (Chiu et al., 2021).

7.5.3. Reduction to Halting Problem

To simplify a problem with the Halting problem, consider the following steps:

i. Suppose that there exists a reliable procedure, such as a Turing machine and any other algorithm, capable of solving problem P.
ii. Demonstrate the use of the program over P in addressing the Halting problem.
iii. It can be concluded that problem P is unsolvable (Barmpalias & Lewis, 2017).

7.5.3.1. State Entry Problem

The problem, also known as the "dead code problem," involves determining if a given Turing machine M, as provided with input w, will ever reach state q. When a Turing machine M comes to a state q where its transition function $\delta(q_i, a_i)$ is undefined, that's when it finally comes to a halt. Include a new state called z in the Turing machine and ensure that all the necessary transitions are added to direct to state z. Now, utilize the presumed state-entry process to determine if state z is ever reached when M is provided with input w. This will help us determine whether the original device M will stop or not. Based on our analysis, it seems unlikely that the believed state-entry process can be constructed (DeYoung et al., 1998).

Here are a few problems that cannot be solved:

i. Would the specific Turing machine model M halt on all input?

ii. Would Turing machine M terminate for any input?

iii. Is the language of machine M finite?

iv. Is there a string for length k within $L(M)$, for a specific value of k?

v. Are the languages accepted by Turing machines $M1$ along with $M2$ the same?

The existence of an algorithm to determine whether the Turing machine M accepts an input such as string w is not guaranteed. These issues, in which algorithms do not exist, are commonly referred to as "undecidable" or "unsolvable" (Impullitti et al., 2013).

Did you know?

It is widely acknowledged in academic circles that the halting issue, which pertains to the determination of the following statement: 'if a Turing machine can stop on a specific input, is undecidable'. The issue of halting cannot be solved by any algorithm across all machine-input pairs.

7.5.3.2. Post's Correspondence Problem

Consider a finite alphabet, denoted by Σ. Suppose one has two lists, A and B, consisting of empty strings.

Σ, alongside $|A| = |B|$, i.e.,

$A = (w_1, w_2, w_3, \ldots\ldots w_k)$

or $B = (x_1, x_2, x_3, \ldots\ldots x_k)$

The problem at hand is known as the Post's Correspondence Problem.

Is it possible to identify an order of integers $i_1, i_2, \ldots\ldots i_m$ like $m \geq 1$ and

Is there an order of integers that exists? $i_1, i_2, \ldots\ldots i_m$

$w_{i_1} w_{i_2} w_{i_3} \ldots\ldots w_{i_m} = x_{i_1} x_{i_2} x_{i_3} \ldots\ldots x_{i_m}$?

1. **Example:** Consider $A = (a, abaaa, ab)$ or $B = (aaa, ab, b)$. The sequence for integers needed was 2, 1, 1, 3, resulting in

abaaa a a ab = abaaa aaa b.

There is a solution to this instance. In overall, it will be found that the Post's correspondence issue is unsolvable (Myasnikov et al., 2014).

ACTIVITY 7.1

Objective: To understand the operation of a Turing machine by simulating one on paper.

Materials: Grid paper, pencils, erasers.

Instructions:

- Draw a grid representing the tape of a Turing machine. Label each cell with a number.
- Create a set of states and define a transition function for a simple task, such as recognizing a string of alternating 1s and 0s.
- Use the grid to simulate the movement of the tape head, state transitions, and symbol manipulations as defined by your transition function.
- Record each step of the simulation, noting the state, tape contents, and tape head position.

Discuss the results with your peers, highlighting any challenges encountered and how they were addressed.

7.6. RICE'S THEOREM

A machine designed by Turing (TM) is a method for describing a language, and the issue of choice can be seen as falling into the broader category of problems.

"Does the language recognized by the Turing machine possess property P?

Regarding this case, P denotes the property of including the null string (Rice, 1968).

- **Theorem:** "If there exists a property P that can be fulfilled by certain recursively enumerable languages yet not through all of them, then the choice is a problem."
    - **D:** It is impossible to determine whether the language recognized by a Turing Machine possesses a certain property."
- **Proof:** Consider P as a nontrivial speech property. Beginning with a Turing machine TM, we have an arbitrary example of Accepts (∧). One must locate an instance TM′ of D where the response matches that of TM

The machine that executes TM′ is designed to initially move the tape head beyond the input string when executing TM on a specific input. What TM′ provides with the initial input after that is determined by the result of Accepts (∧).

One wants TM′ to continue with the initial input as if its objective were to accept a specific language L_A only halting when the original input exists in L_A. Additionally, we would like TM' to behave just like it was recognized as a distinct language L

To ensure accuracy, one desires L_A to have a language that fulfills P,

While L_B should have a language that does not fulfill P. This guarantees that when TM′ is a positive example of D, then TM is also a positive example of Accepts (∧), and vice versa.

There is an issue that arises in this situation where, if the Turing Machine does not accept a certain input, it will enter an infinite loop. Then TM′ would be unable to accept anything. Thus, L_B is a language that contains no elements. So, if TM crashes upon input ∧, the next TM′ likewise crashes. If an empty set ⊠ occurs to have a language that does not satisfy the requirement P, the next one had precisely what one wants (Roginsky, 1991).

The selection of a language L_A is completely up to us, if L_A meets the requirement of satisfying P. Fortunately, we have found a language L_A that fulfills this condition, as P is not a trivial matter. Thus, it is demonstrated if P is a nontrivial property that even an empty language does not satisfy, then D is unresolved thereby establishing the validity of Rice's Theorem.

SUMMARY

- This chapter delves into the concept of Turing machines, an essential model in the theory of computation. A Turing machine consists of a finite-state machine and an infinite tape, divided into cells, each capable of holding a symbol. The machine operates based on a set of rules defined by its transition function, which dictates its state changes and movements along the tape.
- We examine the distinction between deterministic and non-deterministic Turing machines, focusing on the deterministic type. Programming a Turing machine involves defining its transition rules, allowing it to solve specific computational tasks. The chapter also explores the idea of Turing machines as both acceptors, which produce binary outcomes, and transducers, which generate more complex outputs.
- Furthermore, we discuss the equivalence of various Turing machine modifications, such as multi-tape, multi-dimensional, and non-deterministic versions, demonstrating their computational power. The Church-Turing thesis posits that any computation that can be performed by a digital computer can also be executed by a Turing machine. The chapter concludes by addressing the concepts of recursive and recursively enumerable languages and the significance of the halting problem, which underscores the limits of computational predictability.

REVIEW QUESTIONS

1. Define a Turing machine and describe its main components.
2. Explain the difference between deterministic and non-deterministic Turing machines.
3. Describe how the transition function works in a Turing machine.
4. What are the different types of Turing machines discussed in this chapter?
5. Explain the concept of recursive and recursively enumerable languages.
6. What is the halting problem, and why is it significant in computation theory?
7. Discuss the implications of the Church-Turing thesis.

MULTIPLE CHOICE QUESTIONS

1. **What is the primary difference between a Pushdown Automaton and a Turing Machine?**
    a. Type of state machine
    b. Input alphabet
    c. Transition function
    d. Storage mechanism

2. **What symbol is commonly used to represent a blank in a Turing machine's tape?**
    a. #
    b. $
    c. *
    d. @
3. **In a Turing machine, what does the transition function define?**
    a. State changes and tape movements
    b. Input and output symbols
    c. Initial and final states
    d. Tape alphabet
4. **Which of the following statements is true about the Church-Turing thesis?**
    a. It has been mathematically proven
    b. It states that all effective procedures can be computed by a Turing machine
    c. It only applies to non-deterministic Turing machines
    d. It limits the computational power of Turing machines
5. **What happens if a Turing machine enters an infinite loop?**
    a. Accepts the input
    b. Rejects the input
    c. Never halts
    d. Moves to the initial state
6. **Which type of language is accepted by a Turing machine that always halts for all input strings?**
    a. Recursive language
    b. Context-free language
    c. Regular language
    d. Recursively enumerable language

Answers to Multiple Questions

1. (d); 2. (a); 3. (a); 4. (b); 5. (c); 6. (a)

REFERENCES

1. Ambos-Spies, K., & Lerman, M. (1986). Lattice embeddings into the recursively enumerable degrees. *The Journal of Symbolic Logic, 51*(2), 257–272.
2. Arrighi, P., & Dowek, G. (2012). The physical Church-Turing thesis and the principles of quantum theory. *International Journal of Foundations of Computer Science, 23*(05), 1131–1145.

3. Asperti, A., & Ricciotti, W. (2015). A formalization of multi-tape Turing machines. *Theoretical Computer Science, 603*, 23–42.
4. Aspnes, J., Herlihy, M., & Shavit, N. (1994). Counting networks. *Journal of the ACM (JACM), 41*(5), 1020–1048.
5. Barmpalias, G., & Lewis-Pye, A. (2017). Computing halting probabilities from other halting probabilities. *Theoretical Computer Science, 660*, 16–22.
6. Bedregal, B. C., & Figueira, S. (2008). On the computing power of fuzzy Turing machines. *Fuzzy Sets and Systems, 159*(9), 1072–1083.
7. Benioff, P. (1980). The computer as a physical system: A microscopic quantum mechanical Hamiltonian model of computers as represented by Turing machines. *Journal of Statistical Physics, 22*, 563–591.
8. Böhm, C., & Jacopini, G. (1966). Flow diagrams, Turing machines and languages with only two formation rules. *Communications of the ACM, 9*(5), 366–371.
9. Burnett, M. M., & McIntyre, D. W. (1995). Visual programming. *Computer, 28*, 14.
10. Carpi, A., D'Alessandro, F., Ibarra, O. H., & McQuillan, I. (2021). Relationships between bounded languages, counter machines, finite-index grammars, ambiguity, and commutative regularity. *Theoretical Computer Science, 862*, 97–118.
11. Caucal, D. (2003). On the transition graphs of Turing machines. *Theoretical Computer Science, 296*(2), 195–223.
12. Chiu, T. K., Meng, H., Chai, C. S., King, I., Wong, S., & Yam, Y. (2021). Creation and evaluation of a pretertiary artificial intelligence (AI) curriculum. *IEEE Transactions on Education, 65*(1), 30–39.
13. Culik, K. (1979). A purely homomorphic characterization of recursively enumerable sets. *Journal of the ACM (JACM), 26*(2), 345–350.
14. Dash, T., & Nayak, T. (2012). Comparative analysis on Turing machine and quantum Turing machine. *Journal of Global Research in Computer Science, 3*(5), 51–56.
15. De Benedetto, M. (2021). Explication as a three-step procedure: The case of the Church-Turing thesis. *European Journal for Philosophy of Science, 11*(1), 21.
16. Devienne, P. (1990). Weighted graphs: A tool for studying the halting problem and time complexity in term rewriting systems and logic programming. *Theoretical Computer Science, 75*(1, 2), 157–215.
17. DeYoung, R., Hasan, I., & Kirchhoff, B. (1998). The impact of out-of-state entry on the cost efficiency of local commercial banks. *Journal of Economics and Business, 50*(2), 191–203.
18. Findler, R. B., Clements, J., Flanagan, C., Flatt, M., Krishnamurthi, S., Steckler, P., & Felleisen, M. (2002). DrScheme: A programming environment for Scheme. *Journal of Functional Programming, 12*(2), 159–182.
19. Goldin, D. Q., Smolka, S. A., Attie, P. C., & Sonderegger, E. L. (2004). Turing machines, transition systems, and interaction. *Information and Computation, 194*(2), 101–128.
20. Gustafsson, L., & Sternad, M. (2016). A guide to population modelling for simulation. *Open Journal of Modelling and Simulation, 4*(02), 55.

21. Haleem, A., Javaid, M., & Khan, I. H. (2019). Current status and applications of artificial intelligence (AI) in the medical field: An overview. *Current Medicine Research and Practice, 9*(6), 231–237.

22. Hernández-Orallo, J., Insa-Cabrera, J., Dowe, D. L., & Hibbard, B. (2012). Turing tests with Turing machines. *Turing-100, 10*(140–156), 36.

23. Hickey, T., & Cohen, J. (1983). Uniform random generation of strings in a context-free language. *SIAM Journal on Computing, 12*(4), 645–655.

24. Hjelmfelt, A., Weinberger, E. D., & Ross, J. (1991). Chemical implementation of neural networks and Turing machines. *Proceedings of the National Academy of Sciences, 88*(24), 10983–10987.

25. Hooper, P. K. (1966). The undecidability of the Turing machine immortality problem. *The Journal of Symbolic Logic, 31*(2), 219–234.

26. Hudak, P. (1989). Conception, evolution, and application of functional programming languages. *ACM Computing Surveys (CSUR), 21*(3), 359–411.

27. Ibarra, O. H. (1971). Characterizations of some tape and time complexity classes of Turing machines in terms of multihead and auxiliary stack automata. *Journal of Computer and System Sciences, 5*(2), 88–117.

28. Impullitti, G., Irarrazabal, A. A., & Opromolla, L. D. (2013). A theory of entry into and exit from export markets. *Journal of International Economics, 90*(1), 75–90.

29. Inoue, K., Ito, A., Kamiura, T., Petersen, H., & Zhang, L. (2004). A note on rebound Turing machines. *International Journal of Foundations of Computer Science, 15*(05), 791–807.

30. Jack Copeland, B., & Shagrir, O. (2011). Do accelerating Turing machines compute the uncomputable? *Minds and Machines, 21*, 221–239.

31. Jain, S., Lange, S., & Nessel, J. (2001). On the learnability of recursively enumerable languages from good examples. *Theoretical Computer Science, 261*(1), 3–29.

32. Kamarianakis, Y., & Gao, H. O. (2010). Accounting for exhaust gas transport dynamics in instantaneous emission models via smooth transition regression. *Environmental Science & Technology, 44*(4), 1320–1326.

33. Kapoutsis, C. (2005). Non-recursive trade-offs for two-way machines. *International Journal of Foundations of Computer Science, 16*(05), 943–956.

34. Kleinschmidt, D. F., & Jaeger, T. F. (2015). Robust speech perception: Recognize the familiar, generalize to the similar, and adapt to the novel. *Psychological Review, 122*(2), 148.

35. Malekmohamadi Faradonbe, S., Safi-Esfahani, F., & Karimian-Kelishadrokhi, M. (2020). A review on neural Turing machine (NTM). *SN Computer Science, 1*(6), 333.

36. Manin, Y. I. (2012). Renormalisation and computation II: Time cut-off and the halting problem. *Mathematical Structures in Computer Science, 22*(5), 729–751.

37. Marion, B. (1994). Turing machines and computational complexity. *The American Mathematical Monthly, 101*(1), 61–65.

38. Myasnikov, A., Nikolaev, A., & Ushakov, A. (2014). The Post correspondence problem in groups. *Journal of Group Theory, 17*(6), 991–1008.

39. Ogheneovo, E. E. (2014). Turing machine and the conceptual problems of computational theory. *Research Inventy: International Journal of Engineering and Science, 4*(4), 53–60.

40. Peterfreund, L. (2023). Enumerating grammar-based extractions. *Discrete Applied Mathematics, 341*, 372–392.

41. Prokopenko, M., Harré, M., Lizier, J., Boschetti, F., Peppas, P., & Kauffman, S. (2019). Self-referential basis of undecidable dynamics: From the Liar paradox and the halting problem to the edge of chaos. *Physics of Life Reviews, 31*, 134–156.

42. Rice, S. O. (1968). Uniform asymptotic expansions for saddle point integrals—Application to a probability distribution occurring in noise theory. *Bell System Technical Journal, 47*(9), 1971–2013.

43. Roginsky, J. (1991). Derivation of closed-form expressions for the T matrices of Rayleigh–Rice and extinction-theorem perturbation theories. *The Journal of the Acoustical Society of America, 90*(2), 1130–1137.

44. Rogozhin, Y. (1996). Small universal Turing machines. *Theoretical Computer Science, 168*(2), 215–240.

45. Sayama, H. (2008). Construction theory, self-replication, and the halting problem. *Complexity, 13*(5), 16–22.

46. Shannon, C. E. (1956). A universal Turing machine with two internal states. *Automata Studies, 34*, 157–165.

47. Sherry, D. (1986). On instantaneous velocity. *History of Philosophy Quarterly, 3*(4), 391–406.

48. Shore, B. W. (2014). Two-state behavior in N-state quantum systems: The Morris–Shore transformation reviewed. *Journal of Modern Optics, 61*(10), 787–815.

49. Wegner, P., & Goldin, D. (2003). Computation beyond Turing machines. *Communications of the ACM, 46*(4), 100–102.

50. Žák, S. (1983). A Turing machine time hierarchy. *Theoretical Computer Science, 26*(3), 327–333.

51. Zenil, H. (2013). Turing patterns with Turing machines: Emergence and low-level structure formation. *Natural Computing, 12*, 291–303.

52. Zylberberg, A., Dehaene, S., Roelfsema, P. R., & Sigman, M. (2011). The human Turing machine: A neural framework for mental programs. *Trends in Cognitive Sciences, 15*(7), 293–300.

CHAPTER

8 Computability and Undecidability

LEARNING OBJECTIVES

After studying this chapter, you will be able to:

- Understand the concept of the Church-Turing thesis and its implications for computational procedures.
- Differentiate between decidable and undecidable problems.
- Describe the concept of Turing machine (TM) languages and their classifications.
- Explain the distinction between recursively enumerable languages and recursive languages.
- Learn the principles and rules of unrestricted grammar.
- Understand the construction of Turing machines for various language recognition tasks.
- Analyze the properties and operations of recursive and recursively enumerable languages.
- Explore the concept of undecidability and its impact on computational theory.
- Understand the process of reducibility and its application in solving computational problems.

KEY TERMS FROM THIS CHAPTER

Church-Turing thesis
Kuroda normal form
Recursive languages
Semi-decidability
Decidable problems
Modified Chomsky hierarchy
Recursively enumerable languages
Turing machine (TM)

UNIT INTRODUCTION

The Church thesis states that the Turing machine (TM) may represent an algorithm associated with any computational procedure. Are there any issues that are unsolvable by algorithms? This issue categorizes the set of challenges into two distinct groups: decidable and undecidable. An issue is considered decidable if there is an algorithm available to solve it. Conversely, if no algorithm exists, the problem is classified as undecidable. Prior to delving into the concept of undecidability, it is imperative to have an understanding of the languages that are deemed acceptable by the Turing Machine (TM) (Velupillai, 2009).

This section delves into the fundamental concepts of computability as well as undecidability, starting with the Church-Turing thesis. According to this thesis, any computing process may be expressed using a Turing machine (TM). The categorization of problems is analyzed as either decidable or undecidable, which is determined by the presence of algorithms capable of solving them (Mackenzie, 1996). This unit explores the languages that Turing Machines (TMs) can accept, specifically differentiating between recursively enumerable versus recursive languages. In addition, the notion of unconstrained grammar and its connection to Turing Machines (TMs) is also presented. Finally, an analysis of undecidability and the approach to reduction employed to address intricate computational problems is also provided (Basti & Perrone, 1995).

8.1. TM LANGUAGES

A string w is considered to be acknowledged by a Turing Machine if it reaches the halt state (H). What are the consequences if it does not come to a halt? In certain cases, it is possible that there is no stated transitional function or the process may continue indefinitely without halting for the present state q and the current input symbol. In the initial scenario, the string w is not a valid input for the Turing Machine. However, the second case presents a compelling scenario (Schjoldager & Christensen, 2010).

Examine a Turing Machine with the transition functions described as follows:

$$\delta(q_0, a) \rightarrow (q_1, X, R)$$

$$\delta(q_1, a) \rightarrow (q_4, X, H)$$

$$\delta(q_1, B) \rightarrow (q_2, B, L)$$

$$\delta(q_2, X) \rightarrow (q_3, a, L)$$

$$\delta(q_3, B) \rightarrow (q_0, B, R)$$

$$\delta(q_0, B) \rightarrow (q_f, B, H)$$

Consider null, '*aa*', and '*a*' as 3 input strings:

i. The null string is recognized since the computer receives the input '*B*', transitions to state q_f, and stops execution.

ii. When the string '*aa*' is traversed, the initial '*a*' is replaced with *X*. Upon encountering the second '*a*', the system transitions to state q_4 and ceases further execution. The defined Turing Machine rejects the input '*aa*' (Dillon & Fraser, 2006).

iii. When the string '*a*' is inputted, the machine continues running indefinitely without stopping. The Turing Machine does not determine the outcome of the string '*a*'.

Based on the information provided above, it can be inferred that there exist two distinct categories of languages for a TM.

i. A TM is considered acceptable or, otherwise, recursively enumerable.

ii. Recursive language or, otherwise, Turing decidable (LeBlanc, 2013).

8.1.1. Turing Acceptable

A language L is classified as Turing recognizable, acceptable, or recursively enumerable if there exists a Turing computer that can either pause and accept L, halt and reject L, or continue running indefinitely (Vorobiev & Samsonovich, 2018).

It can be expressed in notation as follows. Regarding a given string w,

w ∈ L

or

w ∉ L

In the case of a Turing acceptable language, it is a possibility that a Turing Machine (TM) will stop on a significant number of input strings *w*, where *w* belongs to the language *L*. However, it is necessary for there to be at least one string *w* in *L* for which the TM does not stop as can be shown in Figure 8.1.

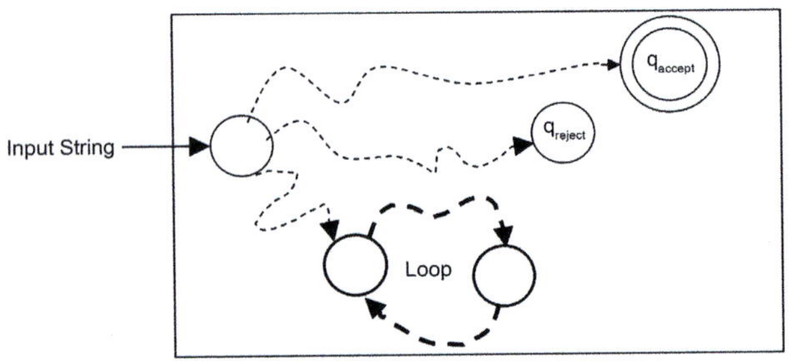

Figure 8.1. *Illustration of Turing acceptable language.*

Source: Hopcroft, Creative Commons License.

Occasionally, there may arise a scenario where it is possible to confidently assert that a string is accepted in certain instances, but it is undecidable if the string is not accepted (Berrar et al., 2013).

Examine a Turing Machine that locates a symbol *X* in the tape and then stops. The system will locate the symbol *X* by navigating through the symbol *B*.

If it is located, it will come to a stop. The transitional functions refer to specific processes or actions that facilitate the shift from one state or condition to another:

$\delta(q_0, B) \rightarrow (q_0, B, R)$

$\delta(q_0, X) \rightarrow (q_f, H)$

When given the string *BBXBBB*, the machine can readily identify the sign and stop. However, in the absence of any occurrence of *X* on the input tape, the machine will continue to run indefinitely. The property being referred to is known as the semi-decidability of the Turing Machine (Ujhelyi et al., 2022).

8.1.2. Turing Decidable

L is considered Turing decidable, or simply decidable, when there happens a Turing machine *M* that, when given an input *x*, recognizes if $x \in L$, and refuses otherwise. An *L* is deemed undecidable if it cannot be determined (Hooper, 1966). The decision issues always yield a binary answer, either yes or no. Another crucial characteristic of choice problems is that the Turing Machine must come to a stop for the task (Ehrenfeucht, 1975).

Consider the task of determining whether a given integer *X* is prime or composite. The methodology for solving the problem is as follows:

1. Input *X*.
2. Divide *X* by all integers from 2 to the square root of *X*.
3. If any number is a factor of *X*, reject. Alternatively, agree.
4. Cease

In this scenario, given an input of an integer *X*, it may be determined if the integer is prime or not, and the answer can be expressed as either yes or no. This can be depicted in Figure 8.2. A language *L* is considered to be recursively enumerable if and only if it is recursive. TM halts and recognizes a string if it is a member of *L*, and halts and denies the string if it is not a member of *L*.

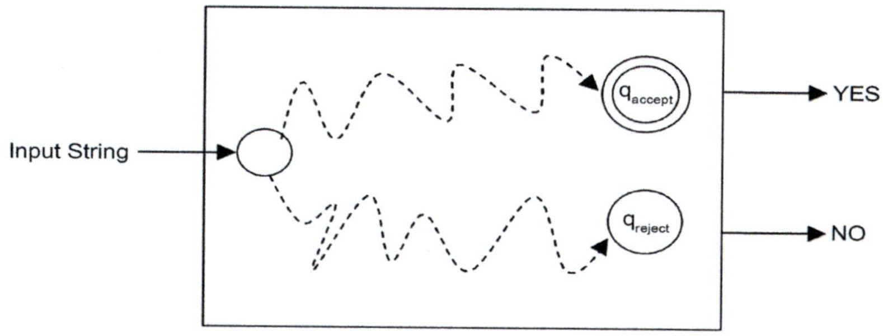

Figure 8.2. *Turing decidable language.*

Source: George H, Creative Commons License.

These prerequisites are also met for a recursively enumerable language. Therefore, it may be concluded that every recursive language is also recursively enumerable (Delvenne et al., 2006).

The distinction separating recursive from recursively enumerable languages lies in the behavior of Turing Machines (TM).

This information can be found in Figure 8.3.

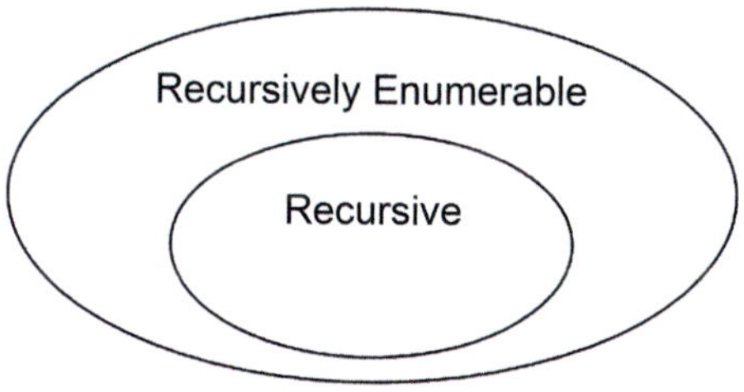

Figure 8.3. *Relation of recursive and recursively enumerable.*

Source: Lewis M, Creative Commons License.

Did you know?

Alan Turing introduced the notion of the Turing machine in 1936. This is a conceptual machine that has the ability to carry out any calculation that can be algorithmically stated. The Turing machine, albeit simple in design, possesses sufficient computational capacity to emulate the logical operations of any computer algorithm.

8.2. UNRESTRICTED GRAMMAR

The phrase was initially introduced in the chapter on language and grammar. In the chapter on Turing machines, it was discovered that Turing machines can accept unconstrained grammars. The term 'unrestricted' indicates that the grammar does not have any limitations or restrictions. In this context, "restriction" refers to the presence of non-terminal versus terminal symbols on both sides (Buttelmann, 1975).

An unrestricted grammar is defined as a grammar (VN, Ó, P, S) where all of its productions belong to the type $LS \to RS$, where $LS \in (V_N \cup Ó)$ and $RS \in (V_N \cup Ó)$ *.

In context-free grammar, there are no restrictions on the types of symbols that can appear at either end of a production rule. Both terminal and non-terminal symbols can be used interchangeably.

The sole limitation is that the empty string (λ) is prohibited from appearing on the production rule left side (Harris, 1987). According to the Chomsky hierarchy, type 0 as well as unrestricted grammar encompasses all grammars and so encompasses more languages compared to type 1 or other grammars. As previously stated, a Turing machine (TM) can take an unbounded grammar, and the language recognized by a TM is referred to as a recursively enumerable language. This part will explore the connection of unrestricted grammar with recursively enumerable language (Kuhlmann, 2013).

8.2.1. Turing Machine to Unrestricted Grammar

This means that a Turing machine is able to comprehend languages that are classified as type 0 languages. Language of type 0 is the result of grammar of type 0 being used. It is possible to directly derive a Type 0 language from the transitional functions of a Turing Machine. The rules will be described in further detail below (Currin et al., 2017).

Let the string that is traversed by a Turing Machine *M* be denoted as *S*, which is encompassed between two end markers (Watumull, 2012), represented as $\psi S\$$. Let's presume that the transitional table is provided as follows:

Input State	a_1	.....	a_j
q_1			
⋮			
q_i			

8.2.1.1. No Change in Length

- **Right Move:** If there exists a transitional function:
  - $\delta(q_i, a_j) \rightarrow (q_k, a_l, R)$

of the TM, the corresponding production rule is:

$q_i a_j$ ®$a_l q_k$

- **Left Move:** If there exists a transitional function:
  - $\delta(q_i, a_j) \rightarrow (q_k, a_l, L)$

of the TM, then the corresponding production rule of the grammar is (Chomsky, 1959):

- $a_p q_i a_j$ ®$q_k a_p a_l$ for all$a_p \in G$

8.2.1.2. Change in Length

- **Left Bracket '[' at the Left End**: For a production

  $\delta(q_i, a_j) \rightarrow (q_k, a_l, L)$

TM will cross the left boundary '[', and then execute the production:

$[q_i a_j \rightarrow q_k B a_l$

An element is appended to the production rule (in this context, the letter B is used to denote a missing or unknown value). If the letter B is adjacent to the left bracket, it can be eliminated using the production rule.

$[B \rightarrow [$

The right bracket ']' is located at the right end. If the letter B is immediately followed by the closing bracket ']', it can be removed using the production rule:

$a_p B] \rightarrow a_p]$ for all $a_p \in G$

If the Turing Machine moves to the right of the symbol ']', the length of the sequence is increased as a result of inserting the symbol B. The productions exist:

$q_i] \rightarrow q_i B]$ for all $q_i \in Q$

The string is delimited by two end markers. The subsequent productions are added to introduce the final markers (Calude & Păun, 2004).

$[q_i \, \psi \rightarrow [q_i$ for all $q_i \in Q$

Remember

Remember that the Church-Turing thesis asserts that any function that can be computed by any mechanical procedure can be computed by a Turing machine. This forms the foundation for understanding the limits of what can be computed.

$a_p\$$ ®a_p for all a_p (≠B) ∈ G

In order to eliminate the braces '[' and ']' from [qfB], the subsequent production is included,

$[q_f B] \rightarrow S$

The initial symbol of the grammar is denoted by S.

8.2.2. Kuroda Normal Form

This is associated with unrestricted yet context-sensitive grammar.

- **Explanation:** It is said that grammar is in Kuroda Normal Form when each of its production rules adheres to the form that is defined:

AB → CD

A → BC

A → B

A → *a*

Where A, B, C are non-terminal symbols, and '*a*' is a terminal symbol (Kuroda & Tvergaard, 2001).

ACTIVITY 8.1

Objective: To design and simulate a Turing machine that accepts a given language and to analyze its behavior.

Instructions:

- Choose a language that is recursively enumerable but not recursive (e.g., the language of all strings over {a, b} containing equal numbers of *a's* and *b's*).
- Design a Turing machine (TM) that accepts this language. Define the states, input alphabet, tape alphabet, transition functions, and the start and accept states.
- Write a detailed description of the TM, including the transition table and state diagram.
- Simulate the TM on different input strings (both accepted and not accepted) and observe its behavior.

Analyze the results and discuss whether the TM halts on all inputs and how it demonstrates the properties of recursively enumerable languages.

8.3. MODIFIED CHOMSKY HIERARCHY

An understanding of the Chomsky hierarchy was gained in the chapter that was devoted to grammar and language. It is mentioned that the type 0 language, which is sometimes referred to as an unconstrained language, is a language that is accepted by the Universal Language. It was learned about the Turing language that it is a recursively enumerable language. This was something that was discovered while talking about it (Jäger & Rogers, 2012). In the context of recursively enumerable languages, a recursive language is a legitimate subset of other languages. Recursively enumerable and recursive language are the two unique categories that can be used to classify type 0 languages based on their respective characteristics. Figure 8.4 displays the revised Chomsky hierarchy (Krivochen, 2021).

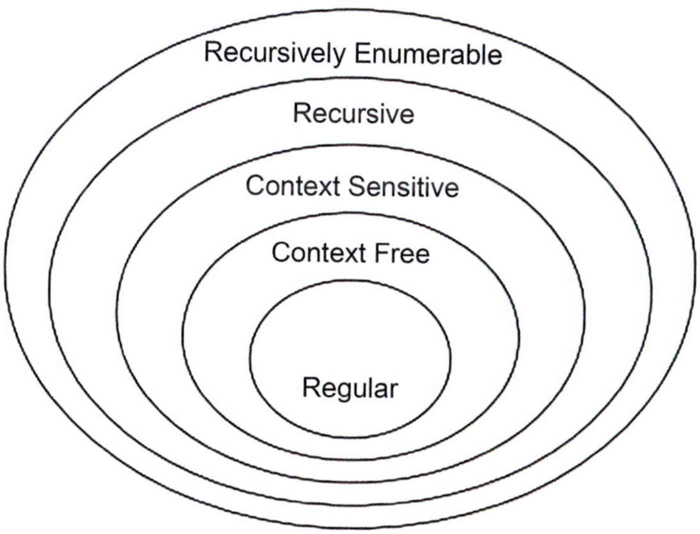

Figure 8.4. *Modified chomsky hierarchy.*

Source: Hopcroft, Creative Commons License.

8.4. PROPERTIES OF RECURSIVE AND RECURSIVELY ENUMERABLE LANGUAGE

8.4.1. The Union of Two Recursive Languages is Recursive

1. **Proof:** Consider two recursive languages, *L1* and *L2*. This suggests the presence of two Turing Machines, *T1* and *T2*, that recognize *L1* and *L2*, respectively. A new Turing Machine (TM) named *M* is constructed by combining *T1* and *T2*, as depicted in Figure 8.5. If a string *w* is input to *T1* and it is accepted, then *M* also accepts it. If *T1* rejects the input, the same input is then given to *T2*; if *T2* accepts the input, then *M* accepts the input (Amadio & Cardelli, 1993). From this reasoning, it is clear that *M* accepts the union of *L1* and *L2*.

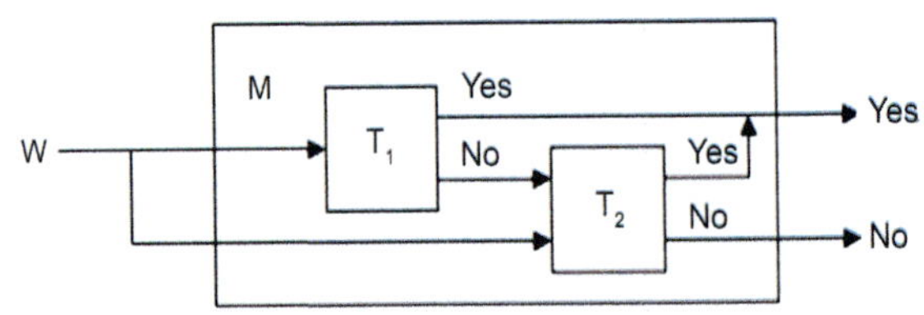

Figure 8.5. *Union of two recursive languages.*

Source: S. Y. Kuroda, Creative Commons License.

Since there is a TM for the union of *L1* and *L2* that is guaranteed to halt, it can be concluded that the union of *L1* and *L2* is recursive (Lange et al., 2008).

8.4.2. The Union of two Recursively Enumerable Languages is Recursively Enumerable

- **Proof:** Consider two recursively enumerable languages, *L1* and *L2*. This implies the existence of two Turing Machines, *T1* and *T2*, which accept *L1* and *L2*, respectively (Turakainen, 1978). A new Turing Machine, *M*, is created by joining *T1* and *T2*, as shown in Figure 8.6.

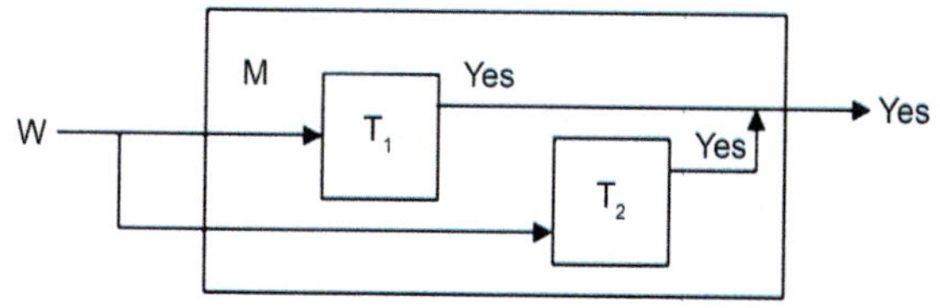

Figure 8.6. *Union of two recursive enumerable languages.*

Source: S. Y. Kuroda, Creative Commons License.

A string *w* is considered acceptable by machine *M* if it is accepted by either *T1* or *T2*. Acceptance by either *T1* or *T2* means accepting the union of *L1* and *L2*. If the input *w* is not accepted by both Turing machines *T1* and *T2*, then machine *M* does not guarantee halting. This shows that the union of languages *L1* and *L2* is recursively enumerable (Rice, 1953).

8.4.3. The Intersection of Two Recursive Languages is Recursive

- **Proof:** Consider *L1* and *L2* as two recursive languages. This suggests the presence of two Turing Machines, denoted as *T1* and *T2*, that accept *L1* and *L2*, respectively (Roeper, 2011). A new Turing Machine, *M*, will be created by merging *T1* and *T2*, as illustrated in Figure 8.7.

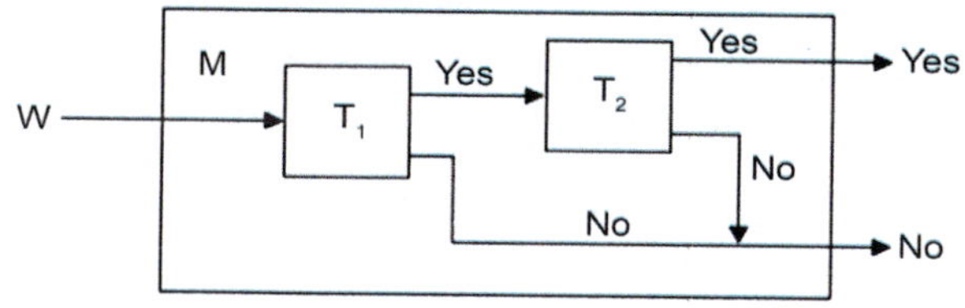

Figure 8.7. *Intersection of two recursive languages.*

Source: Michel Sipser, Creative Commons License.

A string *w* is deemed acceptable by machine *M* if it is deemed acceptable by *T1*, and *T2*, and it is deemed unacceptable if any of them deems it unacceptable.

Based on the discussion, it is evident that *M* acknowledges the intersection of *L1* and *L2*. Since there is a TM that guarantees to halt the intersection of languages *L1* and *L2*, this proves that the intersection of *L1* and *L2* is recursive (Hull & Su, 1998).

8.4.4. The Intersection of Two Recursively Enumerable Languages is Recursively Enumerable.

The similarity to the previous feature can be demonstrated, with the exception of the rejection component, as illustrated in Figure 8.8.

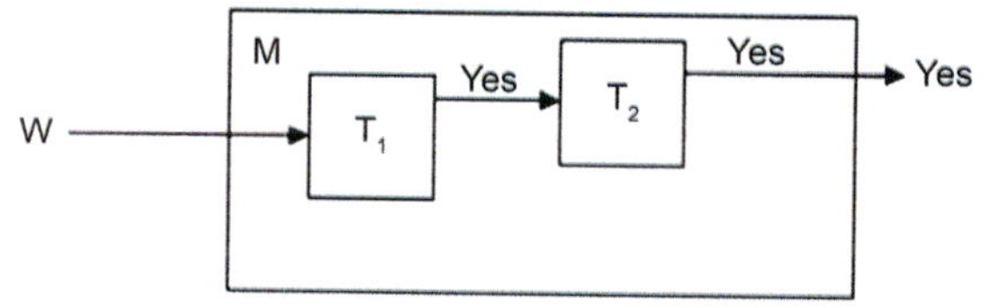

Figure 8.8. *Intersection of two recursively enumerable languages.*

Source: S. Y. Kuroda, Creative Commons License.

8.4.5. If a Language and Its Complement Both are Recursively Enumerable, then Both the Language and its Complement are Recursive

- **Proof:** Let *L* and its complement *L'* be recursively enumerable languages, indicating the existence of Turing Machines *T1* and *T2* that accept *L* and *L'* respectively.

One can construct a new Turing Machine, *M*, which concurrently simulates *T1* and *T2*. TM *M* accepts a string *w* if *T1* accepts it and rejects *w* if *T2* accepts it. Therefore, *M* is guaranteed to halt for every input, providing a definitive 'yes' or 'no' response. This halting property establishes *L* as recursive. Furthermore, since the complement of a recursive language is also recursive, this demonstrates that *L'* is recursive as well (Paap & Partridge, 2014).

8.4.6. The Concatenation of Two Recursive Languages is Recursive

- **Proof:** Let both *L1* and *L2* denote two recursive languages, which signifies the existence of Turing Machines *T1* and *T2* that individually recognize *L1* and *L2*. The objective is to devise a machine *M* capable of accepting the language *L1L2* using the following algorithm (Ushakova & Legalov, 2018).

Let $W \in L1L2$. Select a number, *n*, from the range of 0 to the absolute value of *W*. Divide the string *W* into two parts, *W1* and *W2*, so that $W = W1W2$.

The length of *W1* is *n*, and the length of *W2* is equal to the length of *W1W2-n*. Initialize the counter *i* to 0 and increment it until it reaches the length of *W*. Execute algorithm *W1* on input *T1* for *n* iterations. Check if *T1* terminates and accepts *W1*.

Execute the algorithm *W2* on the input *T2* for the next $|W|$ iterations, given that *T2* terminates and accepts *W2* (Ryoo & Aggarwal, 2009).

8.4.7. The Kleene-Star Operation on a Recursive Language is Recursive

- **Proof:** Just by making a few adjustments to the algorithm, it is possible to apply the same proof approach as was used in the previous scenario. If *T* does not accept any of the values that are associated with *wi*, then the process will reject the value (Jipsen & Moshier, 2016).

8.4.8. The Intersection of Recursive and Recursively Enumerable Language is Recursively Enumerable

- **Proof:** Assume that *L1* is a recursive language and that *L2* is a recursively enumerable language. *T1* and *T2* are the names of the two Turing Machines that are capable of understanding languages *L1* and *L2*, respectively. Create *M* that can accept $L1 \cap L2$, using the following reasoning for its operation (Jain et al., 2001).

Given an input $w \in L_1 \cap L_2$. Execute a simulation of the variable "*w*" on the *T1* system.

If *T1* comes to a stop and accepts *w*, then the contents of *M's* tape should be erased and a duplicate of *w* should be used in their stead (Ehrenfeucht et al., 1981).

The variable "*w*" should be simulated on the system "*T2*" in order to be performed.

In the event that *T2* comes to a standstill and accepts *w*, then *M* can accept *w*.

8.4.9. If L is a Recursive Language, then Σ* – L is Also Recursive

- **Proof:** As L is recursive, there is a TM T_m which accepts L. Whereas Σ* – L is the set of all those languages excluding L which have the terminal symbols through which L is created (Fairtlough & Wainer, 1998).

A further TM T¢m is created as depicted below (Figure 8.9).

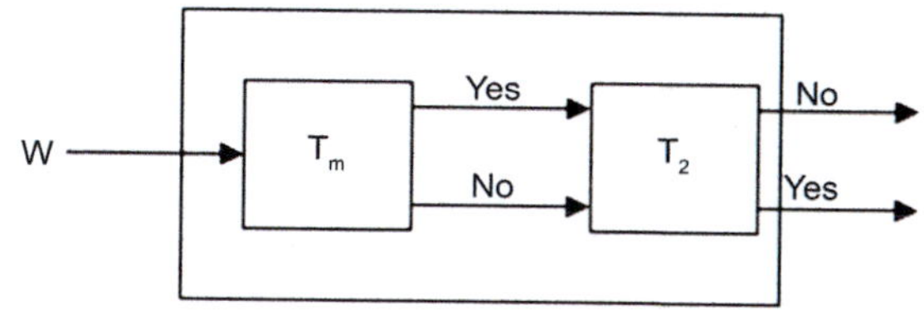

Figure 8.9. *Illustration of TM for Ó * – L.*

Source: Lewis M, Creative Commons License.

The new machine comprises two Turing Machines, *Tm* and *T2*. The design of the system ensures that if a string is accepted by Tm, it will be refused by *T2*, and conversely.

It works as string $w \in \Sigma^*$ be provided as input; it forwards it to T_m. Given that $w \in L$, T_m receives and is forwarded to T_2 which rejects (Barthe et al., 2004).

Types / Operations	Regular	Context Free	Recursively Enumerable	Recursive
Union	Yes	Yes	Yes	Yes
Intersection	Yes	No	Yes	Yes
Concatenation	Yes	Yes	Yes	Yes
Complement	Yes	No	No	Yes
Closure	Yes	Yes	Yes	Yes

8.5. UNDECIDABILITY

The previous section affirmed that if there exists an algorithm capable of solving a problem, then that problem is decidable. According to the Church-Turing thesis, any computational procedure is not considered an algorithm unless it can be represented by a Turing machine. For a problem to be classified as decidable, there must exist a Turing Machine (TM) that can effectively solve it. Decidable problems, also known as solvable problems, are those that can be effectively addressed by a computer. Given the existence of problems that can be solved, it logically follows that there are also problems that are undecidable and cannot be resolved by a computer. Prior to delving into the intricacies of undecidability, it is necessary to address the many categories of problems (Landi, 1992).

- **Decidable or Solvable:** A language L is classified as decidable if there exists a Turing Machine M that accepts and halts on every string in L, and rejects and halts on every string not in L. A computational problem is deemed decidable or solvable if its associated language can be decided by such a Turing Machine (Norval, 2004).
- **Recognizable:** The language L is deemed to be correctly recognized if there is a Turing machine M that accepts every string in the language L and either rejects or does not terminate on every string that is not in the language L. In other words, the language L is perfectly recognized. Assuming that the language that is associated with a computing problem is also recognizable, the problem is considered to be recognized or, according to Turing, acceptable (Robinson, 1971).
- **Undecidable:** Something that cannot be decided or determined in any way is referred to as "undecidable," and the term "undecidable" is used to describe this. Undecidable languages are languages for which there is no decider, which is a Turing computer that can determine whether or not a given input belongs to the language. In other words, an undecidable language does not have a decider. The language cannot function correctly without these deciders, which are essential to its usage. A Turing machine cannot accept the language and stop for each individual string that is entered; nevertheless, it may stop for some strings regardless of whether or not it stops for all strings. This is because it is not possible for a Turing machine to comprehend the language (Urquhart, 1984).

In the event that the language that corresponds to a computer problem cannot be determined, then the problem itself is referred to as undecidable or unsolvable (Moore, 1991).

8.6. REDUCIBILITY

The process of reducing one problem into another problem that has already been solved is referred to as a reduction. This transformation takes place in such a way that the solution to the second problem can be utilized to solve the first problem. This observation is gained from experiences that occur on a daily basis (Ruiz et al., 2017). For example, a person is traveling to a city that they are not familiar with and does not have any information on the transportation route. The individual makes use of a travel guidebook, which contains information such as the numbers of buses, the numbers of routes, and the locations of destinations. One could consider the book to be a solution to the problem. Finding the right bus to take in order to arrive at the specified location is the difficult part. Utilize a problem that has been solved in the past, specifically the tour guidebook, in order to find a solution to the difficulty (Jones, 1975). There is a challenge involved in determining the regular expression that is recognized by a finite automaton. Resolution of the Arden theorem has been accomplished with success. It is necessary to simplify the first problem by reducing it to the second problem using the Arden theorem in order to find an answer to the first problem (Pitt & Warmuth,1990). There are two challenges that are included in the concept of reducibility: one of them has already been resolved, while the other one is still being worked on. The characteristics listed below are possessed by reducibility (Bournez & Branicky, 2002).

1. If *A* is transformed into *B*, the difficulty of solving *A* cannot exceed the difficulty of solving B.
2. If problem *A* can be transformed into problem *B* and problem B can be solved, then problem *A* can also be solved.
3. If problem *A* is undecidable and can be reduced to problem *B*, then problem *B* is also undecidable. This property is crucial in showing the undecidability of a problem (Appel et al., 1977).

8.7. POST'S CORRESPONDENCE PROBLEM (PCP)

This problem is widely recognized as an undecidable problem. PCP is highly valuable in demonstrating the undecidability of numerous other problems through the use of reducibility. Prior to delving into the idea of PCP, a game is considered. Consider a set of N cards, each of which is divided into two pieces. Every card is comprised of an upper string and a lower string (Mateescu et al., 1995).

- **Example:** If N is equal to five, then the cards will be as follows:

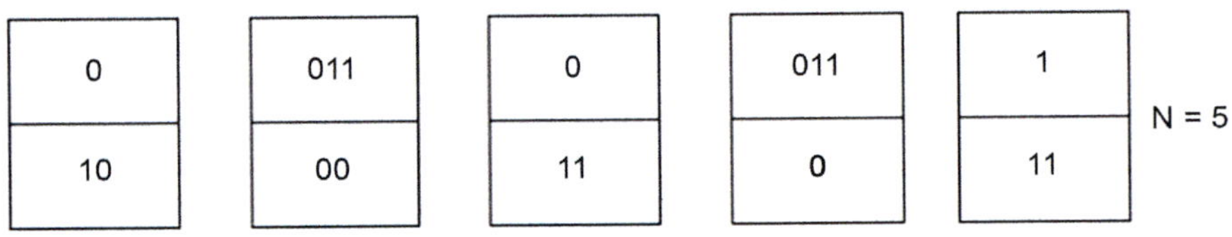

- **Aim of the Game:** The objective is to organize the cards in a way that the upper and bottom strings are identical.
- **Solution:** The sequence is 4 3 2 5 1, and there is a possibility of a solution (Halava & Harju, 2020).

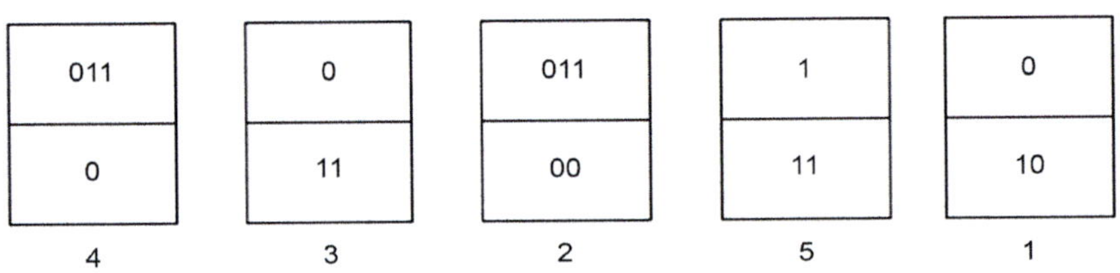

8.8. MODIFIED POST CORRESPONDENCE PROBLEM (MPCP)

MPCP is a PCP where the first substrings utilized in all cases are denoted as w_1 and x_1.

Take into consideration two sequences of strings, namely w_1, w_2,..., w_n and x_1, x_2,..., x_n, spread out across the alphabet Σ. To answer the problem, one must locate a series of numbers i_2, i_3,..., i_k that is not empty. This sequence must be such that the product of the components that correspond to two sequences, $w_{i1}w_{i2}w_{i3}...w_{ik}$ and $x_{i1}x_{i2}x_{i3}...x_{ik}$, are equal (Li & Yousefi'zadeh, 2009).

MPCP is a method that can be utilized to simplify the process of deriving a string that is acceptable by a specific grammar (Cain, 2006). Sets *A* and *B* are the two sets of strings that are required for the MPCP to function properly. A simplified method of derivation can be achieved by the utilization of MPCP, with the assistance of the table that is presented below (Zhang et al., 2007).

Top A	Bottom B	Grammer G
FS→	F	S: Start symbol F: Special symbol
a	a	For every symbol ∈ Σ
V	V	For every non-terminal symbol
E	→wE	String w E: Special symbol
y	x	For every production x → y
→	→	

8.8.1. Reduction of MPCP to PCP

1. Taking into consideration two sequences of strings, namely w_1, w_2,..., w_n and x_1, x_2,..., x_n, it is important to take into account the alphabet λ. A sequence of numbers i_2, i_3,..., i_k exists in such a way that the product of w_1, w_{i2}, w_{i3},..., w_{ik} is equivalent to the product of x_1, x_{i2}, x_{i3},..., x_{ik}. Also, there is a series of numbers i_2, i_3,..., i_k.

2. It is suggested that a new sign, represented by the symbol *, be implemented. Following each symbol in the first list, which is symbolized by w_i (where i can range from 1 to n), the symbol * is added before the next symbol. Each symbol in the second list, which is symbolized by the symbol x_i (where i can range from 1 to n), has the symbol * added in front of it (Shibahara et al., 2008).
3. Choose the beginning pair w_1 and x_1 from the MPCP that has been handed. The next step is to incorporate an additional pair into the PCP instance, where the *s are maintained in the same manner as they were adjusted in step (ii), but an additional * is added to the beginning of w_1.
4. It is necessary to add an additional pair of $ and *$ to the PCP instance since the initial list has an additional * at the closing position (Xing et al., 1993).

SUMMARY

- This chapter explores the fundamental ideas of computability and undecidability, starting with an analysis of the Church-Turing thesis. This thesis posits that every algorithmic procedure may be expressed through a Turing machine (TM), which acts as a foundational framework for computation. The chapter examines the categorization of problems into decidable and undecidable classifications. Decidable problems are those that can be solved using an algorithm, while undecidable problems cannot be solved using any technique.
- The discussion on Turing machine (TM) languages presents two fundamental types: recursively enumerable and recursive languages. Recursively enumerable languages are characterized by the property that a Turing Machine can either pause and accept strings, halt and refuse strings, or continue to loop indefinitely. In contrast, recursive languages are characterized by Turing Machines (TMs) that terminate for every input, resulting in a definitive acceptance or rejection outcome.
- The chapter also discusses unbounded grammar, which refers to a sort of grammar that Turing Machines can recognize. The process of converting Turing Machines (TMs) into unconstrained grammars and describing production rules is elucidated. In addition, the text explores the features and operations of recursive and recursively enumerable languages, emphasizing their closure properties when subjected to different operations. The notion of undecidability is introduced, highlighting problems that are impossible to answer using any Turing Machine (TM). The reduction methodology is then offered as a mechanism to transform unresolved problems into solved ones, thereby offering a thorough comprehension of these fundamental computational concepts.

REVIEW QUESTIONS

1. Explain the Church-Turing thesis and its significance in computational theory.
2. Differentiate between decidable and undecidable problems with examples.
3. Describe the concept of Turing machine languages and the distinction between recursively enumerable and recursive languages.
4. What is unrestricted grammar and how is it related to Turing machines?
5. Discuss the properties and operations of recursive and recursively enumerable languages.
6. Explain the concept of semi-decidability with an example.
7. What is the importance of the Kuroda normal form in the context of unrestricted grammar?
8. How does the reduction process help in solving complex computational problems?

MULTIPLE CHOICE QUESTIONS

1. **What does the Church-Turing thesis assert?**
   a. Any problem can be solved by a computer.
   b. Any computational procedure can be represented by a Turing machine.
   c. All problems are decidable.
   d. Turing machines are faster than modern computers.
2. **What is a decidable problem?**
   a. A problem with no known solution.
   b. A problem that can be solved by a Turing machine.
   c. A problem that cannot be represented by an algorithm.
   d. A problem that can be solved by a finite state machine.
3. **What is a recursively enumerable language?**
   a. A language that a Turing machine can accept but not necessarily halt on.
   b. A language that can be accepted by a finite state machine.
   c. A language that can only be accepted by a human.
   d. A language with no strings.
4. **What is the main characteristic of a recursive language?**
   a. The Turing machine halts on all inputs.
   b. The Turing machine never halts.
   c. The language contains only terminal symbols.
   d. The language has no production rules.
5. **Which of the following is an example of a semi-decidable problem?**
   a. Determining if a number is prime.
   b. Determining if a string contains a specific symbol.
   c. Finding the shortest path in a graph.
   d. Solving a quadratic equation.
6. **What is an unrestricted grammar?**
   a. A grammar with no production rules.
   b. A grammar where non-terminal and terminal symbols can appear on both sides of the production rules.
   c. A grammar used only in human languages.
   d. A grammar that is limited to context-free languages.

Answers to Multiple Questions

1. (b); 2. (b); 3. (a); 4. (a); 5. (b); 6. (b)

REFERENCES

1. Amadio, R. M., & Cardelli, L. (1993). Subtyping recursive types. *ACM Transactions on Programming Languages and Systems (TOPLAS), 15*(4), 575–631.
2. Appel, K., Haken, W., & Koch, J. (1977). Every planar map is four colorable. Part II: Reducibility. *Illinois Journal of Mathematics, 21*(3), 491–567.
3. Barthe, G., Frade, M. J., Giménez, E., Pinto, L., & Uustalu, T. (2004). Type-based termination of recursive definitions. *Mathematical Structures in Computer Science, 14*(1), 97–141.
4. Basti, G., & Perrone, A. L. (1995). Chaotic neural nets, computability, and undecidability: Toward a computational dynamic. *International Journal of Intelligent Systems, 10*(1), 41–69.
5. Berrar, D., Konagaya, A., & Schuster, A. (2013). Turing test considered mostly harmless. *New Generation Computing, 31*, 241–263.
6. Bournez, O., & Branicky, M. (2002). The mortality problem for matrices of low dimensions. *Theory of Computing Systems, 35*, 433–448.
7. Buttelmann, H. W. (1975). On the syntactic structures of unrestricted grammars I. Generative grammars and phrase structure grammars. *Information and Control, 29*(1), 29–80.
8. Cain, A. J. (2006). Cancellability is undecidable for automatic semigroups. *Quarterly Journal of Mathematics, 57*(3), 285–296.
9. Calude, C. S., & Păun, G. (2004). Bio-steps beyond Turing. *Biosystems, 77*(1–3), 175–194.
10. Chomsky, N. (1959). On certain formal properties of grammars. *Information and Control, 2*(2), 137–167.
11. Currin, A., Korovin, K., Ababi, M., Roper, K., Kell, D. B., Day, P. J., & King, R. D. (2017). Computing exponentially faster: Implementing a non-deterministic universal Turing machine using DNA. *Journal of the Royal Society Interface, 14*(128), 20160990.
12. Delvenne, J. C., Kůrka, P., & Blondel, V. (2006). Decidability and universality in symbolic dynamical systems. *Fundamental Informaticae, 74*(4), 463–490.
13. Dillon, S., & Fraser, J. (2006). Translators and TM: An investigation of translators' perceptions of translation memory adoption. *Machine Translation, 20*, 67–79.
14. Ehrenfeucht, A. (1975). Practical decidability. *Journal of Computer and System Sciences, 11*(3), 392–396.
15. Ehrenfeucht, A., Rozenberg, G., & Ruohonen, K. (1981). A morphic representation of complements of recursively enumerable sets. *Journal of the ACM (JACM), 28*(4), 706–714.
16. Fairtlough, M., & Wainer, S. S. (1998). Hierarchies of provably recursive functions. In *Studies in Logic and the Foundations of Mathematics* (Vol. 137, pp. 149–207).
17. Halava, V., & Harju, T. (2020). On the steps of Emil Post: From normal systems to the correspondence decision problem. *Acta Cybernetica, 24*(4), 613–623.

18. Harris, L. A. (1987). SLR (1) and LALR (1) parsing for unrestricted grammars. *Acta Informatica, 24*, 191–209.

19. Hooper, P. K. (1966). The undecidability of the Turing machine immortality problem. *The Journal of Symbolic Logic, 31*(2), 219–234.

20. Hull, R., & Su, J. (1998). Deductive query languages for recursively typed complex objects. *The Journal of Logic Programming, 35*(3), 231–261.

21. Jäger, G., & Rogers, J. (2012). Formal language theory: Refining the Chomsky hierarchy. *Philosophical Transactions of the Royal Society B: Biological Sciences, 367*(1598), 1956–1970.

22. Jain, S., Lange, S., & Nessel, J. (2001). On the learnability of recursively enumerable languages from good examples. *Theoretical Computer Science, 261*(1), 3–29.

23. Jipsen, P., & Moshier, M. A. (2016). Concurrent Kleene algebra with tests and branching automata. *Journal of Logical and Algebraic Methods in Programming, 85*(4), 637–652.

24. Jones, N. D. (1975). Space-bounded reducibility among combinatorial problems. *Journal of Computer and System Sciences, 11*(1), 68–85.

25. Krivochen, D. G. (2021). Mixed computation: Grammar up and down the Chomsky hierarchy. *Evolutionary Linguistic Theory, 3*(2), 215–244.

26. Kuhlmann, M. (2013). Mildly non-projective dependency grammar. *Computational Linguistics, 39*(2), 355–387.

27. Kuroda, M., & Tvergaard, V. (2001). A phenomenological plasticity model with non-normality effects representing observations in crystal plasticity. *Journal of the Mechanics and Physics of Solids, 49*(6), 1239–1263.

28. Landi, W. (1992). Undecidability of static analysis. *ACM Letters on Programming Languages and Systems (LOPLAS), 1*(4), 323–337.

29. Lange, S., Zeugmann, T., & Zilles, S. (2008). Learning indexed families of recursive languages from positive data: A survey. *Theoretical Computer Science, 397*(1–3), 194–232.

30. LeBlanc, M. (2013). Translators on translation memory (TM). Results of an ethnographic study in three translation services and agencies. *Translation & Interpreting: The International Journal of Translation and Interpreting Research, 5*(2), 1–13.

31. Li, X., & Yousefi'zadeh, H. (2009). MPCP: Multi packet congestion-control protocol. *ACM SIGCOMM Computer Communication Review, 39*(5), 5–11.

32. Mackenzie, A. (1996). Undecidability: The history and time of the universal Turing machine. *Configurations, 4*(3), 359–379.

33. Mateescu, A., Salomaa, A., Salomaa, K., & Yu, S. (1995). P, NP, and the Post correspondence problem. *Information and Computation, 121*(2), 135–142.

34. Moore, C. (1991). Generalized shifts: Unpredictability and undecidability in dynamical systems. *Nonlinearity, 4*(2), 199.

35. Norval, A. J. (2004). Hegemony after deconstruction: The consequences of undecidability. *Journal of Political Ideologies, 9*(2), 139–157.

36. Paap, K. R., & Partridge, D. (2014). Recursion isn't necessary for human language processing: NEAR (Non-iterative Explicit Alternatives Rule) grammars are superior. *Minds and Machines, 24*, 389–414.

37. Pitt, L., & Warmuth, M. K. (1990). Prediction-preserving reducibility. *Journal of Computer and System Sciences, 41*(3), 430–467.

38. Rice, H. G. (1953). Classes of recursively enumerable sets and their decision problems. *Transactions of the American Mathematical Society, 74*(2), 358–366.

39. Robinson, R. M. (1971). Undecidability and nonperiodicity for tilings of the plane. *Inventiones Mathematicae, 12*, 177–209.

40. Roeper, T. W. (2011). The acquisition of recursion: How formalism articulates the child's path. *Biolinguistics, 5*(1, 2), 057–086.

41. Ruiz Puigdollers, A., Schlexer, P., Tosoni, S., & Pacchioni, G. (2017). Increasing oxide reducibility: The role of metal/oxide interfaces in the formation of oxygen vacancies. *ACS Catalysis, 7*(10), 6493–6513.

42. Ryoo, M. S., & Aggarwal, J. K. (2009). Semantic representation and recognition of continued and recursive human activities. *International Journal of Computer Vision, 82*, 1–24.

43. Schjoldager, A. G., & Christensen, T. P. (2010). Translation-memory (TM) research: What do we know and how do we know it? *Hermes, 44*, 89–101.

44. Shibahara, M., Watanabe, M., Iwanaga, T., Matsumoto, T., Ideta, K., & Shinmyozu, T. (2008). Synthesis, structure, and transannular $\pi - \pi$ interaction of three-and four-layered [3.3] paracyclophanes. *The Journal of Organic Chemistry, 73*(12), 4433–4442.

45. Turakainen, P. (1978). On characterization of recursively enumerable languages in terms of linear languages and VW-grammars. In *Indagationes Mathematicae (Proceedings)* (Vol. 81, No. 1, pp. 145–153).

46. Ujhelyi, A., Almosdi, F., & Fodor, A. (2022). Would you pass the Turing test? Influencing factors of the Turing decision. *Psihologijske Teme, 31*(1), 185–202.

47. Urquhart, A. (1984). The undecidability of entailment and relevant implication. *The Journal of Symbolic Logic, 49*(4), 1059–1073.

48. Ushakova, M. S., & Legalov, A. I. (2018). Verification of programs with mutual recursion in Pifagor language. *Automatic Control and Computer Sciences, 52*, 850–866.

49. Velupillai, K. V. (2009). Uncomputability and undecidability in economic theory. *Applied Mathematics and Computation, 215*(4), 1404–1416.

50. Vorobiev, I., & Samsonovich, A. V. (2018). A conceptually different approach to the empirical test of Alan Turing. *Procedia Computer Science, 123*, 512–521.

51. Watumull, J. (2012). A Turing program for linguistic theory. *Biolinguistics, 6*(2), 222–245.

52. Xing, B., McGill, W. B., Dudas, M. J., Hepler, L. G., & Dobrogowska, C. (1993). Thermodynamic parameters for pentachlorophenol sorption on montmorillonite in aqueous suspensions. *Chemosphere, 26*(7), 1311–1324.

53. Zhang, W., Gao, X., Sung, E., Sattar, F., & Venkateswarlu, R. (2007). A feature-based matching scheme: MPCD and robust matching strategy. *Pattern Recognition Letters, 28*(10), 1222–1231.

Index

D

T

U

V

W

Printed and bound by CPI Group (UK) Ltd, Croydon, CR0 4YY

18/09/2026

14965063-0008